Emerging Scriptures

Torah, Gospel & Qur'an in Christian perspective

Published by

Mzuni Press
P/Bag 201
Luwinga, Mzuzu 2, Malawi

ISBN 978-99908-0-399-0 (Mzuni Press)

Mzuni Press is represented outside Africa by:
African Books Collective Oxford (also for e-books)
(orders@africanbookscollective.com)

www.mzunipress.luviri.net
www.africanbookscollective.com

Emerging Scriptures

Torah, Gospel & Qur'an in Christian perspective

Rodney Schofield

Mzuni Press 2014

The cover illustration is from

Codex Aureus (8th century), probably the work of monks in Canterbury. The school of archbishop Theodore (from Tarsus) and of abbot Hadrian (from North Africa) flourished there from the late 7th century.

St Matthew is shown seated in a Temple setting (cf. the Jewish Temple depicted at Dura Europos), receiving angelic inspiration (cf. Muhammad's intermediary Gabriel)

The codex is kept in the Royal Library, Stockholm.

The illustration on the title page is known as

The fall of the idols (13th century), a wall painting in Brook Church near Wye, Kent.

It depicts an episode found in the 6th century apocryphal *Arabic Infancy Gospel* in which temple idols fell when the Holy Family arrived in Egypt (cf. Isaiah 19.1).

The theme of dethroning idols is one held in common by the three Abrahamic faiths. Yet the sacred space remains ...

CONTENTS

Part 3 – Responding to the Qur'an

Epilogue

Biblical quotations
are taken from the Revised Standard Version

Those from the Qur'an
are in the translation by M.A.S. Abdel Haleem
(Oxford World Classics 2010)

References to Early Texts
other than the 'canonical' scriptures are usually *italicised*

Abbreviations
CCTQ: The Cambridge Companion to the Qur'an (2006)
OHCW: The Oxford History of the Classical World (1995)
TQHC: The Qur'an in its Historical Context (Routledge 2008)

INTRODUCTION

Abraham's 'Terebinth' [right of centre]
within the 6th century Holy Land map at Madaba, Jordan

'Everyone venerates this place according to his religion'
[so the early historian Sozomen]

1. Many Roads, One Goal

'In man's present situation, the dialogue of religions is a necessary condition for peace in the world and it is therefore a duty for Christians as well as other communities.'

Those words of Benedict XVI are taken from one of his last major speeches as Pope, on the occasion of his Christmas 2012 address to the Roman Curia. The same theme has motivated the writing of this book, and the series of Lent lectures on which it has been based. A condensed version of several of these has been published in *The Pastoral Review*.

The intention has not been to provide a comprehensive introduction to the three scriptural compilations (the Old and New Testaments, the Qur'an) that are considered in turn, but to offer an overview of literary, historical and theological issues arising in each of them. The approach varies widely, depending on the reader's assumed degree of familiarity with each text. While the majority of those who attended the lectures already had considerable knowledge of most New Testament writings, their acquaintance with Old Testament scholarship was less extensive and – not untypically – with the Qur'an itself was fairly minimal. In places, therefore, a general summary is included before more detailed questions are considered. It is hoped that the latter will be of interest to those from an academic background as well, since (for example) not only are new readings proposed for various biblical and extra-biblical writings, but the crucial question of the 'hierarchy' of texts within the canon is also addressed. Within this context it has seemed appropriate from time to time to examine existing preconceptions and the various doubts to which they give rise. Thus, in the public domain there is a readiness to dismiss scriptural teachings as irrelevant to modern society or riddled with superstitious fictions, while it is apparent that literal readings of some Old Testament passages most certainly clash with Christian principles and that the ideology of fundamentalist Muslim sects all too easily prejudices public opinion against the Islamic faith. Indeed, religious convictions have undeniably been perceived as a mixed blessing down the centuries.

As well as considering the process by which each diverse corpus of texts circulated orally as well as in writing, possibly through different stages of revision, before being collected together within the course of more general dissemination and eventual 'canonisation', attention is given to the range of other writings with which they co-existed or which developed later. Some of these, often labelled 'pseudepigraphic' or 'apocryphal' in a biblical context or known as *hadith* in Islam, may now be identified solely through references or citations elsewhere; but even surviving texts may be incomplete, partially illegible or only available in modified or translated versions. Yet together with the recognised scriptural writings they influenced not only followers of the faith from which they sprang, but to some extent became part of the (often oral) inheritance of the other 'Abrahamic' traditions. Indeed, some documents are only known to us because of this:

> The rabbis of the first and second centuries CE had not permitted religious writings of that epoch to go down to posterity unless they conformed fully to their ideas, and although some of these texts were preserved by Christians ... the fact that they had served as a vehicle for Church apologetics caused their textual reliability to be suspect.[1]

Much later on, although to a lesser degree, even stories from the *hadith* fed back into medieval Christian tradition. This continuing overlap and cross-fertilisation is a reminder that all three faiths share much in common – supremely a belief in monotheism, but also many ethical ideals.

The conviction underlying this book is that, certainly at the present time, there is a pressing need to promote greater understanding among Christians of the heritage of faith that is shared with Jews and with Muslims. This book offers a partial contribution viz. by encouraging deeper knowledge both of the Christian canon as well as the foundational documents of Judaism and Islam. It is not the intention to delve here into broader issues of religious belief and practice e.g. to survey how Rabbinic Judaism developed or to consider the changing face of Islam in today's world. The focus is above all on the recognised scriptures, even though ultimately these cannot be detached from the traditions which interpret them and so bring them to life. Jews refer at this point to the prime importance of their so-called Oral Torah, Christians to Church Tradition, and

---

[1] Geza Vermes: *The Complete Dead Sea Scrolls in English* (London 2011, 24)

Muslims to the *suhuf* (the teachings of God's messengers, 'the earlier scriptures' cf. Q 53.36; 87.18) as well as their *hadith*.

While the texts are examined mainly in English translation, there is occasional reference to the Hebrew, Greek or Arabic originals. In any deeper dialogue, Jews and Muslims alike would of course emphasise the limitations of using translated versions of their scriptures. Christians would certainly agree with them in the further insistence that in any case it is not merely the text that needs to be properly understood, but the divine revelation that illumines it. Inevitably, therefore, some of the textual interpretations offered here will fall short of more profound meanings found in them by the faithful of each religion.

It is important to acknowledge that I do not approach the task as an 'impartial' commentator; indeed, any reading of texts must always depend to some extent upon the reader's own religious and intellectual orientation. So it would be misleading to deny that in treating the sacred scriptures of the three Abrahamic faiths they are subjected here to similar critical interrogation i.e. my understanding (which not all would share) is that their veracity or otherwise needs to be established by examining the evidence for their insights and beliefs using the same canons of reason. The principle is in fact enunciated in all three traditions:

> If a prophet arises among you or a dreamer of dreams, and gives you a sign or a wonder, and if the sign or wonder which he tells you comes to pass, and if he says, 'Let us go after other gods,' which you have not known, 'and let us serve them,' you shall not listen to the words of that prophet or to that dreamer of dreams. [Deut 13.1-3]
>
> Beloved, do not believe every spirit, but test the spirits to see whether they are of God. [1 Jn 4.1]
>
> This is what He commands you to do: so that you may *use your reason* ... There are signs in all these *for those who use their minds* ... There truly are signs in this *for people who reason* ... The disbelievers invent lies about God. *Most of them do not use reason*. [Q 6.151; 2.164; 13.4; 5.103]

Profound philosophical claims about human destiny should not, in other words, be accepted solely as unquestionable assertions, but need to be supported by adequate testimony and other evidence. It is indeed essential to ask of any purported divine revelation that appropriate corroboration be provided, such as its coherence with beliefs and practices that commend themselves to people intent on seeking holiness. Undoubtedly such questioning may sit uncomfortably with some received attitudes, but – as the above citations illustrate – my contention is that all three traditions, including the Qur'an, encourage 'the use of the mind' in preference to unsustainable speculation. This reflects the classical convention that belief is fostered by the convergence of the *logos* (the teaching itself), the *ethos* (the milieu in which it arises), and the *pathos* (the response made to it).

Further, 'testing' (the biblical term) with 'reason' (mentioned in the Qur'an) must today surely take account of historical scholarship and its growing appreciation of the circumstances which gave birth to these revered scriptures. The possibility of unsustainable assertions or legendary accretions should not be dismissed *a priori*; new evidence, for example the discovery of previously unknown texts or inscriptions, should be appraised carefully. Jesus himself taught that 'the truth will make you free' [Jn 8.32].

My guiding principle as a Christian is that the key to life's mystery lies above all in Jesus' death and resurrection. Chapter 7 discusses the contemporary evidence supporting the historicity of these happenings, which I happen to find compelling. That is not to say that the acceptance of this evidence will necessarily lead others to others into Christian belief, for, as John Henry Newman expressed it in his *Essay in Aid of a Grammar of Assent*, much depends on 'the cumulation of probabllities' – including what he obscurely termed 'antecedent' probability, perhaps indicating the need for an 'expectant' heart and mind. Nor does it mean that all the theological implications of the Easter event have been adequately expressed within the Christian tradition, and it is clear from (e.g.) the centuries of Christological and Trinitarian dispute that no form of words will ever prove sufficient. The emperor Constantine achieved a degree of compromise among the bishops at the Council of Nicaea in 325 CE, but this did not stem the continuing debate which resulted in further church divisions. Most Christians now accept Trinitarian language as the orthodox norm, yet many seem to interpret it in somewhat unorthodox ('tritheistic') ways: the corresponding accusations levelled in his day by Muhammad were seemingly not without justification. (Even today it can be advisable to explain that the Holy Trinity does not consist of two persons and a bird, despite such representation in medieval art.)

So in promoting the growth of mutual understanding between different religions, it is not a matter of reiterating even deeply held convictions. Dialogue is necessary, both to understand other faiths better and also to discover what is of greatest value in one's own tradition. In the end, while shared insights and brotherly feelings can make a tremendous difference to the way we live together in God's world, it is the search for truth that must remain paramount. The goal may never be fully attained in this life, and it is not one to be grasped by human intellect alone. Hence all three Abrahamic traditions certainly emphasise the importance of revelation, a sense of truth being gifted to us from above, even if it then requires appropriate reception and evaluation. Here it is recognised that 'reason' alone is insufficient: 'the use of the mind' needs to be complemented by an openness of the human heart. In the words of a recent papal encyclical:

> One who loves realises that love is an experience of truth, that it often opens our eyes to see reality in a new way in union with the beloved.
> [*Lumen Fidei* 27]

The task, however, is not one to be left solely to religious leaders. To foster any meeting of hearts and minds, an atmosphere of trust and respect must first be created, which depends very much upon appropriate gestures and attitudes at every level. Soon after becoming bishop of Rome in 2013, Pope Francis washed the feet of a Muslim woman; this reminded me of a parish visit many years ago when I was invited in to a Muslim household, who interrupted their family prayers to give me refreshment together with a footstool on which to rest my feet. That memory has always encouraged me to think that such fellow-believers have much to contribute to the well-being of Western society, whereas all too often since then I have encountered suspicion and hostility towards them, even from established churchgoers. Four years spent in Malawi where there is a significant Muslim minority, with whom one had most cordial daily dealings, demonstrated that it remains possible today as often in the past for different religions to co-exist harmoniously: indeed, it was sometimes posited that Muslim colleagues were more trustworthy than fellow Christians! One of Jesus' best known parables also offers profoundly relevant ecumenical teaching. In his day there was a long-standing rift between Jews and Samaritans, which more than once had erupted into violence. Yet both parties looked to

Abraham as their father and held at least some of the scriptures in common. It no doubt surprised Jesus' audience to be reminded that a Samaritan's compassion – and on another occasion, his gratitude for being healed – might outweigh their own, and may have challenged at least a few to search their consciences and revise their attitudes.

Hence, the belief that motivates this book is that it is both necessary and possible for Christians, Jews and Muslims to journey together towards the same goal. If there remain profound differences between us, let them be discussed in relation to the scriptures we venerate, rather than 'used as an excuse for violent separation'.[2] A further insight from *Lumen Fidei*, although of broader application, seems germane in the context of scriptural knowledge and understanding:

> We can speak of a massive amnesia in our contemporary world. The question of truth is really a question of memory, deep memory, for it deals with something prior to ourselves and can succeed in uniting us in a way that transcends our petty and limited individual consciousness.[3]

'Deep' memory is surely one that explores below the surface to discover layers of textual meaning[4] and to bring to light the deep resonances of spiritual truth that may indeed have been forgotten within the contemporary world. In so doing, it may prove possible to dispel some at least of the apparent disparities and inconsistencies between the different traditions – and those that are found too within each separate corpus of scripture. Perhaps indeed we have neglected our common roots in 'our father Abraham', and can rediscover a symbolic meeting point at his

---

2 Rowan Williams: *Faith in the Public Square* (London 2012, 291)

3 *Lumen Fidei* (Vatican 2013, 25)

[4] There is nonetheless a perpetual danger of *eisegesis* (implanting into the text one's own ideas and preconceptions) in the place of *exegesis*. Oscar Wilde, in his play *The Importance of Being Earnest*, satirises this in the person of Dr Chasuble: 'My sermon on the meaning of the manna in the wilderness can be adapted to almost any occasion, joyful, or, as in the present case, distressing. I have preached it at harvest celebrations, christenings, confirmations, on days of humiliation and festal days. The last time I delivered it was in the Cathedral, as a charity sermon on behalf of the Society for the Prevention of Discontent among the Upper Orders.'

famous terebinth which is prominent on the ancient Madaba mosaic (illustrated on the opening page, above).

PART 1

Reflecting on the Hebrew Scriptures

*A section of the Great Isaiah Scroll found at Qumran (Cave 1)
dated to the later 2nd century BCE
and now kept in the Shrine of the Book, Jerusalem.*

*Scriptural usage in other Dead Sea Scrolls
exhibits many resemblances to that of the early Church.*

2. The Jewish Inheritance of Jesus and the Early Church

Inherited traditions

The first gatherings of Christians were held in Jerusalem. At that time the Temple was intact and the daily round of sacrifice and prayer was still offered. In 70 CE, as a result of the first Jewish revolt, the Temple was destroyed by the Romans. The Christian community then relocated to Pella across the Jordan. Yet if they had sometimes 'attended' the Temple [Acts 2.46; 3.1] there is no suggestion that they participated in its sacrifices: Paul's description of Jesus as 'an expiation by his blood' [Rom 3.25] expressed the universal Christian understanding that their Lord was himself the new temple [e.g. Mark 14.58]. Hence, their much treasured Jewish inheritance was something different, as indeed it had been for centuries for those Jews living outside Jerusalem or in the Diaspora. Even in the city itself synagogues already existed where Jewish communities met for study and prayer, and the spreading network of Christian 'house' churches seems a related development. There is a reference in the book of Acts to 'the synagogue of the Freedmen' [Acts 6.9], and the contemporary 'Theodotus' inscription records another 1st century synagogue in Jerusalem:

> Theodotus, son of Vettenus, priest and archisynagogue, son of an archisynagogue, grandson of an archisynagogue, built the synagogue for the reading of the Law and the teaching of the commandments, and guest-house and the rooms and the water supplies for the lodging of strangers in need, which his fathers founded and the Elders and Simonides.

Synagogues no doubt varied in their facilities, but each would certainly have been equipped with an 'ark' housing scrolls of the sacred Hebrew scriptures. Ideally this should have been a full complement of texts, but in places there may have been little more than the basic five books of the Law. Literary and archaeological evidence shows that the Torah chest typically held from 2 to 9 books but might contain as many as 21.

Jesus himself had voiced criticism of Jewish practices and attitudes, clashing with the Pharisaic party over matters of ritual purity. He argued that they exalted 'the precepts of men' into doctrines which were far less important than God's more fundamental concerns [Mk 7.7-8 cf. 2.15-17].

Similarly his attitude to sabbath observance was more relaxed than theirs; rigid legalism did not necessarily promote God's restorative purposes [Mk 2.23-28; 3.1-6]. In Jerusalem he physically challenged what he saw as the commercial desecration of the temple [Mk 11.15-17] and predicted its destruction [Mk 13.2 cf. 14.58]. Yet he still attended synagogue worship [Mk 1.21; 3.1; 6.2], on one occasion addressing the congregation with what was perceived as 'authority'. Likewise he taught in the temple [Mk 11.27ff; 12.35ff], and expounded the scriptures as the very word of God [e.g. Mk 12.24ff]. His approach, and indeed subsequently that of the early Church, might be described as one of critical engagement, in which a key feature was the notion of 'fulfilment'. This is summarised in the Sermon on the Mount:

> Think not that I have come to abolish the law and the prophets; I have come not to abolish them but to fulfil them. [Mt 5.17]

The same idea is expressed in John's Gospel:

> If you believed Moses, you would believe me, for he wrote of me. [Jn 5.46]

Differences do, however, surface within the New Testament over the applicability of the Jewish law: how far did this still need to be observed? Was it the letter or the spirit of the law that mattered? Certainly Paul sat light to some of its ritual requirements, which in any case required eventual revision after the destruction of the Temple by the Romans in 70 CE. Thus, he regarded circumcision as an unnecessary burden on his Gentile converts. In Jesus' discussion with a scribe about the 'first' commandment of all, the Markan version [Mk 12.28-34] leans towards the Pauline interpretation, that 'love is the fulfilling of the law' [Rom 13.10], which suggests a certain abrogation of its detailed regulations. By contrast, in Matthew's Gospel there is a briefer conversation which concludes with the uncompromising statement:

> On these two commandments depend all the law and the prophets. [Mt 22.40]

A further text in the Sermon on the Mount dispels any residual ambiguity in the minds of Matthew's readers:

Not an iota, not a dot, will pass from the law until all is accomplished. [Mt 5.18]

The letter of James also advocates full observance of the 'perfect law' [Jas 1.25]. One may conclude that, while Jews and Christians have many scriptures in common, the value placed upon them may well be quite diverse – and potentially a cause of dispute not only between the different faiths, but even between their own parties.

It is perhaps also worth noting that when towards the end of the 1st century John the Seer insisted that his prophecy should be recorded 'in a book' [Apoc 1.3, 11; 22.9-10, 18-19] and was not to be altered, he was effectively fulfilling a need to supplement ancient scripture with an equally firm deposit of Christian teaching, as inviolable as the Jewish Torah:

You shall not add to the word which I command you, nor take from it. [Deut 4.2 cf. 12.32]

There is undoubtedly much within the New Testament, in terms of content and imagery, which relies upon the Hebrew writings, even if in a Greek translation which is usually that of the Septuagint. Prior to the circulation of the letters and Gospels, largely written in the later decades of the first century, that comprise such an additional corpus, it is clear that passages from 'the law and the prophets' were already read in Christian assemblies, and were the subject of explanation and commentary. The practice followed naturally from the continuing association of Christian believers with their local synagogue. Paul, for example, – or Saul, as he then was – clearly expected to find 'any belonging to the Way, men or women' in 'the synagogues at Damascus' [Acts 9.2]. He confessed later:

Lord, they themselves [the Christian believers] know that in every synagogue I imprisoned and beat those who believed in thee. [Acts 22.19 cf. 26.11]

After his dramatic change of heart Paul and those with him maintained the association:

On the Sabbath day they went into the synagogue and sat down. After the reading of the law and the prophets, the rulers of the synagogue sent to

12

them, saying, 'Brethren, if you have any word of exhortation for the people, say it.' [Acts 13.14-15 cf. 13.5]

It seems likely that when separate gatherings had to be held [as in Acts 19.8], the pattern continued, although with prophecies and other charismatic gifts the structure of worship might be quite variable:

When you come together, each one has a hymn, a lesson, a revelation, a tongue, or an interpretation. Let all things be done for edification. [1 Cor 14.26]

By the time of Justin Martyr, well into the second century, the 'common assembly' (according to his account) has a familiar Eucharistic structure:

And on the day called Sunday, all who live in cities or in the country gather together to one place, and the memoirs of the apostles or the writings of the prophets are read, as long as time permits; then, when the reader has ceased, the president verbally instructs, and exhorts to the imitation of these good things. Then we all rise together and pray, and, as we before said, when our prayer is ended, bread and wine and water are brought ... [1 Apol 67]

'The writings of the prophets' is probably a reference, not just to prophetic texts, but to whatever Jewish scriptures were available; while 'the memoirs of the apostles' suggests one or other of the Gospels.

Responding to scripture

If Justin's account above is typical, the Eucharistic offering was preceded by the ministry of the word. At first, assuming the practice of the synagogue, the readings will have been from the Jewish scriptures. Although he doubts that all are prophets or teachers [1 Cor 12.29], Paul does seem to leave open the possibility that commentary, or prophecy, was in principle welcome from any (male?) believer present, although it was more edifying to limit the number contributing to just two or three [1 Cor 14.29-33]. This is not contradicted in his letter to the Colossians:

Teach and admonish one another in all wisdom, and sing psalms and hymns and spiritual songs. [Col 3.16]

In synagogues it was the elders [Lk 7.3] or the 'rulers' [Lk 13.14; Acts 13.15] who were responsible for discipline, and for the provision of teaching: the elders and overseers, however chosen or appointed for the house-churches, no doubt had a similar role. There were sometimes visiting prophets, who in principle were to be welcomed [Matt 10.41]; yet expounding scripture was too important to be left entirely to chance, and needed careful supervision:

> Take heed to yourselves and to all the flock, in which the Holy Spirit has made you overseers, to care for the church of God ... I know that after my departure fierce wolves will come in among you, not sparing the flock; and from among your own selves will arise men speaking perverse things, to draw away the disciples after them. Therefore be alert. [Acts 20.27-31]

For the Gospel writers the model exegete is Jesus. Mark demonstrates on several occasions Jesus' mastery of scripture [Mk 10.1ff; 11.17; 12.14-37]. According to Luke, he had been an accomplished interpreter from much younger days [Lk 2.46-7]. In John's Gospel Jesus rebukes 'a teacher of Israel' for his inadequate understanding [Jn 3.10] as he does other Jews more generally:

> If you do not believe [Moses'] writings, how will you believe my words? [Jn 5.47]

In fact, in this Fourth Gospel Jesus is himself God's living Word. The same is apparent in the account of Jesus' walk with two disciples to Emmaus (which is in embryo a Christian Eucharist). The discussion must have lasted for a good hour, which with a meal at the end meant a couple of hours at least were spent in the Lord's presence – possibly what the early Church expected in its own gatherings. Before the meal there is the ministry of the Word:

> Beginning with Moses and all the prophets he interpreted to them in all the scriptures the things concerning himself. [Lk 24.27]

Luke reiterates this point later in Jesus' parting words:

These are my words which I spoke to you, while I was still with you, that everything written about me in the law of Moses and the prophets and the psalms must be fulfilled. [Lk 24.44]

'Everything written about me' is then the main agenda for the apostolic preaching in the book of Acts. In Peter's opening sermon [Acts 2.14-36] there are quotations from the prophets (Isaiah and Joel) and from the psalms; in his next address [Acts 3.12-26] he mentions texts from four of the five books of Moses. It is left to Stephen to include references to the missing book of Numbers [Acts 7.36, 39]. Luke concludes with Paul teaching all who came to his lodging in Rome:

He expounded the matter to them from morning to evening, testifying to the kingdom of God and trying to convince them about Jesus both from the law of Moses and from the prophets. [Acts 28.23]

The historical point is not how far this is an accurate summary of all that was said; but rather the clear indication that 'prophets and teachers' now reinterpreted the Jewish writings for a potentially Christian audience – as did Philip for the Ethiopian eunuch on the road to Gaza [Acts 8.26-40]. In Paul's words:

Whatever was written in former days was written for our instruction, that by steadfastness and by the encouragement of the scriptures we might have hope. [Rom 15.4]

There was, therefore, no need to jettison elements of the written inheritance. If it seemed outdated or irrelevant, a new meaning must be found. Those who wrote in Paul's name upheld similar teaching:

All scripture is inspired by God and profitable for teaching, for reproof, for correction, and for training in righteousness, that the man of God may be complete, equipped for every good work. [2 Tim 3.16-17]

This view was widespread: thus, Clement of Rome, writing at the end of the 1st century, called scripture 'the authentic voice of the Holy Spirit', a description not seriously challenged until Marcion appeared on the scene in the mid 2nd century.

It may nevertheless be observed that in the NT there is frequent recourse to particular psalms, to particular texts from Isaiah, to figures such as Abraham and Moses, while certain writings get little or no attention. Hence it seems that in practice the Church, at least in its earliest phase, exercised some selectivity. Given that these same OT texts are used frequently in 2nd century writings as well, it seems possible that at an early stage compilations of certain scriptural 'testimonies' were made to help travelling preachers. Written on folded sheets of parchment they would have been easily portable. They were effectively notebooks, whose use may in time have suggested wholesale replacement of papyrus scrolls by codices, that is, books.

> When you come, bring the cloak ... also the books, and above all the parchments. [2 Tim 4.13]

House-churches were no doubt anxious to expand their own collections of biblical writings. Without some of these, there would be no sense in the instruction to Timothy:

> Till I come, attend to the public reading of scripture, to preaching, to teaching [1 Tim 4.13]

Imitation of synagogue practice cannot, of course, be assumed to have taken place everywhere; nor must it be overlooked that public reading requires at least one or two competent readers, who may sometimes have been in short supply. Since, at the time of the early Church, Greek texts were written in 'continuous script' which lacked punctuation and spaces between words, it meant that any reading was an acquired skill, needing the charism of interpretation. In Christian assemblies readings may at times have been intoned as they were in synagogues, making for clearer articulation. The principal evidence for first century church usage is found within the NT, particularly in Paul's writing. He mentions the use of psalms in the worship at Corinth, which according to *The Acts of Paul* still happened a century later:

> Each one partook of the bread and feasted ... amid the singing of psalms of David and of hymns. [7.10]

Paul's widest selection of scriptural citations is in his letter to the Romans. He stresses that the events of Easter were 'in accordance with the scriptures' [1 Cor 15.3-4], but since this was the tradition he inherited and then shared 'as of first importance' in Corinth, no doubt he could assume familiarity with the relevant texts [e.g. Isa 53.3; Hos 6.2; Jon 1.17-2.2]. Elsewhere there are frequent allusions to OT events, ideas, and practices, with pertinent meaning found even in difficult texts. Thus, 'allegory' unveils the significance of Abraham's two sons [Gal 4.24], while the disasters recorded in the book of Numbers are plain morality tales [1 Cor 10.11]. Scriptural reminiscences abound in the gospels and in the Apocalypse (often despite explicit quotations), but less so in the Johannine letters and Paul's brief letter to Philemon. It remains fair to conclude: the study and comprehension of scripture was among the major occupations of the primitive church.

If, however, such knowledge was not to be the sole preserve of those previously instructed as Jews, public reading and exegesis of the scriptures was essential within church worship, accompanied by any available Christian literature. We may note Paul's instruction about his letter to the Colossians: it was 'to be read among you' [Col 4.16] – not simply passed from hand to hand. 'Have it read also in the church of the Laodiceans' implies the occasion of their regular gathering for worship. So too Paul can adjure the Thessalonians that his letter to them 'be read to all the brethren', when assembled together [1 Thess 5.27]. There were some known to Ignatius of Antioch who disparaged such recent communications, and laid more weight upon the Hebrew writings:

> If I do not find it in the ancient scriptures, I will not believe the gospel. [*Ep Phil* 8]

Ignatius responded robustly:

> To me Jesus Christ is in the place of all that is ancient: His cross, and death, and resurrection, and the faith which is by him, are undefiled monuments of antiquity; by which I desire, through your prayers, to be justified. [*ibid.*]

Thus, testimony to the life and teaching of Jesus, from eye-witnesses or from those to whom the tradition had passed, was included within the prophecies and teachings within the assembly.

An idea of the 'elementary doctrine of Christ' imparted to initiates is found in the letter to the Hebrews:

> Repentance from dead works and of faith towards God, with instruction about ablutions, the laying on of hands, the resurrection of the dead, and eternal judgment. [Heb 6.1-2]

Much more than these teachings, it is implied, is available to lead believers to maturity; and the gospel tradition gives written accounts of what was earlier delivered orally. It is not clear how soon these accounts gained the status of scripture, but by the end of the first century there were those who regarded Paul's letters in this way:

> So also our beloved brother Paul wrote to you according to the wisdom given him, speaking of this [the opportunity to grow in holiness] as he does in all his letters. There are some things in them hard to understand, which the ignorant and unstable twist to their own destruction, as they do the *other scriptures*. [2 Pet 3.15-16]

No doubt it was the sharing (and by implication the copying) of these letters [Rom 1.7; Gal 1.2; Col 4.16] and other texts [e.g. Jas 1.1; 1 Pet 1.1; 2 Pet 1.1; Jude 1.1] which led to Christian writings being held in collections comparable with those of the Hebrew scriptures, even to some extent supplanting them. While John the Seer included teachings for seven specific churches within the single Apocalypse, it was Polycarp who brought together seven of Ignatius' separate letters:

> The letters of Ignatius written by him to us, and all the rest which we have by us, we have sent to you, as you requested. They are subjoined to this letter. [*Poly Phil* 13]

Others may already have made similar moves with Paul's letters; the author of 2 Peter evidently knew 'all his letters'. The Gospels were more likely to have remained as separate documents, if only because of their greater length but also to facilitate their public use. Papyrus manuscripts seem initially to have contained at most one Gospel. Yet from the time and trouble devoted to their composition it may be deduced that the evangelists intended them for a wide readership. Given that both Matthew and Luke had recourse to written copies of Mark's Gospel, such an aim was demonstrably achievable. It was, however, only around the time of Justin that church communities began to acquire several different Gospels, of which he himself used a so-called 'harmony' version. The most renowned of these was Tatian's *Diatessaron*, which spread rapidly throughout Syriac churches in the later second century (although the original may have been written in Greek). The gradual extension of Christian writings to distant places is indicated in the interrogation of Speratus in North Africa in 180 CE, who confessed to holding 'books, and letters of Paul' [*Acts of Scillitan Martyrs* 19]. Around the same time the 'Muratorian' canon was compiled, listing acceptable Christian writings; and in Asia Minor Melito of Sardis set about discovering the precise number and arrangement of 'the ancient books' as recently agreed by rabbinic authorities.

Lections in 'gentile' churches

Although many house-churches may have originated as offshoots from a synagogue congregation, over the course of the first century the proportion of Jewish Christians declined — a trend that continued in the following century according to Justin Martyr [*1 Apol* 53]. In Paul's greetings to the Romans, it may be significant that only Andronicus, Junias and Herodian are called his 'kinsmen' [Rom 16.7, 11] — presumably those of Jewish origin like himself, suggesting that the remaining long list of names refers to Gentile Christians. There is no reason to suppose that in places where these formed the main body of believers, as perhaps in Thessalonica [1 Thess 1.9-10], the patterns of worship were markedly different. In other words, they too will have listened to Jewish scriptures, and been instructed in their meaning. Some may also have heard what would now be termed Jewish apocryphal writings. When Clement wrote his letter to the Corinthians from Rome he made several such citations or allusions, as if from 'scripture' [e.g. *1 Clem* 17.6; 23.3; 46.2].

1 Peter clearly has Gentile Christians in mind. They are not to be 'conformed to the passions of their former ignorance' since they have been 'ransomed from the futile ways inherited from [their] fathers' [1 Pet 1.14, 18]. They were once 'no people' [2.10], but they must abandon 'human passions' and the licentious lifestyle of the Gentiles [4.2-3]:

They are surprised that you do not now join them in the same wild profligacy, and they abuse you. [4.4]

Despite their unpopularity with former associates, who accuse them of 'wrongdoing', they must 'maintain good conduct among the Gentiles' [2.12]. The letter begins by stressing how the scriptures that they have come to know demonstrate clearly their rightful inheritance of God's promises:

The prophets who prophesied of the grace that was to be yours searched and inquired about this salvation ... It was revealed to them that they were serving not themselves but you, in the things which have now been announced to you by those who preached the good news to you through the Holy Spirit sent from heaven. [1.10-12]

The letter to the Hebrews (a later designation, not in the text itself) is also addressed to Gentile Christians:

Once you were no people but now you are God's people; once you had not received mercy but now you have received mercy. [2.10 cf. Hos 2.23]

Again and again the writer reminds his readers of their 'enlightenment' [Heb 6.4; 10.32] and urges them not to lose faith:

Recall the former days, when after you were enlightened, you endured a hard struggle ... Do not throw away your confidence ... We are not of those who shrink back. [10.32, 35, 39]
See to it ... that no one be immoral or irreligious like Esau, who sold his birthright for a single meal. [12.16]
Do not be led away by diverse and strange teachings; for it is well that the heart be strengthened by grace, not by foods. [13.9]

Of course, as Harnack once observed:

At first, and indeed always, there were naturally some people who imagined that one could secure the holy contents and blessings of   Christianity   as one did those of Isis or the Magna Mater, and then withdraw.

Yet here, the author of Hebrews clearly has a more specific situation in his sights. The root of disaffection with the faith seems to have been certain 'strange' teachings. They apparently urged the resumption of some kind of 'food', which would ease the pressure of 'hostility' – yet would effectively mean deserting the Christian assembly and their church leaders, who have evidently remained loyal from the first [13.7, 17].

What is it that is unsettling the 'wavering' believers – and who is 'abusing' them [13.13]? The food in question seems to be linked to the offering of sacrifices [13.10]. It seems implausible that the affair is connected with events or attitudes arising from the Jewish diaspora: if all this is happening subsequent to the temple's recent destruction, there is no longer any Jewish altar and 'the blood of goats and bulls' [9.13] has by now ceased to flow. The letter to the Hebrews makes no reference to contemporary Judaism, but concerns itself with texts that are increasingly being seen as rightfully the Christian inheritance. A comparison with the first letter of Peter, in which Christians are being abused by their former Gentile associates, reinforces the conclusion that a not dissimilar situation has occurred here. And if some church members have lost confidence and have questioned the accepted teaching, then others will be disturbed as well.

The response to these wavering Gentile Christians suggests how their doubts have arisen. We have here detailed exegesis of texts drawn largely from the Torah, and to a lesser extent from the prophets and the psalms. It is assumed that the addressees are familiar with these texts and are prepared to accord them some authority. So these are former pagans who have listened to scriptures read in church and have heard all about the traditional Jewish sacrifices. They are reminded of what they once practised in sacrificial rituals, aware that the friends they once ate with on those occasions are now abusing them. The issue confronting them is whether those pagan sacrifices are really such a bad thing after all, given the Jewish lections they now hear in church? Since Greco-Roman culture rather readily incorporated new gods alongside the old, could they not do something similar? They have no wish to resurrect the tabernacle liturgies described in Leviticus, but the fact that they have been mentioned in church worship might seem to legitimate aspects of their former (not entirely dissimilar) pagan customs.

It is an issue, already encountered by Paul among believers at Corinth [1 Cor 8] and again at Rome [Rom 14], that has been taken one stage further. What was then at stake was whether meat that had become available in the market after previously being sacrificed in a temple was 'unclean' for

Christians to eat. Now some are beginning to doubt whether there is much harm in the meals associated with those sacrifices. Perhaps the claims made for Christ's 'superiority' [Heb 1.4] have been exaggerated? Perhaps he is merely a 'god' like so many others, in fact like the heavenly beings known as angels? Perhaps the gospel is simply an updating by another angelic being of the Jewish law that was once given by angels to Moses [2.2 cf. Acts 7.38; Gal 3.19]? The letter's opening discussion tackles head-on this fundamental Christological misapprehension.

It was obvious to the early Church that the use of Hebrew scriptures needed careful exegesis. Soon after the writing of this letter others in similar vein followed, such as the Epistle of Barnabas and the letters of Ignatius of Antioch – although they were never recognised as part of the NT canon. As more pagans turned to the Christian faith, and as tensions with the Jewish community continued, the importance of clarifying how the Church should understand its inherited 'word of God' cannot be overstated. Moral behaviour was not the only problem: it was necessary to come to terms with ritual and dietary law, and issues surrounding the priesthood. The choice was either to consider certain texts as superseded, or to exhibit their relevance by the application of new principles – in the end, to discover (as Luke expressed it) teachings about Christ 'in the law of Moses and the prophets and the psalms'. Paul had long since argued that 'when they [the Israelites] read the old covenant ... a veil lies over their minds; but when a man turns to the Lord the veil is removed' [2 Cor 3.14-16].

So, a concluding example may be given from the *Epistle of Barnabas*, written around the start of the 2nd century, which unveiled why various foods (pigs, birds of prey, the hare, the hyena and so on) were forbidden in the scriptures: Moses' intended a 'spiritual' truth, that each animal represented a moral character inappropriate for the Christian believer [*Ep Barn* 10.1-12]. The Jews had 'lost' the proper meaning [4.7]! Ignatius of Antioch – a contemporary of the writer – was a little more generous to God's ancient people. Their prophets, he wrote, were holy men who 'have a place in our hearts' and who 'merit our love and admiration':

> Jesus Christ has borne his own testimony to them, and they are included as participants in the universal gospel hope. [*Ep Phil* 5]

22

In our own day there is a growing recognition in the Christian Church that God's covenant with the Jews has not been abrogated, but how far it is possible for their own traditions to be retained in accepting 'salvation' in Christocentric terms remains the unanswered question. John McDade has recently made this proposal:

> The Church is 'reconfigured' Israel whose boundaries have been enlarged to include potentially all human beings. Its basis, accessible to all through faith, is a practice of Torah-observance, conducted through Christian discipleship and a sacramental sharing in Christ's passion.

At least there is material here for serious discussion, and it remains important – especially because of the many centuries of anti-Semitism – that Christians should not be unmindful of the as yet unresolved tensions with which Paul and many early Christians struggled so much.

3. Valuing the Hebrew Scriptures

Christian concerns

The only scriptures known to the first generation of Christians were those inherited from Jewish tradition. Over the next 50 to 100 years they endeavoured to discover their 'true' meaning, which had been 'veiled' until now. There were many obscurities, but they approached the task with the same assumptions as the Jewish scribes:

(1) The *biblia* – the books or scrolls – are cryptic, and mean far more than is apparent on the surface. Whereas in secular writing truths are usually communicated in plain words, a divine communication has hidden depths not immediately apparent. This is surely implied in the passage cited already from 2 Peter that comments on the letters of Paul:

> There are some things hard to understand, which the ignorant and unstable twist to their own destruction, as they do the other scriptures. [2 Pet 3.16]

The apparent criticism here is actually an affirmation of the letters' spiritual value. If there were no difficulties, it might be a sign of superficiality! Necessarily, therefore, there is an accompanying warning, that it is possible for the uninstructed to read the wrong message. Note too, that at the start of the 2nd century, when 2 Peter was written, the existing corpus of scripture was being expanded by the addition of new Christian writings, so what later came to be called the 'canon' (i.e. rule) of scripture – the officially authorised Bible – was not yet in existence. The process which led to this was chiefly one of common usage.

(2) A second assumption, also noted in the previous chapter, is expressed in another late letter included in the New Testament:

> From childhood you have been acquainted with the sacred writings which are able to instruct you for salvation through faith in Christ Jesus. All scripture [*which here means the OT*] is inspired by God and profitable for teaching, for reproof, for correction, and for training in righteousness. [2 Tim 3.15-16]

So, although initially there may have been a selection of so-called proof texts which clarified God's purposes in Christ, in principle the scriptures were appreciated collectively as divine teaching of enduring value. Their interpretation might not always be immediately apparent, and indeed might be read differently with the passing of time. Yet no passage, however obscure, was irrelevant to later generations (whether Jewish or Christian). To give one example: prophets often issued warnings about what might happen unless people mended their ways or (more encouragingly) advised that God would not abandon his people for ever in their difficulties. Such messages were invariably delivered in response to contemporary circumstances, and their primary aim was not to foretell events far into the future. Nevertheless, their inspired wisdom was seen to be perennially valid, provided one could unlock its truth. One well-known example occurs in the book of Daniel:

> I, Daniel, perceived in the books the number of years which, according to the word of the Lord to Jeremiah the prophet, must pass before the end of the desolations of Jerusalem, namely, seventy years ... *Seventy weeks* of years are decreed concerning your people and your holy city. [Dan 9.1, 24]

So Jeremiah's message of hope is revived in oppressive circumstances centuries later through the expedient of interpreting a 'year' as 'a week of years'. A precedent is set for Christian commentators too:

> With the Lord one day is as a thousand years, and a thousand years as one day. [2 Pet 3.8]

The re-interpretation of the scriptures for a contemporary audience is found throughout the OT itself, not least in the prophets: for example, while Amos tells us that his visions occurred in king Uzziah's time [Am 1.1], verses in chapter 9 extend his prophecy to a later date when 'the booth of David' has fallen – in other words, to the exilic period. Paul enunciates the key principle, when he observes to the Corinthians:

> Now these things happened to them as a warning, but they were written down *for our instruction*.[1 Cor 10.11]

Or again, he writes to the Romans about Abraham's faith:

The words, 'it was reckoned to him [as righteousness],' were written not for his sake alone, but *for ours also*. It will be reckoned to *us* who believe in ... Jesus. [Rom 4.23]

(3) Thirdly, if the scriptures are indeed God's word, there must be a fundamental harmony in their testimony. So a particular word or phrase need not always be taken at face value – it may sometimes, for example, be better understood through cross-reference to a passage elsewhere in the OT. Details matter, even though their significance may be discovered within an altogether different context. This approach can be very helpful: in the story of Moses in the bulrushes, he is hidden in 'a basket' [Exod 2.3]. That at least is the common, and perfectly valid, English translation of the word. In Hebrew, however, the word is *teba* which means an ark – the very word used in the story of the flood. At once a wealth of meaning is unlocked for us, and the parallels between Noah and Moses become mutually illuminating. The one small detail of language testifies to God's providence in time of need. It can happen, of course, that biblical texts throw up difficulties or anomalies: if God's word speaks with one voice, these challenge the exegete to delve more deeply to uncover the proper meaning of the text. That is not in doubt, but the issue here is: do efforts to find consistency in the scriptures, to find these hidden truths, defy or ignore the obvious literal meaning? In later rabbinic circles, for example, it was shocking to contemplate the description of an ancestral hero as behaving badly. Their *a priori* assumption, sitting in judgement on the text, was that the words could not possibly be taken at face value. So in Genesis, confronted by the sentence 'Rachel stole her father's household gods' [Gen 31.19], the rabbinic interpretation was to deny that stealing had occurred. Rather, it was argued, Rachel took the objects into her own custody in order to prevent her father falling into sin. Or when 'the sons of Jacob answered Shechem and his father Hamor deceitfully' [Gen 34.13], it could not possibly mean that these patriarchs were liars – hence 'deceitfully' must be read as 'prudently' or 'wisely'. Is such re-interpretation, however, simply a rewriting of the text?

For many Christians today, the main stumbling block in accepting the Old Testament in its entirety as God's (perennially valid) teaching is the level of indiscriminate violence – even genocide – that occurs, not in defiance of God's will, but in response to his bidding:

Shout; for the Lord has given you the city. And the city and all that is within it shall be devoted to the Lord for destruction. [Jos 6.16]

There are many vengeful and bloodthirsty psalms as well, for example:

[God] will requite my enemies with evil; in thy faithfulness put an end to them. [Ps 54.5]

The only acceptable explanation of such texts is to understand the 'enemy' in spiritual terms, such as our own evil tendencies or the temptations to which our sinful nature may be attracted.[5] This is the traditional Christian reading, which bypasses the literal meaning of the words in their original setting: yet it provokes the inevitable question, In what sense (or senses) then is the Bible the word of God?

It is worth remembering that various concerns have been raised at other times as well. Here is Aelfric in the 10th century expressing his worries about translating the Bible into the vernacular:

Now it seems to me that this work is very dangerous for me or anyone else to undertake, because I fear that if some foolish man reads it or hears it read, he will think that he is allowed to live now in the new dispensation as the patriarchs lived before the old law was established, or how people lived under the law of Moses. Once I knew a certain priest, who was my schoolmaster at the time, and he had the book of Genesis, and knew a certain amount of Latin. He said of the patriarch Jacob that he had four
wives — two sisters and their two maidservants ... [Or again that] In the beginning of the world, brother had sister as wife, and sometimes even father bred with his own daughter, and many had more than one wife for the increase of the population, and in the early days people could only marry their own close family. If anyone wishes to live in this fashion now,

---

[5] Nonetheless, not all Christians have found scriptural bloodthirstiness so unappetising. 'Jacky' Fisher, operational head of Britain's navy in the early 20th century was, according to Margaret MacMillan, extremely devout and believed that God had chosen Britain to rule the world. His favourite reading was the Bible, 'the Old Testament in particular with its many battles'.

since the coming of Christ, as people lived then before or under the law of Moses, that person is no Christian.

Similar concerns surfaced in the 16th century, at the time of the Reformation, when translations into the vernacular started to multiply. For all its obvious benefits, it was also potentially dangerous to allow free access to the text, given the readiness of people untutored in the ways of Christ, or in the Church's hermeneutic traditions, to misread it. Precisely this problem faced missionaries in 19th century Africa. They knew only too well that, when they encountered widespread polygamy, it was not helpful for the newly converted to know overmuch about the domestic life of David or Solomon, or the biblical heroes who preceded them. Nor for them to discover the prominence given in the OT to marriage dowries, which to this day is a thorny social issue, causing family tension and the avoidance of marriage altogether.

And issues continue to present themselves at the present time. What account, for example, can we give of the many healings and miracles featured in both Old and New Testaments? It is not uncommon for those who face a struggle in life to imagine that such stories are the norm and that biblical faith offers painless remedies to their problems. Or suppose one verse of a psalm is selected for undue emphasis:

I have been young, and now am old; yet I have not seen the righteous forsaken or his children begging bread. [Ps 37.25]

If that is true, it is but a short step for the so-called 'prosperity gospel' to gain a hold, with the tragic consequence that a Christian who fails to prosper may come to the desperate conclusion that they are unrighteous, that they lack true faith, and that they are rejected by God. We know how easily such distortions can arise if but a single verse is misused or taken out of context. To give one final example: anyone who has attempted to discuss the Bible with Jehovah's Witnesses will know their resistance to any interpretative mindset but their own. They are renowned for their refusal to sanction blood transfusions, even in dire medical circumstances. They derive this from a seemingly perverse attachment to the one of the Jewish dietary regulations, namely, the prohibition against eating meat with the blood in it, an ordinance laid upon Gentile Christians at the Council of Jerusalem [Acts 15]; whereas in the recent words of a rabbi:

> In Jewish belief, saving a life is one of the most important commandments overriding nearly all of the others. If a blood transfusion is deemed medically necessary, then it is not only permissible but obligatory.

Evidently for Jehovah's Witnesses one particular regulation has been seen in isolation from what Jesus himself termed 'the weightier' considerations of the law. This surely implies the need to carry out adequate cross-references.

Yet even the People of the Book – orthodox Jews and Christians themselves – may in times past, or in the present, have mishandled its contents. One of the great tragedies of our day might have been avoided if this promise recorded in Genesis had been interpreted differently:

> On that day the Lord made a covenant with Abram, saying, 'To your descendants I give this land, from the river of Egypt to the great river, the river Euphrates, the land of the Kenites, the Kenizzites, the Kadmonites, the Hittites, the Perizzites, the Rephaim, the Amorites, the Canaanites, the Girgashites and the Jebusites. [Gen 15.18-21]

Suppose, for example, other verses had been read alongside it:

> The land shall not be sold in perpetuity, for the land is mine; for you are strangers and sojourners with me. [Lev 25.23]
> I am thy passing guest, a sojourner, like all my fathers. [Ps 39.12]

Or there is this reflection, surprisingly on the lips of king David:

> We are sojourners, as all our fathers were ... and there is no abiding. [1 Chron 29.15]

'The land is mine': if those forgotten biblical words were brought to remembrance, how many disputes, not only in the Middle East, but the world over, might have been resolved more peaceably. Perhaps the current hostility against immigrants in Britain, some of which relies upon an unwritten narrative not dissimilar to that of the Zionists, might also have been mitigated. The Christian ethos is not in doubt – all of us are 'passing guests' on God's earth, none of us with any 'lasting city' here below [Heb 13.14].

Nevertheless, in the aftermath of the Holocaust (or *Shoah*, meaning 'destruction' in Hebrew), might not any alternative reading of the Abrahamic covenant appear insensitive, if not open to the accusation of anti-Semitism? Edward Kessler has pointed out that Jews themselves are much divided on the issue. While for some 'traditional biblical interpretation provides the means to come to terms with the Shoah', for others, such as Emil Fackenstein, 'the Jewish Bible ... must be struggled with, if necessary fought against'. He concludes:

> The majority of Jews are intensely aware ... of the inherent danger in the use of the fulfilment of biblical prophecy as the sole basis for Jewish attachment to the Land of Israel.[6]

This is not to say that the Church herself has not gone astray in her reading of the ancient scriptures. It is only necessary to mention names such as Galileo or Darwin, much criticised in their day, to make clear that for too long the opening chapters of the Bible were not understood adequately as the *theological prolegomena* for all that followed. Rather they were reckoned as divine revelation about 'how things began' – a supposedly privileged account of world history in its earliest phases. Today the myth is still abroad that science and religion are in opposition, and that the biblical view propagated by the Church is out of touch with scientific endeavour. Thus, the misreading of texts has contributed to denigration of those texts, and of the Bible itself. We need therefore to address more thoroughly questions such as: With what genre (or genres) are we dealing – what kind of book is the Bible? And wherein rests its authority, that is to say, its truth?

Biblical authority

There is a range of answers to these questions. In terms of genre, of course, the Bible is really *biblia* – that is, a collection of writings. The OT is a library

---

[6] Edward Kessler: *Judaism* (in The Blackwell Companion to the Bible and Culture, Chichester, 2012, 124-126)

of scrolls, which can be dated over many centuries before Christ, a few having much older origins, but most of them written or re-edited in post-exilic times. They comprise historical records, ancient myths, legal material, wise sayings, religious poetry, prophecies and reflections on the fate of Israel and of the individual. We need to remember too that the contents of this library remained fluid until at least the 2nd or 3rd century CE. This is also true in some degree of the actual text, and is certainly in evidence among the Dead Sea Scrolls. Hebrew writing does not employ vowels, although later insertions attempted to indicate pronunciation and occasionally resulted in altering the meaning. A famous example occurs in Job. Here the Masoretic or vocalised text produces the AV translation, 'Though he slay me, yet will I trust him', whereas the consonantic text used by RSV says 'Behold, he will slay me; I have no hope'. Again, it still remains uncertain how the name YHWH was actually pronounced (bearing in mind that it may have been regarded as too holy to be spoken out loud): Jehovah is one pronunciation, but Yahweh seems more likely.   Since every scroll was handwritten, there were inevitably scribal errors and sometimes changes in a text with ambiguities or obscurities (we shall later discover that the Qur'an complains of this, even if it appears to alter the biblical record itself).

Christians as well as Jews made 'corrections' from time to time. A well-known example is that of Justin Martyr, who in the 2nd century CE objected that the Jews had altered certain texts in Isaiah and in the Psalms: hence (without much justification) he gave a version that suited his purposes better! Sometimes, too, explanatory (or marginal) 'glosses' could become part of the text. Or again whole books might be rewritten from a different perspective, essentially reshaping past history or reformulating Israel's heritage. 1 and 2 Chronicles based on the books of Kings are earlier examples. Similarly Jubilees is a version of Genesis and the opening chapters of Exodus which dates from the 2nd century BCE; yet although widely used (in particular by the Qumran community) Jubilees never became part of the recognised canon. Although prophecy was largely discouraged after the exile – to some extent because it was a questionable, even partisan, activity, in which truth and falsehood were exceedingly hard to distinguish – the existing deposit of written prophecies was mined extensively in the Pesharist tradition, which finds expression in the 1st century BCE in some of the Dead Sea Scrolls. Such interpretations were treated in some communities with the same respect as other scriptures. Indeed, Judaism was always a multi-faceted religion, with different sects existing side by side, not necessarily in harmony. Within these sects, what counted as scripture was quite varied: there were no official lists of recognised biblical books until the Babylonian Talmud was compiled well into the Christian era, although by then a broad consensus had already been reached. Josephus in the 1st century CE reckoned the number of sacred books to be twenty-two [*Against Apion* 1.7] — coincidentally the same as the letters of the Hebrew alphabet, but perhaps carrying the implication that the count was complete.

Yet in fact, new writings abounded in this later period, some of them in an apocalyptic genre, whose authorship was assigned to figures of great antiquity such as Abraham (a 'prophet' according to Genesis 20.7) or Enoch, which was a way of asserting greater authority than that of Moses. Some sects revered them, whereas there were those such as the Samaritans who rejected anything written (or apparently written) after the great apostasy of the golden calf. 'The traditions of the elders' were also often treated on the same footing as the written laws of the Pentateuch, since most Jews (like the Christian Church later cf. John 21.25) were clear that written texts can never in fact be exhaustive of God's truth. In practice, whereas compilations such as the Mishna and the Talmud are studied in the synagogue, they are not read in Jewish liturgy, which gives precedence to the Torah supplemented by the Prophets. The latter category, it should be remembered, was often a fluid category, allowing David to be regarded as a prophet [Acts 2.30] and the Psalms to be interpreted [e.g. at Qumran] as prophecies of things to come.

Jesus himself makes in one place a somewhat different evaluation of the inherited deposit, viz. between God's initial intention and the concession subsequently allowed to human weakness:

For your hardness of heart Moses allowed you to divorce your wives, but from the beginning it was not so. [Mt 19.8]

The same principle of temporal priority is seen repeatedly in John's Gospel:

After me comes a man who ranks before me, for he was before me. [Jn 1.15, 30]
Your father Abraham rejoiced that he was to see my day ... before Abraham was, I am. [Jn 8.56, 58]

Hence, whereas in the modern world it is frequently assumed that 'the latest is the best', to the ancients it was the very opposite: the greatest authority lay with what had endured the test of time. The principle was adopted by the Church when it too had to determine what Christian writings were to be commended for public reading as scripture. One criterion was that of antiquity, meaning apostolic authorship: even though some of the latest works included in the NT almost certainly post-date the apostles, their claim to be Pauline or Johannine in origin can be accepted at least in terms of the continuity of their content.

By now it should be clear that what eventually came to be agreed as the Hebrew Bible and what the Church uses as its own OT are not quite the same. The situation is complicated further by the choice of language. As the Christian faith was carried far and wide, most of its followers came to be found in lands surrounding the Mediterranean where Greek was commonly spoken. In Jewish terms these were also places where the *Diaspora* was located i.e. where Jews resided outside Israel. A sizeable colony of them had existed in Alexandria for several centuries; and it was here that the Septuagint translation (LXX) of the Hebrew scriptures into Greek was made during the 3rd century BCE largely for their benefit; although it seems that Ptolemy Philadelphus, the ruler of Egypt in those days, wanted copies of these scrolls for the famous library in Alexandria. The legend is that 70 (LXX) scribes undertook the work, but this is considered a largely symbolic figure, with some scholars now claiming to have detected only six different hands in the translation. Included among the writings of the Septuagint are a number of works of much less antiquity, probably dating from the 3rd century BCE itself. These were often disregarded by later Jewish commentators; but, since it was principally the Greek Septuagint which was read and studied in the Church, the Christian Bible now includes them, together of course with the NT.

The story does not quite end there, as the usage of the Latin Church, the Syrian Church, the Ethiopian Church (and so on) did vary somewhat – even before the major disruption of the Reformation. Regional variations can be seen in the oldest extant codices, which date back to the 4th century AD: thus, Codex Alexandrinus includes the books of Maccabees and Psalm 151, missing in Codex Vaticanus. Jerome, who resided at Bethlehem and after Origen was one of the earliest Hebrew scholars, preferred the Hebrew canon to that of the Septuagint, and was followed over a thousand years later by Martin Luther, well known for his strong views on biblical writings. He famously dismissed the letter of James in the NT as 'an epistle of straw' – considering it to lay more emphasis on Christian works than on faith – while he also wrote:

> I so hate Esther and Second Maccabees that I wish they did not exist; there is too much Judaism in them and not a little heathenism.

The outcome was the limiting of Protestant Bibles (including in time the King James Version) to the Hebrew canon, the other writings becoming known as the Apocrypha. But once again church usage has modified this reaction; for example, passages from the Wisdom of Solomon or from Ecclesiasticus are commonly read now in Anglican churches, especially at funeral services.

There are therefore various assessments of the Hebrew scriptures found across the spectrum of churches, bearing in mind that verbal or textual inerrancy, from all that has gone before, is certainly not a viable option (and, although it may be a preferred view of the Qur'an, it will need to be examined later) :

(1) The OT is to be revered in its entirety as God's word. Although this is associated with fundamentalist ideas, it should be remembered that not all who hold this position are so literal-minded. The afore-mentioned Origen probably adhered to this position, but he distinguished between different levels of meaning – for example, the literal, the moral and the spiritual. Sometimes all these aspects are of value: the story of Israel's passage through the wilderness can certainly be understood as an historical event, but it can be seen as an allegory of pilgrimage from unbelief to Christian faith, or again as symbolising the ultimate passage of a believer from this world to the next. At other times (such as Israel's conquest of the land of Canaan) some symbolic interpretation is to be preferred. Yet the sacredness

of the text has led some into questionable territory. Origen himself suggested that, even if the listener did not understand what he or she was hearing, there was nevertheless a spiritual benefit. The great Augustine was inclined to think that a headache might be relieved if one rested one's head at night upon St John's Gospel (hopefully a paperback edition?). In line with this, verses from the 1st chapter of John came to be considered particularly efficacious in imparting a blessing at the end of mass.

Again, throughout the Christian centuries the practice known as *sortes biblicae* (biblical 'sortilege') has remained in popular usage: the Bible is opened at random, the finger is pointed at the page, and the words discovered thereby are believed to convey God's special truth for the one who seeks guidance. Undoubtedly, a message is there to be found, but whether it is interpreted at its most profound or challenging level is another question. The danger is that God's word can be manipulated into meaning anything or everything.

(2) A somewhat different view is that the OT should be understood as the record of a progressive revelation of God's purposes. Gregory of Nyssa thought along these lines in the 4th century CE; but it was particularly during the 19th century that the notion of religious development gained a stronger hold, encouraged by evolutionary ideas. So a primitive phase was seen in the Bible, in which were found a few traces of *animism*. Then came a nomadic phase when *theism* grew, and Abrahamic faith in a tribal God Yahweh emerged. This belief then faced new challenges when Israel, as the people came to be known, finally settled in Canaan: other gods competed there for attention, and some lapsed into *polytheism* or *syncretism*. In the end a firm *monotheism* came to prevail, as championed by the major prophets; and in post-exilic times, if not before, this became Israel's normative religion.

We shall discover that this historical summary is really an over-simplification, not wholly borne out by archaeological or literary evidence. But it does correspond to a sense that there are degrees of spiritual insight in the Hebrew scriptures, with some of the most profound texts found in (say) Isaiah or Job, compared with (say) some of the earlier genealogies. It was actually in the late 18th century that German rationalists began to be dismissive of considerable portions of the OT. Georg Bauer notoriously rejected the Pentateuch as primitive and chauvinistic, Joshua and Judges as barbarous, most of the history as crude, many of the prophets as too judaical, and the only spiritual worth to be found in the writings of private individuals who had manage to raise themselves above the prejudices of their countrymen. Those who followed him were a little more generous, but still in agreement that wisdom literature, such as Proverbs, was all that could properly be called 'divinely inspired'. Here, of course, we can note ideas that fed into Nazism.

It should not be forgotten that a similar onslaught had already been made in early Christian times by a wealthy lay Christian at Rome named Marcion. For him, the OT was influenced by false notions of God and was therefore simply superceded by Christian teachings. He favoured an edited version of Luke's Gospel and the writings of St Paul – but was less selective than Thomas Jefferson in his 1820 minimalist version of the Bible, which omitted all miracles, the resurrection and ascension, and the Holy Spirit. Jefferson's work remained in obscurity until recently, but around the mid 2nd century Marcion's proposals were a serious challenge to the Church, which concluded that the Hebrew scriptures were not to be discarded, but – properly interpreted – remained of the greatest value (as did all four Gospels, which in Syrian circles were being neglected in favour of a merged compilation, Tatian's *Diatesseron*). The question of defining the limits of the Old Testament was pursued further when the Hebrew canon came to be closed within Judaism. But even then, it was recognised that guidance was needed in studying it; a couple of centuries later the great Jerome counselled new Christians to read first the wisdom writings, then the gospels, followed by the NT letters, then the Pentateuch and the Prophets, and last of all the Song of Songs.

(3) One acceptable way of expressing what is of most enduring value within the hugely diverse spiritual range of books in the OT may be the phrase 'a canon within the canon'. The idea is familiar from liturgical practice in the Church. The Gospels are recognised as the core texts of the NT, whereas the letter of Jude (say) hardly attracts any attention at all. It is the Gospels that help to shape the interpretation we place upon Jude, rather than vice versa, and for this reason the reading of the Gospel is the highpoint of the ministry of the word. Similarly, in Jewish practice, it is actually the Torah (the Pentateuch) that has pride of place. The Prophets and the Writings, as we now know them, are seen as supplementary to the Law. Christians, as

we have seen, argued that it was Christ himself who was the key to understanding the true meaning of all these books – a point which cannot be urged too strongly against those who think of every part of the Bible, every word or sentence even, as speaking as it were its own divine message. Truth is a contextual matter, where meaning is often discovered by relating passages to each other across the canonical Bible. Nor is our knowledge of Christ drawn wholly from the Bible: it is passed on from generation to generation of Christians in the Church, and there is an enduring tradition of understanding and interpretation. The Reformation catch phrase *sola scriptura* does not do justice to the lived inheritance of faith.

(4) The Hebrew scriptures can certainly be appreciated historically as a major influence upon the lives of Jesus and his earliest followers and hence as the original *preparatio evangelica*. This leaves open the question, however, concerning the most appropriate forms of 'preparation for the gospel' in today's culturally complex world – which might postpone scrutiny of the OT in favour of exploring insights in other religions or cultures that might offer different paths towards Christian faith. Such privileged authority as the OT can claim needs to be seen, therefore, in relation to the merits of a wider range of spiritual writings.

4. Israel's History

The biblical perspective

Until relatively recent times the course of Israel's history presented in the OT was taken at face value: the migration of Abraham – a period of enslavement in Egypt – the crossing of the Red Sea and subsequent conquest of Canaan – transition to kingly rule – the north-south division between Israel and Judah – invasion from the north into Israel and eventually Judah – deportation into Babylon – the return from exile, with continuing subjugation to foreign empires, the longing for messianic deliverance, and the editing of the writings and records that had accumulated down the centuries. So our version of the Hebrew Bible testifies to a faith that sustained the people of God, or Yahweh as they knew him, over a thousand or more years.

Undoubtedly this is how the final editors present the story. The question is, apart from their fervent religious convictions and the teaching they wished to convey, how far does the text in its redacted form correspond to the facts on the ground? We know from other historical examples that sometimes what really happened can be whitewashed or airbrushed away altogether, if it proves more acceptable to the authorities. General Custer never made his famous last stand at Little Bighorn, but his widow who outlived him by many years was ruthless in suppressing any evidence (confirmed recently by archaeologists examining the pattern of bullets left in the ground) that he was actually retreating when he died. David Livingstone was a remarkable man, but very difficult for anyone to live with and extremely unreliable in some of his opinions and reports on Central Africa: it suited the American journalist Henry Morton Stanley to turn him into a saintly hero, and he fed the British public with what they wanted to hear. Similarly there are heroes in the OT, but are their exploits to be taken uncritically? Did the settlement of Canaan happen as dramatically as the Bible suggests, or was it a more gradual infiltration? More importantly, can the Yahwistic faith that motivated the rulers and scribes of 4th century BCE Israel be traced back confidently over the centuries?

In the last few decades there has been a considerable amount of archaeological research complementing textual studies and more holistic or literary approaches to the Bible, with a scholarly consensus now beginning to emerge. It is commonly accepted that Israel's religious traditions reflect the thinking of the end of a process rather than its origins; that the worship of Yahweh alone may have been the programme of a particular faction which *eventually* achieved political dominance; that the OT in its final form is largely a product of the Babylonian exile, and a response to it.

Here, for example, is an unambiguous extract from a recent publication of the Pontifical Biblical Commission:

> Oral traditions about the ancestors of the patriarchal period were recovered and *reinterpreted* ... in a largely theological and symbolic form. The acknowledgement of God as the Creator of all ... is the *fruit* of Israel's history.

So the Hebrew Bible is the fruit, the outcome, of Israel's lived experience over many centuries, and presents a deeply spiritual – a theological - interpretation of all that has gone before. It can further be seen that such 'memories' are not preserved simply as archival records but as guidance and inspiration for times yet to come. Indeed, neuroscientists engaged in the study of human memory would now argue that, although apparently designed to preserve key elements of the past, the core function of the memory system is actually to serve the future, by suggesting ways of engaging constructively with outcomes some of which can even now be envisaged but others which perhaps have no previous parallel (thus bringing into play the increasingly bizarre imagery of apocalyptic writings, struggling to cope with unprecedented divine interventions). At any rate memory is a reconstructive process, in which details may sometimes be modified, intensified, deleted, or replaced.

Independently acquired knowledge of the historical events in question may clearly therefore be of value in discovering the main concerns and perspective of the final redactors. So here is a digest of relevant evidence that has emerged, either in extra-biblical sources or through scrutiny of the texts themselves. Perhaps the earliest clue lies in the El Amarna cuneiform tablets, which were discovered accidently in Upper Egypt in 1887 by a peasant woman digging through the mud. They comprise about 350 letters sent to the Pharaoh in the mid 14th century BCE by kings as far afield as Babylon, but mainly from Canaanite princes, together some of Pharaoh's replies. They mention a group called the *Apiru* or *Habiru*, which existed on the periphery of Canaanite society. This group seems to lack a clear ethnic identity, with no permanent settlements or property. They were a motley crowd of social outcasts, and the word *Apiru* may have been a term of abuse: it may also represent the origins of the word Hebrew. There is also from the same period reference to a God called YHW – similar to the biblical YHW<u>H</u> – who was found in '*shasu*-land', understood to mean nomadic territory to the south of Judaea. There are comparable OT texts, such as the Song of Deborah which declares:

> Yahweh, when you went out from Seir, when you marched from the region
> of Edom, the earth trembled' [Jdg 5.4 cf. Ps 68.7-8]

Or again in Exodus the claim is made that the name Yahweh was revealed to Moses at the mountain of Sinai [Exod 3.1-12]. The indication is that worship of Yahweh may have had its origins in the vicinity of Sinai.

The earliest known reference to Israel, inscribed on a stele erected at Thebes, has been dated approximately to the year 1209 BCE. The pharaoh Merneptah had then carried out a successful campaign in Canaanite territories and boasted `Israel is laid waste, its seed is no more'. The distinctive name YHWH certainly occurs later in the suffix -jah (as, for example, in Judah, Elijah and Micah) but it is probably significant that the suffix used in this inscription is El (the general Semitic term for God), indicating that the tribe of Israel was not yet so distinctive in its beliefs as it would eventually become.

Further, it needs to be appreciated that Merneptah's victory recorded here was in fact only a holding operation in terms of the region's changing political fortunes. In countries surrounding the Eastern Mediterranean there was turmoil at this time (around 1200 BCE). The so-called Sea Peoples, about whom little is known apart from their intent to migrate with families and household goods into new territories, were attacking many coastal regions. They probably accelerated the collapse of palace civilisation in Minoan Crete as well as of the Hittite empire, and certainly with their arrival as 'Phoenicians' in the coastal areas of Canaan contributed to the decline of Egyptian influence. Canaan had for centuries been a buffer zone between empires to the north and to the south, and would later revert to this uncomfortable situation, but in the early 12th century BCE the pressures eased. This may have enabled those living there to assert their independence, and to develop new social and cultural patterns.

So an epoch of change has been reached: but was it a straightforward matter of Israelites escaping from slavery in Egypt, and in time achieving the conquest of their 'promised land' Canaan, into which they then imported a distinctive monotheistic faith in Yahweh? The evidence is problematic:

(1) Although the Egyptians were remarkable for their historical records, there is nothing in them about slaves who might be identified as Hebrews, nor about a mass exit at this time. However, one ancient text in the Bible is thought to be reliable – the Song of Miriam [Exod 15.21] which records the pursuing 'horse and rider thrown into the sea'.

(2) There is a curious silence in what are undoubtedly pre-exilic (i.e. older) texts within the OT about Moses. Only in Micah 6.4 is there a single reference to Moses. There are, however, a string of references to Israel being brought out of Egypt. (It may be observed here that Abraham and Isaac are not mentioned at all in these early writings, although Jacob is.)

(3) So slavery in Egypt may well have been part of Israel's historical memory, but the accounts have surely been exaggerated: 600,000 men on foot with women and children [Exod 12.37] or even 630,550 men [Num 1.46] – a total of two million is implied – could not possibly have crossed the Red Sea and lived a hand to mouth existence in the Sinai peninsula, nor was the later population in Canaan remotely so large.

(4) Yet archaeologists are confident that during the 12th century BCE, while Egyptian influence over central areas of Canaan was weakening, things were certainly happening in the hill country, initially well north of Jerusalem (at this time still a village). This is the Late Bronze Age, but the Iron Age is beginning to be evident. There are new village settlements in the hills, typically farmers and herdsmen numbering a few dozen in each. Their annual population growth has been estimated as 2% per annum during the first half of the 12th century BCE, with further villages developing south of Jerusalem as well. Some 300 sites are known at the moment, suggesting a total population of 50,000 and upwards. There is nothing to suggest that

the bulk of settlers came from outside the land of Israel, as stated in the biblical tradition. Their material culture appears to have developed from a previous pastoralist stage, when the people pursued a semi-nomadic way of life within a tribal system. The settlers had no distinctive traditions of their own in the realms of architecture, pottery, crafts, and art, but mirrored those of their Canaanite neighbours. What may be envisaged is that as Egyptian control of the lowland towns gradually diminished, people moved out into what the unoccupied hill country, joined by 'shasu' or 'apiru' semi-nomads.

(5) So a likely model is of internal resettlement with some degree of infiltration, including perhaps those who crossed from Transjordan. Initially there was no centralised control i.e. no 'state' authority, no specialised artisans or priests, certainly no scribal class. Villagers relied upon their own subsistence farming, with the rituals of 'folk' religion accompanying the seasons of the year. Renowned shrines may have developed, or have already existed, at such places as Bethel or Shechem in the north (associated in the OT with Jacob), or at Hebron in the south (associated with Abraham). This is not, however, where the patriarchs originate. They seem to have migrated from Syria or even Mesopotamia, whither they generally return to find their brides: 'a wandering Aramean was my father' [Deut 26.5]. It is in the post-exilic writings that the patriarchs come into prominence, with Abraham's precedence over Jacob the inevitable preference of scribes in the southern citadel of Jerusalem.

(6) The reality of invasion from elsewhere remains a possibility, although the archaeological evidence offers limited support for this, nor could it have been on the scale suggested in some biblical texts. Archaeologists have recorded a number of towns that were at different times destroyed and subsequently rebuilt. Jericho was one of them, but during these initial phases of Israel's existence it was a ruin. Joshua may have caused some walls to collapse but not at Jericho, although the rubble there may have influenced the subsequent story. The conquest is described dramatically in the first 11 chapters of the book of Joshua:

> So Joshua defeated the whole land, the hill country and the Negeb and the
> lowland and the slopes, and all their kings; he left none remaining, but

utterly destroyed all that breathed, as the Lord God of Israel commanded. [10.40]

If we read on, however, through the rest of the book and into Judges, a rather different picture emerges. Even after Joshua's death, the Israelite tribes were still inching their way slowly towards greater territorial control. Here is a small sample of what is described in Judges:

> And the men of Judah fought against Jerusalem, and took it, and smote it with the edge of the sword, and set the city on fire. And afterward the men of Judah went down to fight against the Canaanites who dwelt in the hill country, in the Negeb, and in the lowland. And Judah went against the Canaanites who dwelt in Hebron (now the name of Hebron was formerly Kir'iath-ar'ba); and they defeated She'shai and Ahi'man and Talmai. [1.8-10]

The record is one of limited success, and of necessary co-existence:

> Asher did not drive out the inhabitants of Acco, or the inhabitants of Sidon, or of Ahlab, or of Achzib, or of Helbah, or of Aphik, or of Rehob; but the Asherites dwelt among the Canaanites, the inhabitants of the land; for they did not drive them out. [1.31-32]

(7) Coexistence implies a certain intermingling of cultures and religions, and while it is feasible that Yahwistic faith migrated northwards from the direction of Sinai its hold upon the allegiance of the emerging population was surely far from complete. In these historical books one can begin to glimpse the difference between how the Yahwist believers would like it to have happened and the reality of cultural plurality. Even when greater centralisation had been achieved two or three centuries later, a wide range of religious practices can still be glimpsed in a telling passage from Isaiah, in which he prophesies the collapse of the established order:

> The Lord is taking away ... stay and staff, the whole stay of bread, and the whole stay of water; the mighty man and the soldier, the judge and the prophet, the diviner and the elder, the captain of fifty and the man of rank, the counsellor and the skilful magician and the expert in charms. [Is 3.1-3]

43

We now turn to the monarchic period – the rise of the 'kingdoms' in the late 11th century BCE, and here the following comments are typical of today's scholarly consensus:

> The picture of 'Israel' in the Old Testament is an idealization. It must be understood as an 'Israel' of literature and not necessarily of historical reality.[7]
>
> Monarchic Israel and Judah and their "traditions" are a creation (though not necessarily entirely from nothing) of a later society and do not correspond to any society that occupied Palestine in the Iron Age.[8]

So once again, the biblical picture appears to exaggerate Israel's territorial extent, and its initial integrity.

One method of assessing its claims is to survey the place names mentioned in the stories, first of Saul, then of David. Predominantly, the sites linked to Saul are to the north of Jerusalem, whereas David's area of activity and influence is further south. According to 1 Samuel, David controls the land south-west of Jerusalem [1 Sam 23.5, 13, 14] as a bandit chief – a typical *'shasu'* or *'apiru'*:

> And everyone who was in distress, and everyone who was in debt, and everyone who was discontented, gathered to him; and he became captain over them. And there were with him about four hundred men. [1 Sam 22.2]

By way of comparison, the account mentions in 2 Samuel that 'Saul's son had two men who were *captains of raiding bands*' [2 Sam 4.2]. But as well as fighting against Philistines, David also collaborated with them:

> Then David said to A'chish, 'If I have found favour in your eyes, let a place be given me in one of the country towns, that I may dwell there; for why should your servant dwell in the royal city with you?' So that day A'chish gave him Ziklag; therefore Ziklag has belonged to the kings of Judah to this day. And the number of the days that David dwelt in the country of the Philistines was a year and four months. [1 Sam 27.5-7]

---

[7] F.H.Cryer: *Magic in Ancient Syria-Palestine – and in the Old Testament* (London 2001, 107)

[8] P.R.Davies: *Scribes and Schools: the Canonization of the Hebrew Scriptures* (London 1998, 3)

1 Samuel 25 indicates that, like most guerrilla leaders, David operated a protection racket, a popular leader who shared out the booty. Where then does his youthful encounter with Goliath fit? There are several indications in the text that this singular story is a later literary construction:

- Elhanan, a Bethlehemite, is credited with Goliath's death elsewhere [2 Sam 21.19]
- In his supposed fight with David, Goliath's armour is described in terms that would match the fashions four centuries later on, as known at any rate in Greek sources.
- David's chosen weapons were 'five smooth stones' from the brook [1 Sam 17.40], of which just one was sufficient. This seems an obviously coded reference to the five books of the Torah, and the message one of trust in God's law: those who keep it will prevail over their enemies, whatever their military strength.

While Saul failed to keep the Philistines out of the northern hill country, David had greater success in the south, and seems to have taken over the Jebusite fortified village of Jerusalem. To describe either of them as 'a king' is misleading, since their territorial control must always have hung in the balance - and in any case there were hardly the resources to develop the apparatus of centralised oversight. Jerusalem, for example, remained as a large village, not even mentioned by Shishak (or Sheshonq 1) in his campaign [1 Kgs 14.25] during the late 10th century, a time when Egypt began to feel threatened by Rehoboam's increasing strength in the north. External political fortunes changed, of course, which allowed the rise of Omri as king of Israel in the 9th century. There is a famous 'Mesha' stone, erected in 840 BCE by the then king of Moab, which included these words:

Omri was king of Israel and he oppressed Moab for many days because Kemosh was angry with his land.

The claim is made [1 Kgs 15.24] that Omri established Samaria as his capital, and archaeologists confirm that massive building works were undertaken there in his reign. It is Omri (far later than David) who must be regarded as having the first real Israelite court. When the Assyrians became the main external threat, it is significant that they referred to Israel as 'the house of Omri' (not of David). It was apparently the marriage of Omri's granddaughter Athaliah to Jehoram of Judah [2 Kgs 8.25-29] that encouraged the two kingdoms to combine forces, enabling the much weaker Judah to develop and fortify certain towns and cities.

Religious development

Whereas Saul is linked with a band of ecstatic prophets [1 Sam 10.10-13], the tradition credits David with bringing to Jerusalem the ark of the covenant [2 Sam 6]; this was a cult object that had at one point been captured by the Philistines [1 Sam 4.4]. The ark was possibly a visible symbol of Yahweh's warlike presence among his people, which had been brought to Palestine by *shasu* groups. These different connections point to two features that were to be formative in the development of Israel's faith: a northern prophetic element, and the establishment of the worship of Yahweh in Jerusalem, hence a priestly element. How far they impacted upon the generality of people is hard to discern, but there is some evidence from personal names, from extra-biblical inscriptions, and from artistic representations on seals and amulets.

- The evidence from personal names is not easy to handle because of textual variations between parallel passages (King Abijam in 1 Kgs 14-15 is Abijah in the parallel account in 2 Chr 12-13) and also differences between the Hebrew and Greek versions of the text. It is striking though that the recorded names of the kings of Israel and Judah begin by having no element of the name Yahweh, and that this element only gradually becomes more common. The first northern king whose name has an element of Yahweh is Ahaziah (853-852), the first southern king (assuming that Abijam rather than Abijah is correct) is Jehoshaphat (871-848). Of the 19 kings of Israel, only 7 contain an element of Yahweh while of the 20 kings of Judah (not counting David and Solomon) 14 contain this element. The discrepancy probably owes much to the cult of Yahweh in Jerusalem, while of the 7 names with Yahweh elements in Israel5 follow one after the other from 853 to 782, the period of major activity by the prophetic groups led by Elijah and Elisha, both fiercely loyal to Yahweh [2 Kgs 9].

46

- Hebrew inscriptions, bearing in mind that their survival is haphazard, indicate the presence of personal names combined with Yahweh from the 8th century onwards (not much is available any earlier). From the available information, there are roughly 13 such names from sites in Judah in the 8th century, 8 from the 7th century, and 20 from the late 7th to early 6th centuries – plus various names ending in -yah. On the other hand, the Samaria ostraca, dated from the late 8th century, contain 7 personal names with the element ba'al, the name of the 'Canaanite' god of the storm. This supports the view presented in the books of Kings that Israel was more open to 'Canaanite' influences.

Much interest was aroused when two inscribed jars were found in the late 1970s at Kuntillet-Ajrud, a caravanserai in the Negev. Dated around 800 BCE, they were evidently written and painted on by travellers, and among the inscriptions are references to Yahweh of Samaria, Yahweh of Teman, and Yahweh and his Asherah. So for the travellers Yahweh was worshipped as a localised deity in Samaria and in Edom. The reference to Yahweh's Asherah probably means that a fertility symbol, the Asherah pole or tree, was linked with Yahweh's worship in some places – a practice obviously condemned in the OT [1 Kgs 15.13]. Also, until the late 7th century official seals show the influence of Egyptian and Assyrian religious symbols – but from then on, they are completely absent, suggesting a religious purge, presumably that of Josiah [2 Kgs 22-23].

In summary, it appears that prior to the Exile there were three main religious strands: the official Yahwism sometimes upheld by the court, the prophetic Yahwism which often spoke from marginalised positions, and (the no doubt syncretistic) folk religion. There were, however, differences between Israel and Judah:

- Israel was more open to syncretism at the official level, with the result that prophetic groups frequently clashed with the kings of Israel, and encouraged soldiers and administrators with prophetic sympathies either to subvert official policies (e.g. Obadiah in 1 Kgs 18.3-4) or to attempt *coups d'etat* (e.g. Jehu at Elisha's behest in 2 Kgs 9).
- In Judah, whose territory was much smaller and hence where Jerusalem was the dominant influence, prophets such as Hosea and

47

Amos directed their attention to Israel. Micah by contrast was bitterly critical of Jerusalem towards the end of the 8th century, as were Jeremiah and Ezekiel just over a century later.

These named prophets clearly had sufficient following for their words to be remembered, indeed fairly soon to be written down – with literacy becoming more common from the 8th century onwards. The two factors that promoted this were *first*, the growth of a scribal class belonging to the court establishment dating back to Omri, which was perhaps influenced by the long established scribal tradition in Egypt (Solomon's scribe mentioned in 1 Kings 4.3 had an Egyptian name Elihoreph); and *secondly*, the invention of the alphabet, apparently by the Phoenicians some three hundred years earlier (as discovered at Ugarit). The latter simplified writing and gave rise to local variations such as the Hebrew alphabet. When Israel was overrun by the Assyrians in 722 BCE, royal chronicles and other written or oral traditions, such as the Book of the Wars of Yahweh [Num 21.14], the Book of Jashar [Josh 10.13; 2 Sam 1.17], the Book of the Chronicles of the Kings of Israel [1 Kgs 14.19, 29], the Song of Deborah [Judg 5] or smaller fragments of ancient song, were taken south to Judah by scribes and prophetic groups seeking refuge – and it was probably during Hezekiah's reign (727-698 BCE) that the first steps were taken towards coordinating the records (including the no doubt considerable oral patrimony), hence laying the foundations for a unified national epic.

But Judah too was invaded by the Assyrians under Sennacherib in 701 BCE. For the next 60 years Judah was a vassal state of Assyria and 'pagan' religious elements were allowed to flourish again. Then Assyrian power weakened and in 640 BCE those who favoured Yahwism enthroned the 8-year old Josiah [2 Kgs 21.19-22.2]. During his reign, under the influence of what became known as Deuteronomic theology, Jerusalem became a national, not just a royal, sanctuary. It was held that past disloyalty to Yahweh was responsible for previous setbacks and disasters, hence an exclusive Yahwism was religiously and politically essential. However, Josiah's death in 609 BCE at the hands of the pharaoh Necho II meant that Judah became a vassal state to Egypt. Twenty years later, Babylonian forces took control in 587 BCE, with massive deportations which marked the beginning of 70 years in exile, especially for the literate classes. These reverses allowed popular religion to be freed from official control, and the books of Jeremiah and Ezekiel contain abundant evidence that ordinary people turned back to 'pagan' deities and away from the austere Yahwism that had apparently failed. Much was destroyed at this time, not least the temple in Jerusalem along with the monarchy. What survived were a priestly caste and a scribal class, together with their traditions and their written records. In effect, Judah was on the way to becoming a faith based upon writings that were now held in regard as scripture and which during the period of exile were undoubtedly developed further.

In 539 BCE fate intervened in the person of Cyrus, king of the Persians, who brought an end to Babylonian supremacy. It became possible for the Jews, as they began to be known, to return from exile. It was Cyrus' successor Darius who appointed governors or 'satraps' to the conquered territories, and allowed them the freedom to administer law according to local custom. So Ezra's introduction of the Jewish law had official sanction:

> And all the people gathered as one man into the square before the Water Gate; and they told Ezra the scribe to bring the book of the law of Moses which the Lord had given to Israel. [Neh 8.1]

This Mosaic lawbook is therefore now seen as a colonial programme (under Persian suzerainty) that moves power towards the Levites and enjoins the creation of a temple-centred society in the midst of the 'people of the land':

> The traditional leaders are feuding among themselves, their authority is defunct, local shrines are the focus of fierce doctrinal conflict. What are colonial administrators supposed to do then?[9]

The context is 'the aftermath of war … picking up the pieces and trying to restore order', given that the old social framework has largely disappeared'. The overriding objective would have been 'a call to solidarity', with a radical reconstruction of religious practice and the abolition of potentially divisive teachings. Promotion of state authority is thus a fundamental feature of the Deuteronomic reforms endorsed by Nehemiah. In post-exilic times, any disturbing religious influences would have posed an unwelcome threat to centralised authority:

---

[9] M.Douglas: *Leviticus as Literature* (Oxford 2000, 106)

Since the beginning of the Persian period ... there are no figurines and no remains of any other pagan cultic objects. This is in sharp contrast to the late Judaean monarchic period.[10]

To the Persian period (539-333 BCE) can be assigned the editing of the Pentateuch into its final form (with the creation stories forming a guiding theological preface) together with the substantial completion of the prophets, which included Joshua, Judges, Samuel, and Kings known together as the Former Prophets since their message was essentially also a religious one. By the middle of the 4th century BCE the chronicler's revised and updated history (Chronicles, Ezra, and Nehemiah) was produced along with other Writings. Wisdom compilations seem to have continued into the Greek period, inaugurated in 333 BCE by Alexander the Great's conquests. The advent of the Greek language, the founding of free Greek cities, especially in Transjordan, and the general spread of Greek culture had a noticeable effect upon the last stages of the genesis of the OT. Job and Ecclesiastes seem to have been written in response to a growing scepticism, produced not only by the need to respond to Greek philosophy, but by individuals among the aristocracy who questioned aspects of official Yahwism. Ecclesiastes always uses the general Hebrew word El for God rather than Yahweh, and makes no mention of Israel being specially chosen and commissioned by God, although it accepts that human beings live in a world created by God, to whom their spirits return at death. Its scepticism arises from the need to relate Israelite monotheism to the sufferings of innocent people and to the many injustices that go unpunished (there being as yet no belief in the afterlife), issues simply not answered in the prevailing Deuteronomic theology.

---

[10] E. Stern: *Archaeology of the Land of the Bible Vol II* (New York 2001, 479)

5. Theological Perspectives of the Hebrew Bible

The significance of Genesis 1-3

Israel's self-understanding was of a people chosen by God to be a blessing to the nations [cf. Gen 12.1-3]. Christians see Jesus as the one in whom that hope was fulfilled, and the Church as the inheritor of Israel's calling. At times this has led to disparagement of the Jews and to neglect of their scriptures – with Marcion around the year 150 CE calling for complete abandonment of the Hebrew Bible. His call was rejected, but although the Old Testament has continued as part of the Church's inheritance it has predominantly been valued as prefiguring Christian truth. What surely needs to complement this valuation is an appreciation of its achievement more on its own terms – from the perspective of a thousand years or more of Jewish history, the end result of mature reflection upon what has passed before. As a corpus of edited religious writings, the fruit of much painful experience, intense discussion and spiritual insight, it stands out as a monumental accomplishment. How many other nations have gained so much wisdom from their history as did ancient Israel?

As indicated already, the key moment of truth for Israel came in the 6th century BCE when hopes of achieving an independent, viable state finally collapsed. Her temple was destroyed, her monarchy disappeared, many – including the ablest among them – were taken into captivity in Babylon. Living in a 'buffer zone' of the so-called Fertile Crescent, her existence had always been precarious, with frequent attacks and incursions from bordering countries or from the major powers to the north and to the south. The perception of a few, those remarkable men known as prophets, had been that national well-being could not be bought by an abundance of sacrificial offerings, even to Yahweh himself; but hinged upon the moral integrity of the people and their leaders. As times grew more desperate in the 7th century (following the defeat of the northern kingdom) a 'Deuteronomic' reform movement gained a powerful following in Jerusalem. Jeremiah seems to have lent his support in its earlier stages, but as time went on he perceived that its political achievements (notably, the centralising of the cult in Jerusalem) were not matched by the more important deepening of faith and morality: this suggests that the law book's supposed discovery and implementation at that time [2 Kgs 22-23] were, if not fabricated, certainly exaggerated.

There proved to be ample opportunity to reflect upon all this in exile:

> By the waters of Babylon, there we sat down and wept, when we remembered Zion ... How shall we sing the Lord's song in a foreign land? [Ps 137.1,4]

One profound answer came from the scribal poet who enlarged the recorded oracles of Isaiah, Deutero-Isaiah, as he is known. He perceived that there is but one God, to whom no land therefore may be described as foreign; and further, that his purposes may mature in unexpected ways – for example, through suffering patiently borne to heal the wounds of others, or through the agency of people not previously thought to be in God's service. So he implicitly found Deuteronomic ideas too simplistic – and too limiting. If there is one God then his people are those of any race or tribe who choose to follow him:

> I will pour my Spirit upon your descendants, and my blessing on your offspring. They shall spring up like grass amid waters, like willows by flowing streams. This one will say, `I am the Lord's,' *another* will call himself by the name of Jacob, and *another* will write on his hand, 'The Lord's,' and surname himself by the name of Israel. [Isa 44.3-5]

Apart from Deutero-Isaiah, there were critics too who perceived the weakness of Josiah's reforms to be the lack of a properly moral dimension; and it was this scribal party who came into their own when return from exile became possible and probably had a decisive hand in shaping the Pentateuch and the historical books into something approaching their present form. Obviously the Torah, accompanied by the oral law which interprets it, then started to govern the life of the Jewish people – but it is actually far more than a legal code. It displays a theological perspective that has been influenced by the experience of loss and deportation and by reflections such as those of Deutero-Isaiah. It presents 'paradigms for thinking about the present or hoping for the future', in the words of a seasoned biblical scholar (James Barr). The post-exilic redaction of the Pentateuch was 'a deliberate attempt to turn it from a collection of stories

52

and laws into the foundation document of Judaism, which could act as a guide to every aspect of life within the covenant'. However ...

(1) The above assessment has yet to impact fully upon many who read (or comment on) the Old Testament. 50 years ago the prevailing textual criticism considered the Pentateuch to consist of different strands of tradition that had been (as it were) 'copied and pasted together' to comprise a single work. These strands were lettered J (a Yahwist document composed in Jerusalem perhaps in the 8th century), E (an overlapping version which referred to God as El or Elohim that had been brought south from Israel or Samaria), D (the Deuteronomists' 7th century revisionist programme) and P (emphasising Priestly regulations, especially in the post-exilic book known as Leviticus, which calls for holiness – and separation from the unclean and ungodly). Yet, while various sources were undoubtedly used in the final redaction of the Pentateuch, it is now recognised as a unified literary work, and not simply as a patchwork of texts. In particular, whereas the early chapters of Genesis (1 to 11) were at one time seen as a mythological preamble to the supposedly 'historical' account of Israel's origins, it is now regarded more highly as a theological preface to the whole Pentateuch. Its placement by the post-exilic editors at the head of the canon is no accident.

Further, their retention of different names for God, such as Yahweh, El, El Elyon, El Shaddai, may be a deliberate way of drawing attention to the important truth that he is the same God by whatever name he is called – rather than a clumsy retention of names used in the different sources. This is expressed in other ways too: he can be encountered in many different places (by Abram in Haran, by Jacob in Bethel and at the ford of the Jabbok, by Joseph in Egypt); Melchizedek can offer his blessing, which can generously be promised to Ishmael and imparted to Esau, despite their severance from Israel's stock. Of course 'foreign gods' must be 'put away' [Gen 35.2] because Yahweh is above all, the one God who created heaven and earth and everything within them, as the opening chapters of Genesis make clear.

Again, Deutero-Isaiah's perception that Yahweh's universality opens the doors of Israel to other nations is expressed frequently in the Pentateuch by the willingness of the patriarchs to take wives from beyond their native stock. So when Abraham marries Egyptian or Arab women [Gen 16.2; 25.1], when Joseph has an Egyptian wife [Gen 41.45], when Judah takes a Canaanite [Gen 38.2], and when Moses marries first Zipporah a Midianite [Exod 2.21] and then a Cushite woman [Num 12.1], the redactors are repudiating Ezra's coercive divorce of foreign women [Ezra 9-10] – making this quite explicit in the account of Miriam's punishment by God for criticising the Cushite (who is probably from Sudan or even Ethiopia).

(2) If Yahweh is now understood to be the only creator God, his beneficent activity does not cease. In particular, Israel's expectations can be renewed beyond the exile. There are in fact always new beginnings, even outside the Garden of Eden; such as Eve's conception [Gen 4.1] and then the birth of Seth in place of the murdered Abel, the blessing of Noah (whose ark was a partial recapitulation of Eden), the call of Abram, the fruitfulness of Jacob, the providential rescue of Joseph. Following the first beginnings of life mentioned in Genesis 1 and 2, there is a refrain in the chapters that follow [5.1; 6.9; 10.1; 11.10; 11.27; 25.12; 25.19; 36.1; 37.2] of successive 'generations'. This suggests that the incidents recorded 'in the beginning' and the truths imparted thereby have a perennial validity. In other words, what is told about Adam and Eve might well be told about men and women in any subsequent age; and although they are expelled from Paradise, life does not end for them there and then.

(3) Yet while God himself is characteristically creative and redemptive, human beings – even the worthiest among them – are characteristically flawed: Noah falls into drunkenness [Gen 9], Abraham is duplicitous [Gen 12; 20], Jacob is a cheat [Gen 27], Joseph is arrogant [Gen 37] and practices divination [Gen 44], Moses wavers [Num 20], Aaron apostatises [Gen 32]. There is an important emphasis here upon the role of *individuals*: the first book of the Hebrew Bible is not so much a record of the Jews' primaeval history as the story of how particular named people shaped that history in response to God's promptings and by their infidelities. Later, the books of the Kings continue the story, exhibiting the same ambiguity: Saul is a charismatic figure, indeed one of the prophets – but he exceeds his powers, first when he offers sacrifice [1 Sam 13] and again when he indulges in necromancy [1 Sam 28]; David is a hero – but after he seduces Bathsheba [2 Sam 11], a whole catalogue of misfortunes descends upon him and his family; Solomon is a wise man under whom the nation prospers – but he sows the seeds of its division and downfall, first by conscripting forced

labour [1 Kgs 5], then by permitting the worship of false gods [1 Kgs 11]. These men therefore typify and anticipate those who will follow after – and certainly men are shown faltering as much as women (such as Rachel, Rebekah, or Tamar, none of whom is flawless).

Eve, it must be stressed, is not solely to blame, despite chauvinist readings of the text. Her inclusion in the story illustrates how people stand before God both in their individual dealings and as persons-in-relationship. 'Male and female' are mentioned together first of all [Gen 1.27]. Then it is a 'man' in the singular who is formed from dust and given God's instructions; but in Genesis 3 'the man and his wife' are once again paired together and jointly bear responsibility for what transpires. The couple Adam and Eve reappear in Genesis in the dynamics between other husbands and wives; recalling that Eve is also presented as Adam's offspring, their uncertain relationship can be seen too in the tensions between parents and children e.g. within Isaac's family, while sibling pairs recur of course throughout the Bible. The final redactor would seem to be indicating that Israel's future hinged not only upon the behaviour of each individual, but also upon their dealings with each other and before God.

(4) The account of the Fall in Genesis 3 is open to diverse interpretations: here it should be noted that it relates not only to the narrative of chapter 2 but also to God's ordinance of chapter 1, and as a result leads to the blessings promised there being impaired. In Genesis 1 the words 'God said' occur ten times, making an obvious parallel with the Decalogue. The redactors thus see God's teaching, not simply as a revelation via Moses to a particular people at a formative stage of their history, but as embedded in creation and expressive of God's intention for all human beings – in line with their understanding of his universal sovereignty. A particular command is specified in Genesis 2.16-17:

> You may freely eat of every tree of the garden; but of the tree of the knowledge of good and evil you shall not eat.

When the serpent speaks to the woman, she draws attention to this command but in the end listens to him – a mere creature over whom she should have exercised 'dominion' [Gen 1.28] – rather than to God. Both human fertility and the earth's fruitfulness that were promised in chapter 1 then become more difficult to realise [Gen 3.16-19], and as the narrative unfolds barrenness and hunger recur frequently. This is the human situation, not just Israel's plight, and it may be traced to the failure to heed God's wisdom for humankind. The Fall is thus seen as a paradigm of human behaviour generally. The redactors mention specifically that the following generation – in the person of Seth [Gen 5.3] – is 'in Adam's likeness'; and this surely implies that Seth and all who come after him will be like Adam in his potential for good and for evil. If indeed Israel herself has had a chequered history, its roots lie here. The message is not unlike the sentiment expressed by Cassius in Shakespeare's Julius Caesar:

> The fault, dear Brutus, is not in our stars, but in ourselves, that we are underlings.

The result of the Fall was exclusion from the Garden – the loss of Eden. The longing for such a place, the search for an earthly Paradise, is common to most human beings. So urgent, or so misplaced, can be this longing that inhuman acts sometimes result from its pursuit. Thus, the Bible depicts the conquest of Canaan as a sequence of bloodthirsty massacres. Indeed, no sooner do Adam's sons find it necessary 'to eat bread in the sweat of their faces', than violence is born – Cain kills his brother [Gen 4.8]. Several generations later the violence has intensified:

> If Cain is avenged sevenfold, truly Lamech seventy-sevenfold. [Gen 4.24]

(5) So the earth is 'corrupt in God's sight', and 'filled with violence' [Gen 6.11]. It is saved from destruction because in each generation there are the few who find favour with God. Deutero-Isaiah expressed this in his 'servant' songs:

> It was the will of the Lord to bruise him; he has put him to grief; when he makes himself an offering for sin, he shall see his offspring, he shall prolong his days; the will of the Lord shall prosper in his hand; he shall see the fruit of the travail of his soul and be satisfied; by his knowledge shall the righteous, my servant, make many to be accounted righteous; and he shall bear their iniquities. [Isa 53.10-11]

Noah is one such person, and Abraham is another, recognised as one who intercedes effectively for the well-being of others i.e. he helps to bring about their change of heart [Gen 20.7]. There is the same stress upon the righteous few in Abraham's own pleading with God in Genesis 18, which In more technical language would be termed 'remnant theology'. Essentially it is the recognition of God's merciful goodness, who never quite despairs of the people he has made.

It is perhaps in the story of Abraham's near-sacrifice of Isaac that the heart of this mystery is glimpsed. His opening dialogue with God draws attention to the bond of love between father and son, so that Isaac's reprieve is then a witness to the enduring character of the love that God bears towards those made in his image. God's mercy is enacted too by Esau, in respect of Jacob; while Joseph refuses the opportunity to take revenge upon his brothers. Even Cain is allowed to live, protected by God's 'mark' upon him [Gen 4.15]. Like the Jewish people, however, he is not destined to live permanently flourishing in one place, but to be 'a fugitive and a wanderer on earth':

> Cain went away from the presence of the Lord, and dwelt in the land of Nod [which means 'wandering'], east of Eden.

In the Pentateuch this is the typical fate even of the apparently good and great. The last words of Genesis read:

> Joseph died ... and they embalmed him, and he was put in a coffin in Egypt. [Gen 50.26]

At the end of Deuteronomy we find Moses buried 'in the valley in the land of Moab opposite Beth-peor; but no one knows the place of his burial to this day' [Deut 34.6]. Although in post-exilic days (when these lines were written) there were strong anti-monarchic views contrasting the humility of Moses, as exhibited here, with the destructive hubris of many of Israel's kings, the obscurity of his grave in a foreign land suggests the very elusiveness of the Promised Land. After all the squandered opportunities of Israel's past life, the redactors seem to suggest that, despite God's gracious promises and his boundless mercy (of which one further reminder is the rainbow), the realisation of human dreams will forever remain elusive. In

Jewish synagogues, once this point has been reached in reading through the Pentateuch, the lectionary turns back each time to start again with Genesis.

The rise of wisdom literature

The Decalogue mentioned above in Genesis 1 was spoken at the onset of creation, long before God's teaching was given to Moses on mount Sinai. This conforms to the redactors' belief in Yahweh's universal domain, but one consequence is that, in Paul's much later words:

> Ever since the creation of the world [God's] invisible nature, namely, his eternal power and deity, has been clearly perceived in the things that have been made. [Rom 1.20]

In principle, therefore, the Hebrew scriptures do not hold a monopoly on God's truth, even though pagan cultures may have failed fully to grasp the opportunities for wisdom that God provided, having become 'futile in their thinking'. The 'wisdom' for which Solomon was renowned was in fact found in other cultures of the Ancient Near East, and it is evident that some of the material eventually collected in the book of Proverbs was sourced outside Israel herself – in Massa, which may have once been associated with the Ishmaelites [Gen 25.14]. This wisdom literature (according to a recent publication of the Vatican's International Theological Commission, entitled *'In Search of a Universal Ethic'*) 'deals with the place of man in the world. It develops the conviction that there is a correct way, a wise way, of doing things and conducting one's life ... This wisdom is not so much found in history as in *nature* and *everyday life.*' Thus, 'Go to the ant, O sluggard; consider her ways, and be wise' [Prov 6.6] is a typical piece of advice based on observation of the natural world; whereas 'A fool gives vent to his anger, but a wise man quietly holds it back' [Prov 29.11] comes from a seasoned observer of human relationships.

Even though the muted pessimism of Ecclesiastes (the Speaker) strikes many as bordering on irreligion, his conclusions are not so very different from those exhibited in the Pentateuch itself:

All the toil of man is for his mouth, yet his appetite is not satisfied. [Eccles 6.7]

This is an evil in all that is done under the sun, that one fate comes to all. [Eccles 9.3]

That which is, already has been; that which is to be, already has been. [Eccles 3.15]

There are, however, some mistaken beliefs that arise from natural observation, and here the Pentateuch's prologue [Gen 1-3] is at pains to correct them. In Babylon the Jews would have become especially aware of the importance attached to astrology, and the misreading of the cosmos. Genesis 1 places study of the heavenly bodies firmly within the context of the worship of Yahweh, ruler of the universe, emphasising that knowledge of their movements is solely to facilitate accuracy in the religious calendar:

And God said ... let [lights in the firmament] be for signs and seasons and for days and years. [Gen 1.14]

'The two great lights' [v16] are not even accorded their familiar names of 'sun' and 'moon' in a further effort to distance Israelite belief from any erroneous tendency to worship them as deities. A contrast may be observed too between v18, which allows the lights 'to rule over the day and over the night', and v28, which gives human beings 'dominion ... over every living thing that moves upon the earth', as a further reminder that the heavenly bodies are restricted in their sphere of influence. This clear teaching finds expression too in Psalm 148:

Praise him [that is, the Lord], sun and moon, praise him all you shining stars. [v2]

His name alone is exalted; his glory is above heaven and earth. [v13]

In passing, it can also be observed how a more indigenous threat to God's sovereignty is countered: the importance attached in Judaean society to omens observed in the natural world. Folk religion never really died out; and one of its features was the belief that the rustle of leaves in a tree might, at least to skilled diviners, reveal something of the future. Thus, when David inquired of the Lord, he was told:

> When you hear the sound of marching in the tops of the balsam trees, then bestir yourself; for then the Lord has gone out before you to smite the army of the Philistines. [2 Sam 5.24]

Diviners usually sat under green trees, partly because they afforded plenty of shade for their customers, but also because there was movement in them, of birds or from the wind. Their reputation depended upon reading these natural signs – hence in Genesis 2 the man is commanded:

> Of the tree of the knowledge of good and evil [an idiom for all truth – good and evil, and all that lies between] you shall not eat.

Essentially it was a prohibition against divination, to be set alongside the ban on astrology. The point being emphasised was that the future cannot be known, and is not to be manipulated: it lies in God's hands. This is the conclusion that Job (in one of the greatest wisdom writings) struggles to discover for himself. God rebukes him for his arrogance:

> Who is this that darkens counsel by words without knowledge ... Where were you when I laid the foundations of the earth ... Can you bind the chains of the Pleiades, or loose the cords of Orion ... Do you know when the mountain goats bring forth ... [and so on]?

Finally Job abases himself:

> I have uttered what I did not understand, things too wonderful for me, which I did not know. [Job 42.3]

Here is a pertinent comment from the document already cited, from the International Theological Commission, which has the subtitle 'A new look at the Natural Law':

> The sages do not underestimate the lessons of history and their value as divine revelation, but they have a vivid awareness that the connections among events depend on a coherence that is not itself an historical event ... Wisdom searches for principles and structural laws rather than precise historical perspectives. In so doing, wisdom literature concentrates on protology, namely, on creation at the beginning along with what it implies. In fact, protology attempts to describe the coherence that is found behind

historical events ... History describes these elements in a successive manner: wisdom goes beyond history towards an a-temporal description of what constitutes reality at the time of creation, 'in the beginning', when human beings were created in the image of God.

In this sense, the early chapters of Genesis can be seen as a foundational exercise in wisdom literature, setting out fundamental patterns that will recur throughout history, governing the way God has made the world.

From this same perspective the Torah, the five books of God's teaching are [so the ITC document argues] 'like the incarnation of Wisdom':

If you desire wisdom, keep the commandments, and the Lord will supply it for you. [Sir 1.26]

Indeed, for ben Sira wisdom was God's greatest blessing, as fruitful as Eden itself [Sir 24.25-27]. But wisdom, as noted already, is not found only in the Torah; it is also the result of discerning observation of nature and of human behaviour. Above all, it is gifted from God himself:

I called upon God, and the spirit of wisdom came to me. [Wis 7.7]

Postscript: the perennial search for 'the Promised Land'

The enduring value of these ancient scriptures is not simply as a precursor to the Christian gospel. The issues explored in these writings, whether through narratives, poetry, or the mature conclusions of wise commentators, continue to arise generation after generation. I offer one example here – the human quest for a 'Promised Land'.

In Matthew Kneale's novel *English Passengers* the year is 1857. The Reverend Geoffrey Wilson charters a ship to verify his belief that

The Garden of Eden was not, as supposed, located in the region of Arabia, but was instead in Australia, on the island of Tasmania.

The aboriginals whom he meets on arrival have already been decimated, and to a degree brutalised, by British colonial forces. A young captive named Peevay has acquired a little English and for the benefit of his mother (bearing the symbolic name of Mary) explains what Eden means:

> Eden Garden was made by white man's God long long ago, to put two white
> men inside, till he got hateful and made them eat special fruit and go away.

Wilson's expedition then sets off up the Derwent river, taken to be the biblical Euphrates, into the interior for what proves to be the inevitable fruitless search. A disbelieving companion named Potter protests,

> Can't you see, you ninny? There is no Garden of Eden here. There never was.

But Wilson presses on convinced that Potter is the devil incarnate and that 'Eden would yet be found'. After near disaster the party is forced to abandon its mission and to return to England. Wilson muses,

> Was Eden here, in England, all along? Is this the answer? Has all of this
> venture merely been some kind of grand test?

He ends his days in cheerful imbecility on the Isle of Wight, where the locals call him the Messiah:

> When a visitor appears the Messiah delights in showing him a little
> overgrown patch of land, close beside his simple home, where the pigs used
> to bask in the sun, and which he quite insists is the Garden of Eden!

The biblical allusions here are many: the finding of a place of primeval innocence, emptied of its original people and now guarded by British soldiers against their return; Wilson's blind faith opposed by a demonic Potter, who attempts to give him the benefit of scientific knowledge and open his eyes; then the messianic discovery of a tiny, promised land from which, we note, the pigs (animals forbidden to the Jews) have been excluded; and all of these in a context of arduous journeys like those of the patriarchs (and the Jewish people as a whole) which test Wilson, the upholder of the established religion, to the limit, until at last he returns from exile. His final self-delusion is brought home to us by the 'overgrown' state of his garden, evidently no Eden but a place where thorns and thistles flourish (cf. Genesis 3.18). Yet perhaps that is where our Edens are really to be found, this side of heaven? Is this the thesis behind the Pentateuch as well (in which a heavenly Paradise is not an option)?

The story is not historically implausible. Many interpreters have sought a location for Eden as somewhere that either once existed (as in Genesis 2, where it is described as being 'in the east', perhaps Mesopotamia) or may yet be found (as in the promise to Abraham). In the later book of Jubilees (and in Sirach 24) Eden is mentioned as towards Arabia. Early Christian writers also tried their hand with Eden's rivers: the Gihon was generally held to be the Nile, but the Pishon attracted various solutions – for Ephrem the Syrian it was the Danube, but for Ambrose it was the Ganges. The rabbinic conclusion was finally that 'Eden ... is a special place and no mortal knows where it is'. But perhaps Augustine of Hippo should have the last word: scripture, he explained, may be understood 'in several ways, all of which may yet be true' including meanings which the writer never had in mind.

6. Messianic Expectations

God's new age

Notwithstanding Israel's long history of hopes defeated or deferred, and despite the theological realism (or even pessimism) that emerged in the later stages of the Hebrew Bible's evolution, there were those who refused to accept that subjugation to occupying powers was inevitable and immutable. There was, after all, scriptural warrant for a far more peaceful and prosperous future. It was claimed that a divine promise had been made to Abraham:

> I will make of you a great nation, and I will bless you. [Gen 12.2]

Likewise king David had apparently been assured by God (as no doubt others with dynastic ambitions might be tempted so to assert):

> I will build you a house. [2 Sam 7.27 cf. 22.51; Ps 89.4]

If the exile in Babylon had been merited on account of Israel's failings, the Pentateuch itself witnessed to many justly deserved setbacks that had been reversed in due time by God's mercy. Hence, as Alexander Pope was much later to express it in his poem *An Essay on Man* in 1734:

> Hope springs eternal in the human breast;
> Man never is, but always to be blessed:
> The soul, uneasy and confined from home,
> Rests and expatiates in a life to come.

The emphasis certainly lay for a long time much more on 'the life to come' than on any human agent through whom it might be achieved. It may reasonably be described as a 'messianic' expectation, a longing for the day of the Lord when he would bring deliverance, rather than the more explicit hope for a Messiah. Although the experience of exile intensified this longing, there are intimations to be found in pre-exilic writings [e.g. Isa 2.2-4] – yet there were warnings too that 'the day of the Lord' might be 'darkness' rather than light [Amos 5.18]. It is, however, never easy to be confident about dating specific oracles, since the prophetic collections were often modified and augmented over the years.

The desire for an upright ruler (modelled on David) was sometimes expressed in what would later be interpreted as 'messianic prophecies':

> For to us a child is born, to us a son is given; and the government will be upon his shoulder, and his name will be called 'Wonderful Counsellor, Mighty God, Everlasting Father, Prince of Peace.' Of the increase of his government and of peace there will be no end, upon the throne of Davidand over his kingdom, to establish it, and to uphold it with justice and with righteousness from this time forth and for evermore. The zeal of the Lord of hosts will do this. [Isa 9.6-7 cf. 11.1-5]
>
> But you, O Bethlehem Eph'rathah, who are little to be among the clans of Judah, from you shall come forth for me one who is to be ruler in Israel, whose origin is from of old, from ancient days. And he shall stand and feed his flock in the strength of the Lord, in the majesty of the name of the Lord his God. [Mic 5.2, 4]

Such hopes were reiterated as the land faced an increasingly bleaker future:

> Behold, the days are coming, says the Lord, when I will raise up for David a righteous Branch, and he shall reign as king and deal wisely, and shall execute justice and righteousness in the land. [Jer 23.5]

It comes as a real surprise, therefore, to realise that at a crucial point in Israel's history, when her leaders and men of substance were in Babylonian captivity, the first person to be acclaimed as the 'anointed' one (Heb. *mashiah* Gk *christos*, in English *anointed* or sometimes *Messiah / Christ*) was a foreigner viz. Cyrus, founder of the Achaemenid Empire which now included Babylon:

> Thus says the Lord to his anointed, to Cyrus, whose right hand I have grasped ... [Isa 45.1 cf. 2 Chron 36.22; Ezra 1.1-3][11]

The initial euphoria may have been heightened by the recognition that Cyrus' religion – presumably a form of Zoroastrianism – was not altogether

---

[11] In the 2nd century BCE *Sybilline Oracles* [3.652] there is a similar reference to a foreign overlord who would intervene at the behest of 'the great God'.

incompatible with Israel's own beliefs: indeed, over time certain 'cross-cultural' exchanges are likely to have occurred. The mood undoubtedly changed, however, after a good number were then allowed to return, only to discover the sorry condition of their ravaged homeland. Joel, who seems to date somewhat later, following the Temple's delayed restoration, makes no mention of a king but sees the day of the Lord in more apocalyptic terms. It will be a 'terrible' day of judgement, followed by an outpouring of God's spirit 'on all flesh' [2.28 cf. Isa 32.15; 44.3]:

> And Jerusalem shall be holy and strangers shall never again pass through it.
> [3.17 cf. Isa 35.8-10]

In the messianic age, therefore, it is not only Israel's leaders who will be radically different; the same will be true of all God's people, potentially inclusive of others who acknowledge his sovereignty [e.g. Zech 8.20-23; 14.16]

The apocalyptic current grew much stronger, no doubt because of the increasingly adverse political circumstances at first under the Hellenistic king Antiochus Epiphanes (175 to 164 BCE), but subsequently under the Romans and their oppressive Hasmonean regents from the later 2nd century BCE onwards. In Daniel 7.13, the 'night vision' is recorded of 'one like a son of man', coming 'with the clouds of heaven' to be God's earthly ruler. Supernatural agents of deliverance i.e. angels are also seen at work:

> At that time shall arise Michael, the great prince who has charge of your people [Dan 12.1]

Following this, *The Psalms of Solomon* (mid 1st century BCE) has a fuller account of the expected Messiah than almost any other Jewish writing. It draws upon texts already noted from 2 Samuel and the Book of Psalms:

> Behold, O Lord, and raise up for them their king, the son of David, at the time which you choose, O God, to rule over your servant Israel.
> And gird him with strength, to shatter unjust rulers, to purge Jerusalem from nations that trample her down to destruction;
> in the wisdom of righteousness to thrust out sinners from their inheritance
> ... to crush all their substance with a rod of iron;
> to destroy the lawless nations with the word of his mouth ...

And he will purge Jerusalem and make it holy as it was from the beginning,
for nations will come from the ends of the earth to see his glory ...
There will be no unrighteousness among them in his days, for all shall be
holy,
And their king shall be the Lord Messiah. [*Ps Sol* 17.21-24, 30-32]

One specific target within Jerusalem to be 'purged' was the high priestly
dynasty itself, regarded by many as lacking in true zeal for God's law, if not
actually corrupt. This was the position of the Pharisaic party, and certainly
of the Essenes who withdrew into monastic seclusion at Qumran by the
Dead Sea, according to archaeologists in the 2nd century BCE.

The Dead Sea Scrolls, the first of which were discovered by chance in
1947 in earthenware jars hidden for safety within a cave, with subsequent
searches revealing hundreds of similar finds in another ten caves, suggest
that the community was established by the Teacher of Righteousness ('to
whom God made known all the mysteries ... of his servants the prophets')
who fled from Jerusalem after clashing with the so-called Wicked Priest.
Among the manuscripts are copies of most books of the Hebrew Bible,
together with apocryphal or pseudepigraphical writings such as Sirach,
Tobit, 1 Enoch, Jubilees (which – with its vision of a messianic age about to
dawn – was especially important, to judge by the fourteen or more copies
that were found). In addition, documents composed at Qumran were also
discovered, and these provide considerable knowledge about their
community life and aspirations. Of particular interest to our present theme
is *The War of the Sons of Light against the Sons of Darkness*, which depicts
the community preparing for the battle to end all battles:

On the shield of the Leader of the whole nation they shall write his name,
the names Levi, Israel and Aaron, and the names of the twelve tribes of
Israel. [*1QM* 5.1]

As well as specifying details for the conduct of the battle, the document
offers further teaching contrasting the spirits of truth and perversity, as
found elsewhere in *The Rule of the Community* (formerly known as *The
Manual of Discipline*). It envisages a long drawn-out 'holy war' between the
forces of good and evil, with spiritual forces ranged alongside the earthly
combatants. A messianic being is indicated in several of the scrolls, but a

debate continues as to his envisaged role – and indeed as to whether two different Messiahs were expected. The key verse, found in *The Rule*, reads as follows:

> ... until there shall come a Prophet and the Messiah of Aaron and Israel. [*1QS* 9.11]

The difficulties of interpretation are manifold: (1) texts used for purposes of comparison may be very fragmentary; (2) the community's ideas evolved during their years at Qumran, which lasted until 68 CE when their settlement was destroyed by the Romans;[12] (3) the word *mashiah* does not necessarily refer to a Messiah each time it appears – an 'anointed' priestly or kingly figure may sometimes be indicated;[13] (4) earlier biblical (but possibly non-messianic) verses may have influenced the phraseology used e.g. Zechariah 4.14 (cf. 6.11-12) mentions 'the two anointed who stand by the Lord of the whole earth', while Hebrew parallelism as in Numbers 24.17 ('a star ... and a sceptre') or in Deuteronomy 33.8 ('Levi ... thy godly one') may also lie in the background.[14]

So the Messiah's role envisaged by the Qumran community remains uncertain: is he projected as a war leader, as a prophet, as a teacher of God's law, as a ruler of the new Israel, as a priest – or as God's agent is he *sui generis*, beyond any conventional expectation? In the heralded fulfilment of the role by Jesus a document popularly known as the *Messianic Apocalypse* is of particular interest. It includes a variation on the verse from Isaiah also cited in Jesus' 'manifesto' at Nazareth [Lk 4.18]:

> [The Messiah] will heal the wounded, and revive the dead and bring good news to the poor. [*4Q521*, 12 cf. Isa 61.1]

---

[12] J.Fitzmyer: *Essays on the Semitic Background of the NT* (Missoula 1974, 55) notes 'there is no evidence at Qumran of a systematic, uniform exegesis of the OT'.

[13] L.D.Hurst: *Did Qumran Expect Two Messiahs?* (Bulletin for Biblical Research 9, 1999, 157-180)

[14] J.J.Collins: *The Scepter and the Star* (Grand Rapids 2010, 95-96) suggests that the 2nd century BCE composition *Jubilees* – evidently popular at Qumran – in which 'two of Jacob's sons are singled out for special blessing: first Levi, and then Judah' [31.14,18] anticipates a Messiahship of both priest and prince.

'Messiahs' of the 1st century CE

Other writings emerged in the 1st century CE, sometimes featuring a messianic figure but more generally expressing longings for a radically different messianic age. Nevertheless, there were a number of individuals who claimed a messianic role, or who might be seen in that light, most of whom (according to the Jewish writer Josephus, the chief source of historical information about this period of Judaean life) were seen as a threat by the ruling authorities. When Herod the Great died in 4 BCE he was succeeded by his son Herod Archelaus, although in the end the Romans allowed his brothers to rule adjacent territories beyond Judaea. During this time of instability, various opportunists are mentioned by Josephus:

> At Sepphoris in Galilee Judas, son of Hezekiah [a 'robber chief' during Herod the Great's reign], collected a considerable force, broke into the royal armoury, equipped his followers, and attacked the other seekers after power. In Peraea Simon, one of the royal slaves, considered that his good looks and great stature entitled him to set a crown on his own head. Then he went round with a band of robbers and burnt down the palace in Jericho and many magnificent country residences, securing easy plunder for himself out of the flames … The palace at Betharamatha near the Jordan was burnt down by another gang from Peraea. A third claimant to the throne was a shepherd called Athrongaeus, whose hopes were based on his physical strength and contempt of death … He set a crown on his own head, but continued for a considerable time to raid the country with his brothers … they were harrassing all Judaea with their brigandage. [*The Jewish War* 2.1]

Sometimes these insurrections were responses to provocations by the Romans themselves, such as the census 'when Quirinius was governor of Syria' [Lk 2.2] which was regarded as a direct challenge to God's own sovereignty, or when Pilate 'secretly and under cover conveyed to Jerusalem the [graven] images of Caesar' which certainly defiled the sanctity of the holy city. 'Claimants to the throne' were not necessarily settting themselves up in a messianic role, but the general instability so engendered no doubt contributed to heightened messianic expectations.

Josephus mentions other figures active in the early 1st century CE who may have been perceived by their followers as messianic because of the prophetic mantle that they wore. These are found in his later work *Antiquities of the Jews*. There was, for example, Theudas (also mentioned in Acts 5.36, although there are discrepancies between Josephus' chronology and Luke's):

> A certain charlatan, whose name was Theudas, persuaded a great part of the people to take their effects with them, and follow him to the Jordan river; for he told them he was a prophet, and that he would, by his own command, divide the river, and afford them an easy passage over it. Many were deluded by his words. However, Fadus did not permit them to make any advantage of his wild attempt, but sent a troop of horsemen out against them. After falling upon them unexpectedly, they slew many of them, and took many of them alive. They also took Theudas alive, cut off his head, and carried it to Jerusalem. [*Ant* 20]

He writes too of John the Baptist:

> [He] was a good man, and commanded the Jews to exercise virtue, both as to righteousness towards one another, and piety towards God, and so to come to baptism; for that the washing would be acceptable to him, if they made use of it, not in order to the putting away of some sins [only], but for the purification of the body; supposing still that the soul was thoroughly purified beforehand by righteousness. Now when others came in crowds about him, for they were very greatly moved by hearing his words, Herod, who feared lest the great influence John had over the people might put it into his power and inclination to raise a rebellion (for they seemed ready to do anything he should advise), thought it best, by putting him to death, to prevent any mischief he might cause. [*Ant* 18]

The presentation here differs somewhat from the references found in the Gospels, which suggest that his message may have been seen more in 'messianic' terms than as a call to moral revival:

> In those days came John the Baptist, preaching in the wilderness of Judaea, 'repent, for the kingdom of God is at hand.' [Mt 3.1-2]

John's recorded location in the Jordan valley, not so far from Qumran, makes it likely that he was aware of Essene teachings and expectations. The

Gospels present him as a prophet sent to 'prepare the way of the Lord' [Mk 1.3 cf. Isa 40.3]:

> And John, calling to him two of his disciples, sent them to the Lord, saying, 'Are you he who is to come, or shall we look for another?' [Lk 7.19 cf. Mt 11.3]

While a number of John's disciples were undoubtedly drawn to follow Jesus [e.g. Andrew according to John 1.41], it seems that John the Baptist himself never quite committed himself, despite his claimed identification of Jesus as 'the Lamb of God' in the Fourth Gospel [Jn 1.36]. Apollos features in the book of Acts as an apparently later convert, who completed his Christian formation in Ephesus. On arrival there, however,

> He spoke and taught accurately the things concerning Jesus, though he knew only the baptism of John. [Acts 18.25]

Hence, while John's mission was endorsed by Jesus in his symbolic baptism in the Jordan, his role came to be interpreted by Christians as that of the Messiah's 'predicted' forerunner [e.g. Mal 3.1]. However, his identification as the new Elijah [Mt 11.14 cf. Mal 4.5] is not entirely consistent with Malachi's message that 'Elijah' would be sent 'before the great and terrible day of the Lord'.

We shall return shortly to the question of Jesus' understanding of his own role, but it will by now be clear that during the 1st century CE Judaea experienced political and religious unrest sufficient to foster a wide variety of responses. Josephus' narratives [cf. Acts 21.37-38] include further armed uprisings that culminated in the Great Revolt that broke out in 66 CE and lasted for several years. In his view, messianic beliefs were the root cause of this rebellion:

> But what more than all else incited them to the war was an ambiguous oracle also found in their sacred writings, that 'At about that time, one from their country would become ruler of the habitable world.' This they took to mean one of their own people, and many of the wise men were misled in their interpretation. This oracle, however, in reality signified the government of Vespasian, who was proclaimed Emperor while in Judea. [*The Jewish War* 6.5]

The destruction of the Temple in 70 CE led to the composition of further apocalypses, especially *2 Baruch* (featuring the appearance of a Messiah) and *4 Ezra* (with a vision of the heavenly Jerusalem). Of uncertain date may be mentioned too *The Similitudes of Enoch*, which has an interesting correspondence with the Matthaean parable of the sheep and the goats. In both Matthew's Gospel and *The Similitudes* the Son of Man appears as the messianic King who comes with the angels [cf. Dan 7.13-14] to sit on a glorious throne, where he judges the nations. The mutual interaction between Jewish and Christian apocryphal literature gradually becomes more evident from this time onwards (and may later have influenced some of the traditions lying behind the Qur'an). Many apocalyptic themes were taken up in the explosion of rabbinic texts and commentaries over the ensuing centuries, although these are not usually the main focus of interest. It should be noted that where a Messiah features in them, he is God's agent of salvation or judgement, but not a divine being to be worshipped.

Jesus' self-references

One thing stands out from the Gospel narratives: Jesus resisted attempts to be labelled by his contemporaries, knowing that they would too readily categorise him according to pre-conceived ideas. This surely lies behind the Markan passages often referred to as exhibiting a secrecy motif e.g.

'See that you say nothing to anyone.' [Mk 1.44]
He strictly ordered them not to make him known. [Mk 3.12]

On a later occasion Jesus is shown apparently refuting the common idea that 'the Christ is the son of David' [Mk 12.35]. Although this might seem to align him with the Samaritan idea that the Messiah would be a prophet like Moses [Deut 18.18] and would bring restoration (including true worship) to Israel – meaning the northern territory – that notion is also disabused [Jn 4.19-25]. It is very clear in the Gospels that all who encounter him need to set aside their inherited assumptions. Even when (in the Fourth Gospel) he appears to admit his messianic identity, his answer has a clear resonance with his 'I am' sayings elsewhere:

Jesus said to (the woman): 'I who speak to you am he.' [Jn 4.26]

The reader is therefore reminded of the enigmatic 'I AM WHO I AM' in conversation with Moses [Exod 3.14], whose reply to 'wrestling' Jacob is similarly elusive, 'Why is it that you ask my name?' [Gen 32.29].

The disciples themselves are on a learning curve, and from time to time are reproached for their lack of understanding. Although Peter identifies Jesus as 'the Christ', the disciples are then charged 'to tell no one about him' [Mk 8.29-30]. This instruction is demonstrably justified when immediately afterwards Peter finds himself rebuked for resisting the idea of Jesus' suffering and death:

> Get behind me, Satan! For you are not on the side of God, but of men. [Mk 8.33]

A similar misunderstanding of Jesus' mission is in fact common to all the disciples:

> And James and John, the sons of Zeb'edee, came forward to him, and said to him, Teacher, we want you to do for us whatever we ask of you.' And he said to them, 'What do you want me to do for you?' And they said to him, 'Grant us to sit, one at your right hand and one at your left, in your glory.' But Jesus said to them, 'You do not know what you are asking.'
> ...
> And when the ten heard it, they began to be indignant at James and John. And Jesus called them to him and said to them, 'You know that those who are supposed to rule over the Gentiles lord it over them, and their great men exercise authority over them. But it shall not be so among you; but whoever would be great among you must be your servant, and whoever would be first among you must be slave of all. For the Son of man also came not to be served but to serve, and to give his life as a ransom for many.' [Mk 10.36-45]

While the stress here (and elsewhere e.g. Matthew 11.4-5; Luke 11.20) is upon 'service' rather than 'power politics', the reference to 'the Son of man' raises several questions:
(1) Is this frequent self-designation of Jesus his own – or did the early Church, reflecting upon texts such as Daniel 7.13, find it an appropriate ascription? The fact that Jesus' use of the idiom largely coincides with that of the Old Testament (i.e. in the majority of instances it is a simple self-

reference but subsequently took on a specific designation in relation to the approaching last day) suggests that Jesus did indeed speak in this manner; it seems unlikely that the evangelists would extend the 'messianic' application to other apparently 'mundane' uses.

(2) If it was indeed Dominical, why does the title 'the Son of man' hardly occur outside the Gospels (i.e. other than in Acts 7.56 and twice in the Apocalypse)? Since the majority of writings that omit the phrase are Pauline, or deutero-Pauline, the issue is perhaps related to Paul's other omissions e.g. of much of Jésus' teaching material. His letters were usually a response to specific church issues, and his predominant concern was to instil – in a largely gentile context – a Christian pattern of thought that arose from the key truths of Christ's death and resurrection. In fact, it is arguable that the idea of the 'Son of man' is found in Pauline thought in the guise of (Christ as) the 'new' Adam [Rom 5.14; 1 Cor 15.22, 45].

(3) If Jesus thought of himself as 'the Son of man', was it a messianic title? It may be best to think of the phrase as a common idiom appropriated to his own use, with the potential to be both a self-deprecating reference consistent with his vocation of service but also capable of extension to his role in God's salvific plan for humanity. It has been observed frequently in recent years that the use of the definite article (*the* Son of Man) distinguishes this phrase from its many appearances in earlier writings, which suggests that it indicated at least one way of looking at Jesus' unique role. According to Mark, the description was used at a crucial point in Jesus' trial:

> Again the high priest asked him, 'Are you the Christ, the Son of the Blessed?' And Jesus said, 'I am; and you will see the Son of man seated at the right hand of Power, and coming with the clouds of heaven.' [Mk 14.61-62]

So Jesus' acknowledgement of the coming fulfilment of his messianic role is linked by Mark to the imagery used previously in his teaching ministry.

Of course, the truth of who Jesus was cannot be summarised in any single expression. No doubt this is one reason (other than the political folly of being too candid) why Matthew and Luke record even more ambiguous responses to the interrogation he underwent before the Sanhedrin and then Pilate:

[*Before the priests*] You have said so. [Mt 26.64]

If I tell you, you will not believe. [Lk 22.67]

[*Before Pilate*] He gave him no answer. [Mt 27.14]

You have said so. [Lk 23.3]

Similar equivocation is found In the Fourth Gospel, although it is expressed in typical Johannine dialogue:

I have spoken openly to the world ... I have said nothing secretly ... Do you say this of your own accord, or did others say it to you about me? [Jn 18.20; 34]

My kingship is not of this world; if my kingship were of this world, my servants would fight. [Jn 18.36]

'So you are a king?' Jesus answered, 'You say that I am a king.' [Jn 18.37 cf. Mk 15.2]

Jesus appears to have spoken much about the kingdom of God, which on occasion he termed 'my kingdom' [Mt 19.28; Lk 22.30]. This, together with public occasions when he suggested that his personal mission as the Lord's 'anointed' was the fulfilment of prophetic verses [Isa 61.1-2 cf. Lk 4.16-21; Isa 35.5-6 cf. Mt 11.2 and Lk 7.22] – above all, his triumphal entry into Jerusalem 'humble and riding on an ass' [Zech 9.9], recorded in all four Gospels – may have given sufficient ammunition to those who later mocked him as a 'Messiah' [Mt 26.68; Mk 15.32]. The latter event gave place shortly afterwards to the ultimate humiliation of the Cross, which sealed his decisive departure from Jewish messianic paradigms. His crucifixion 'led to a searching of the Scriptures and to a new, creative exegesis of messianic prophecy' – including the confirmation of his divine status.[15]

The evangelists themselves were in no doubt that *properly understood* Jesus was indeed the Messiah e.g. Mark 1.1-3; John 20.31. In later decades, at the time they were writing, this was the issue that in some places was the most contentious:

The Jews had already agreed that if anyone should confess [Jesus] to be Christ, he was to be put out of the synagogue. [Jn 9.22 cf. 12.42]

---

[15] Collins 236-7

Indeed, despite his proclamation of God's coming kingdom as one of life in abundance, Jesus had also warned of such developments e.g. John 16.2.

Jesus' followers were first called Christians, according to the book of Acts, in Antioch [Acts 11.26], which, combined with the only two other New Testament references [Acts 26.28; 1 Pet 4.16], suggests strongly that it was a term of abuse and indeed derision. Josephus states:

> The tribe of Christians, so named from him, is not extinct at this day. [*Ant* 18.3]

Tacitus too, writing towards the end of the 1st century CE, recorded in his *Annals* that 'by vulgar appellation [they were] commonly called Christians'. Yet half a century later, when the majority of Christians now came from non-Jewish backgrounds, the origins of the name had largely been forgotten. It meant simply 'a follower of Jesus Christ', whose second name was a mark of identification – a surname – rather than a messianic title.

When Gregory of Nyssa elucidated the meaning of the word 'Christ' in the 4th century CE, his authority is St Paul:

> He taught us what was meant by the name 'Christ' when he said that Christ was the power and the wisdom of God, and called him 'peace' and the thirty unapproachable lights in which God dwells ... [He then lists roughly other descriptions found in Paul's letters, not one of which is 'the anointed One'] ... He applied to Christ many other such titles and it is not easy to give a list of them all. If you take them all and compare them, contributing to the total picture the meaning of each of the epithets, then you will grasp the full meaning of that word 'Christ' and that will show us, in so far as we can understand it in our soul, his inexpressible greatness ... It follows then that there must be seen in us [Christians] too all the meanings of that word, so that the title is seen not to be false and meaningless but to be proved by our life. [*On Christian Perfection* PG 46, 254-255]

The controversial debate so prominent in Jesus' lifetime and evidently the principal issue at his trial had thus long since been overshadowed by much wider reflections. Indeed, the believer's hope was less focused on the prospects of God's earthly kingdom than on his own life in eternity. We shall consider this theme in the concluding chapter.

PART 2

Assessing the Christian Writings

The earliest known fragment of the New Testament (John18.31-33)
early 2ⁿᵈ century, discovered in Egypt
and now in the John Rylands Library, Manchester.

7. The Earliest Christian Witnesses

Discoveries, doubts and discrepancies

Over the past couple of hundred years archaeologists in the field and researchers in their libraries have discovered a number of early Christian documents, often very incomplete or even in tiny fragments, which were previously unknown – or in some cases were mentioned in ancient texts but otherwise were thought to be lost. Among famous relatively recent finds are the aforementioned Dead Sea Scrolls (although these come from a Jewish sect, the Qumran community) and the Nag Hammadi manuscripts found in the desert of Upper Egypt. Their immensely fragile condition has required much painstaking work before the contents could be deciphered. Hence with such finds there is generally a long gap between discovery and publication – sometimes extended when squabbles over ownership have had to be resolved. Occasionally the media's interest has been aroused, with sensational headlines such as 'Jesus secretly married to Mary Magdalene' or 'Judas Iscariot was rehabilitated after all'. And finally, along comes Dan Brown, whose best-selling titles have persuaded the more gullible members of the public that for two thousand years the Church has conspired to conceal the truth about what really happened.

At the same time, the world of scholarship has not been idle in examining the traditional texts, among them the four Gospels. The so-called 'Jesus Seminar', founded in the USA in 1985, has taken scepticism to extreme limits. The group decides on their collective view of the activities and sayings of Jesus by casting votes. Unconcerned with canonical boundaries, they claim that the *Gospel of Thomas* may have more authentic material than the Gospel of John. They conclude that Jesus was a mortal man, born of two human parents, who did not perform nature miracles nor did he rise bodily from the dead: resurrection experiences can be attributed to the fevered imagination of some of his disciples. Among more reputable scholars there can also be doubtful methodological approaches, where too much reliance is placed upon subjective evaluations of the text or upon a particular theory of its composition. The end result may well be a variety of differing or even incompatible conclusions.

Even without scholarly expertise, a plain reading of the Gospels will discover factual contradictions between them: for example, on such and such an occasion did Jesus cure one man or was it two? What were the names of the twelve chosen disciples, given that the recorded lists differ about the less well known characters? On what day did the Last Supper take place – on the Passover itself or on the evening before? Who really did discover the empty tomb, and how many appearances did the risen Jesus make on Easter Day (and afterwards)? There is also a sharp contrast between the pithy, sometimes poetical, sayings of Jesus recorded in the Synoptic Gospels (Matthew, Mark and Luke) and the often lengthier discourses attributed to him in the Fourth Gospel: so which of these was Jesus' authentic manner of speaking? And if so much weight is attached in these writings to what Jesus said and taught, why does Paul hardly make any reference to such teachings in his letters, focusing as he does on the meaning of his death and resurrection? This is just a sample of features that continue to puzzle us. Yet we are certainly not the first generation of Christians to have noticed them, so perhaps we can take heart that they have not in the end proved an insuperable barrier to accepting the slightly varying testimony offered in the New Testament. The church fathers were well aware of these difficulties, and were often robust in defending the unity and harmony of the Gospels.

A comparison with other historical recollections is not out of place here. In Primo Levi's review of Holocaust memories he wrote:

> It almost never happens that two eyewitnesses of the same event describe it in the same way and with the same words, even if the event is recent and neither of them has a personal interest in distorting it ... It is certain that practice (in this case, frequent re-evocation) keeps memories fresh and alive in the same manner in which a muscle that is often used remains efficient.

Yet a note of caution is in place:

> Among the testimonies, written or heard, there are also those that are unconsciously stylised, in which convention prevails over genuine memory.[16]

Eyewitnesses

---

[16] Primo Levi: *The Damned and the Saved* (London 1988, 11, 53]

It is also easy to assume that those for whom the earliest Gospels were written were entirely uncritical i.e. prepared to accept their 'accuracy' or 'authenticity' without questioning. This is not Luke's own position:

> Inasmuch as many have undertaken to compile a narrative of the things which have been accomplished among us, just as they were delivered to us by those who from the beginning were eyewitnesses and ministers of the word, it seemed good to me also, having followed all things closely for some time past, to write an orderly account for you, most excellent Theophilus, [Lk 1.1-3]

Previous narratives had evidently been attempted, although to describe them as 'many' may perhaps be a conventional stylistic flourish; nevertheless, Luke has arguably made use of the existing works of Mark and of Matthew, even if other early examples of this genre have disappeared without trace. When he affirms that his is an 'orderly' account, the likeliest meaning is that he has tried to arrange his material in better *chronological* order. While it must be accepted that his ordering is not necessarily definitive, it is his concern for fidelity to the reports handed on 'by those who from the beginning were eyewitnesses' that stands out. In the ancient world written sources were sometimes available, but it was invariably oral testimony – what Quintilian, Luke's contemporary, termed 'living voices' – that was preferred. This can be traced as far back as Thucydides:

> He attacks the lack of care others take in ascertaining facts, and asserts that he was not satisfied with any one eyewitness account, but took great pains to correlate and judge between the often differing accounts of different participants.[17]

In the 2nd century BCE Polybius suggested three main methods of inquiry: if the historian was not himself an eyewitness, he should investigate the evidence of those who were, and also be prepared to hear (or read) memoirs of what had taken place:

---

[17] Oswyn Murray: *Greek Historians* (OHCW 1995, 193)

He reconciles these beliefs by a theory centring on the Greek term *emphasis*, which covers the authoritative impression given by a writer, the vivid significance of the events he recounts, and the powerful impression left in the reader's mind.[18]

The object was not simply to provide an accurate record of historical facts, but to bring them to life. So the sources used might be conflated or compressed, or imaginatively paraphrased – especially with a view to the end result being read out loud. Luke and the evangelists who came both before and after him were not documenting events for the archives, but communicating life-giving truths. In Paul's words:

> I would remind you, brethren, in what terms I preached to you the gospel, which you received, in which you stand, by which you are saved. [1 Cor 15.1-2]

The canonical Gospels certainly display a keen awareness that Jesus' disciples were chosen with this task of 'witnessing' in mind:

> He appointed twelve to be with him, and to be sent out to preach. [Mk 3.14-15]
> He said to them, 'To you has been given the secret of the kingdom of heaven. [Mk 4.11]
> You also are witnesses, because you have been with me from the beginning. [Jn15.27]
> Jesus did many other signs in the presence of his disciples, which are not written in this book. [Jn 20.30]

In the book of Acts, the prime witnesses are met together in Jerusalem following Jesus' ascension:

> Peter and John and James and Andrew, Philip and Thomas, Bartholomew and Matthew, James the son of Alphaeus and Simon the Zealot and Judas the son of James, all these with one accord devoted themselves to prayer, together with the women and Mary the mother of Jesus, and with his brothers. [Acts 1.13-14]

---

[18] Andrew Lintott: *Roman Historians* (OHCW 1995, 640)

The named disciples could bear testimony to Jesus' teaching and ministry, but 'the women' are perhaps mentioned particularly as witnesses of the crucifixion. In addition, Mary knew of his birth and 'his brothers' of his upbringing in Nazareth. Collectively, all aspects of his life, death and resurrection were covered.

It should be added that, although the preaching of the gospel was therefore thoroughly resourced, it was never the intention of any of the gospel writers to include everything that was known. 'John' (i.e. the author of the Fourth Gospel) states the purpose of his record:

> These (*omitting the 'many other signs' that had been witnessed cf. Jn 21.25*) are written that you may believe that Jesus is the Christ, the Son of God, and that believing you may have life in his name. [Jn 20.31]

The evangelist is thus indicating the principle lying behind his careful selectivity. Luke likewise wants his reader(s) to know 'the truth concerning the things of which you have been informed' [Lk 1.4], which again suggests not only the weighing of evidence, but also the omission of less reliable or less important facets of Theophilus' information.

We even have a summary of what was considered to be necessary to qualify as a reliable eyewitness. When it came to replacing Judas Iscariot, Peter summarised the required *curriculum vitae*:

> So one of the men who have accompanied us during all the time that the Lord Jesus went in and out among us, beginning from the baptism of John until the day when he was taken up from us - one of these men must become with us a witness to his resurrection. [Acts 1.21-22]

In the event two names are put forward, but the text implies that the field of choice was even wider i.e. that those who accompanied Jesus during his ministry were more numerous than the Twelve. 'Seventy' (or in some manuscripts 'seventy-two') are mentioned by Luke at one point; this may be a symbolic exaggeration, given that in Matthew's Gospel the observation is made that 'the labourers are few', but it corroborates the general picture. Some of these may be named in the accounts of later apostolic activity; thus Mnason is described as an 'early' (literally 'archaic') disciple [Acts 21.16], while Andronicus and Junias are of Jewish stock like Paul, but were 'in Christ' before him, and 'of note among the apostles' [Rom 16.7]. Luke also records a following of women:

> Soon afterward he went on through cities and villages, preaching and bringing the good news of the kingdom of God. And the twelve were with him, and also some women who had been healed of evil spirits and infirmities: Mary, called Mag'dalene, from whom seven demons had gone out, and Joan'na, the wife of Chuza, Herod's steward, and Susanna, and many others, who provided for them out of their means. [Luke 8.1-3]

Of course, not all who journeyed with Jesus or who belonged to the apostolic community in Jerusalem could date their involvement as far back as 'the baptism of John'; Luke's claim is that many were converted at or soon after Pentecost. The most startling assertion comes from Paul:

> [The risen Christ] appeared to Cephas, then to the twelve. Then he appeared to *more than five hundred brethren at one time, most of whom are still alive, though some have fallen asleep*. Then he appeared to James, then to all the apostles. [1 Cor 15.5-7]

This 1st letter to the Corinthians is usually dated to the early 50s CE, in other words, around twenty years after the climactic events of Easter and its immediate aftermath. It has been suggested that this Pauline account of a resurrection appearance to so many at the same time is somehow related to the dramatic outpouring of the Spirit – on 'the day of Pentecost' according to Luke [Acts 2.1ff], but in John's reckoning on Easter day itself:

> Then the disciples were glad when they saw the Lord ... And when he had said this, he breathed on them, and said to them, 'Receive the Holy Spirit'. [John 20.20, 22]

Whatever the occasion, at least it points to a large number of early Christians who could bear personal witness to the central truth of Jesus' resurrection. Paul seems to hint that this was an essential qualification to be 'an apostle' in the wider sense of the term (as in the letter to the Galatians, 'I saw none of the other apostles except James the Lord's brother'):

> Am I not an apostle? Have I not seen Jesus our Lord? [1 Cor 9.1]

83

If so, then Barnabas, who was recognised as Paul's fellow apostle, was surely another such eyewitness. Given Paul's initial opposition to Christian teaching, his personal testimony to the risen Lord is particularly compelling.

There is a possible hint in the 1st letter of Peter that its addressees were among those to have heard other such evangelists, who shared their first-hand knowledge of the Lord:

> You have been born anew ... through the living and abiding word of God. [1 Pet 1.23]

Indeed, the letter is addressed to 'the exiles of the Dispersion' in provinces now included within modern Turkey: this designation is an adaptation to Christians, described shortly as 'aliens and exiles' in this world [1 Pet 2.11], of a term originally applied to the Jewish Diaspora – but it does not preclude the possibility that 'living eyewitnesses' from Judea had earlier fled to these parts as a result of disturbances. The author himself writes as 'a witness of the suffering of Christ' [1 Pet 5.1], unlike his readers who, 'without having seen [Jesus Christ]', nevertheless love him [1 Pet 1.8].

Dispersion, of course, belonged within God's purposes:

> You shall be my witnesses in Jerusalem and in all Judea and Samaria and to the end of the earth. [Acts 1.8 cf. Matt 28.19]

This may have been effected by deliberate planning (as with the commissioning of 'Barnabas and Saul' at Antioch), or by the accidents of history such as the 'great persecution' that scattered the Jerusalem church after Stephen's martyrdom [Acts 8.1], or as a consequence of the Jewish struggles against Rome in the 60s CE. Similarities between Stephen's anti-Temple rhetoric, evidently shared by the Hellenist Christians who were displaced to Samaria, and the conversation held by Jesus with the Samaritan woman [Jn 4.21-24 cf. Apoc 21.22] have suggested to some scholars (notably Oscar Cullmann) that Samaria was later affected by religious upheavals, whence some Christian believers moved on further to the region of Ephesus to become influential in the Johannine churches. It was certainly Luke's perception that the first significant conversion of Gentiles was effected by the Hellenists:

Now those who were scattered because of the persecution that arose over Stephen traveled as far as Phoeni'cia and Cyprus and Antioch, speaking the word to none except Jews. But there were some of them, men of Cyprus and Cyre'ne, who on coming to Antioch spoke to the Greeks also, preaching the Lord Jesus. And the hand of the Lord was with them, and a great number that believed turned to the Lord. [Acts 11.19-21]

Although Luke records the apostles remaining at this time in Jerusalem [Acts 8.1], traditions associate several of them with missionary journeys abroad later; this may explain the unexpected rise to prominence of James, the Lord's brother [Acts 15.13; Gal 1.19], who was outside the circle of the Twelve. Jerome wrote to one Marcella at the end of the 4th century:

Christ, therefore, was at one and the same time with the apostles and with the angels; in the Father and in the uttermost parts of the sea. So afterwards he was with Thomas in India, with Peter at Rome, with Paul in Illyricum, with Titus in Crete, with Andrew in Achaia. [*Letter 59*]

The significance of apocryphal writings in elaborating these exploits will be considered in chapter 10.

Papias' evidence

As time drew on, the eye witnesses who remained alive grew fewer in number. On the other hand, the Church continued to expand; and as Christian communities grew more numerous, their access to first-hand testimony inevitably diminished. These were presumably important factors behind the late 1st century attempts to preserve the vital evidence in writing. It does not, however, mean that those who wrote the gospels did so without any recourse to those who had seen and heard the Lord themselves. While it is clear that James, son of Zebedee, was martyred early on, a victim of Herod Agrippa 1 in Jerusalem [Acts 12.1-3] and that Peter was crucified some twenty years later under Nero in Rome, tradition credits other close disciples as surviving much longer. It was also still possible for Justin in the mid 2nd century to cherish the *agrapha* – the Lord's sayings in continuing oral tradition – as distinct from the written testimony.

Particularly important evidence comes from Papias, bishop of Hieropolis in Asia Minor, whose life (circa 60 – 130 CE) spanned the time when the canonical gospels were written. A lengthy reference to him, together with quotations from his five volume work *The Sayings of the Lord Explained*, occurs in Eusebius' *Ecclesiastical History* written in the early 4th century. Eusebius first cites Irenaeus:

> Testimony is borne to these things in writing by Papias, an ancient man, who was a hearer of John, and a friend of Polycarp. [*Hist Eccl* 3.39]

He follows this with Papias' own words in his Preface, explaining how in his younger days he had verified the essentials of the Christian faith:

> *I shall not hesitate to furnish you, along with the interpretations, with all that in days gone by I carefully learnt from the presbyters and have carefully recalled, for I can guarantee its truth. Unlike most people, I felt at home not with those who had a great deal to say, but with those who taught the truth; not with those who appeal to commandments from other sources but with those who appeal to the commandments given by the Lord to faith and coming to us from truth itself. And whenever anyone came who had been a follower of the presbyters, I inquired into the words of the presbyters, what Andrew or Peter had said, or Philip or Thomas or James or John or Matthew, or any other disciple of the Lord, and what Aristion and the presbyter John, disciples of the Lord, were still saying; for I did not imagine that things out of books would help me as much as the utterances of a living and abiding voice.*

Eusebius continues with comments of his own:

> Papias, whom we are now discussing, owns that he learnt the words of the apostles from their former followers, but says that he listened to Aristion and the presbyter John with his own ears. Certainly he often mentions them by name, and reproduces their teachings in his writings ....
>
> Now we must go on, from the remarks of Papias already quoted, to other passages in which he tells us of certain miraculous events and other matters, on the basis, it would seem, of direct information. It has already been mentioned that Philip the Apostle resided at Hierapolis with his daughters: it must now be pointed out that their contemporary Papias tells how he heard a wonderful story from the lips of Philip's daughters. He describes the resurrection of a dead person [the wife of Manaen] in his own lifetime, and

a further miracle that happened to Justus, surnamed Barsabas, who swallowed a dangerous poison and by the grace of the Lord was none the worse.

So Papias' particular interest was not in any written testimony ('things out of books') – although Eusebius will shortly record what he knew about the Gospels of Mark and Matthew. It was rather his contact with the 'eyewitnesses' Aristion and the presbyter John, as well as with Philip's daughters, that gave him even closer access to the words and deeds of Christ. These disciples were obviously elderly when Papias conversed with them in his younger days; but even if there were now few remaining apostles he was also able to learn directly from those who had heard the others in their lifetime. The testimony reported to him was apparently more extensive than any found in written sources such as the gospels or the book of Acts:

> Papias reproduces other stories communicated to him by word of mouth, together with some otherwise unknown parables and teachings of the Saviour.

Here Eusebius turns to the written deposit on which Papias throws some light:

> I must now follow up the statements already quoted from him with a piece of information which he sets out regarding Mark, the writer of the gospel:
> 'This, too, the presbyter used to say. 'Mark, who had been Peter's interpreter; wrote down carefully, but not in order, all that he remembered of the Lord's sayings and doings; for he had not heard the Lord or been one of his followers, but later, as I said, one of Peter's. Peter used to adapt his teaching to the occasion, without making a systematic arrangement of the Lord's sayings, so that Mark was quite justified in writing down some things just as he remembered them; for he had one purpose only – to leave out nothing that he had heard and to make no misstatement about it.'
> Such is Papias's account of Mark. Of Matthew he has this to say:
> 'Matthew ordered the Sayings in the Hebrew dialect, and everyone interpreted them as well as he could.'
> Papias also makes use of evidence drawn from 1 John and I Peter, and reproduces a story about a woman falsely accused before the Lord of many sins. This is to be found in the Gospel of the Hebrews.

Since Mark was not himself an apostle, his Gospel would not have been held in high regard by the Church unless it was known to have apostolic authority behind it. This is supplied here by Papias — the earliest known evidence that it is essentially Peter's testimony (other than internal evidence from the text itself). 'The Lord's sayings and doings' are not always recorded in chronological order, nor are they necessarily accurate reportage of what was said and done on every occasion.

- They are written in Greek, not in Aramaic, the language Jesus would normally have spoken.
- They are what Mark remembered of Peter's teaching.
- In any case, Peter's presentation was 'adapted to the occasion'.

The only adverse comment that Papias offers is the lack of 'order', which he attributes to the variety of occasions on which Peter spoke. Otherwise Mark is commended for being faithful to what he had heard: there is no hint that this is inconsistent with what Papias has learnt from other sources. It is implicit in his account that Peter was no longer alive i.e. in a position to check and approve what Mark had recorded. Since Peter was martyred in the mid 60s CE in Rome, and because of the emphasis in his gospel upon other Christians being ready to take up their crosses too [Mk 8.34; 13.9], it is likely that Mark was writing for the church in Rome during Nero's reign, shortly after Peter's death. Mark may have deliberately mentioned Peter's name before that of any other disciple [Mk 1.16] and again as the final name recorded in his Gospel [Mk 16.7 – verses 9-20 were added later] as a way of paying special tribute to him. In a later source, *The (Pseudo-) Clementine Recognitions* [2.1], Peter mentions his night-time habit 'of recalling to memory the words of my Lord, which I heard from himself' and then 'arranging them one by one' so as to remember them better. Eusebius dismisses this 'wordy' text as having 'absolutely no mention in the ancients' [*Hist Eccl* 3.28]; nevertheless, the patristic concern for authenticity is quite evident.

As for Papias' isolated remark about Mathew's writing, it seems likely that this is but a brief extract from more extended comments. There is considerable uncertainty about what it means:

- There seems to be an emphasis upon Matthew's *ordered* arrangement, in contrast with the lack of order in Mark. This in turn might imply that Papias knew that Mark's writing preceded Matthew's.

- 'The Hebrew dialect' suggests the Aramaic language, which most readers ('everyone') would therefore need to translate into Greek, the common language of the Roman Empire. If so, however, it should be noted that the Septuagint (rather than an *ad hoc* translation from Hebrew) seems to be the main source of OT quotations cited in the Greek text of Matthew, although of course other 'reminiscences' of the OT cannot be so readily sourced.

- To describe the work as a collection of Sayings may mean that it lacks a continuous narrative, in which case it is not the Gospel as we know it. On the other hand, it is generally recognised that the sayings of Jesus are mainly found thematically grouped together in five sections of the Gospel, perhaps in imitation of the five books of the Jewish Torah. If these were considered the main feature of Matthew's writing, they could have provided a convenient title for the whole work. It seems implausible that Papias has in mind here a different writing by Matthew, given that his Gospel was now becoming widely known.

- The conclusion may therefore be that Papias understood Matthew's Gospel to have been composed originally in Aramaic, before a Greek version rapidly came to be preferred. Alternatively, it may be that the word 'dialect' is simply Papias' term for 'style' or 'idiom'.

Since Matthew's Gospel was a much fuller, and indeed orderly, account of Jesus' life, death and resurrection it rapidly came into widespread usage. Once again, Papias' sources do not lead him to offer any cautionary words about its accuracy, even though to later generations there are a number of obvious discrepancies between his Gospel and that of Mark. That does not imply that they went unnoticed – rather, that such variations were only to be expected in material that was 'adapted to the occasion'. It is only in recent times that evidence for Matthew's literary dependence upon Mark's Gospel has been scrutinised, and widely accepted: this then opens the door to many insights into the way Matthew adapted Mark's text. Once again, however, it should not be supposed that he did this in scholarly isolation:

eyewitnesses, and many recollections of the preached tradition, continued to be as available to him as they were to Papias himself.

Eusebius is clear that Papias' insistence upon the transmission of the Christian heritage through eyewitnesses and their successors is an important principle in the Church. He quotes Irenaeus, writing towards the end of the 2nd century to rebuke a Gnostic heretic Florinus for holding views that were not handed down from the beginning:

> Such notions not even the heretics outside the Church have ever dared to propound.[19] Such notions the presbyters of an 'earlier generation, those taught by the apostles themselves, did not transmit to you. When I was still a boy I saw you in Lower Asia in Polycarp's company, when you were cutting a fine figure at the imperial court and wanted to be in favour with him. I have a clearer recollection of events at that time than of recent happenings - what we learn in childhood develops along with the mind and becomes a part of it - so that I can describe the place where blessed Polycarp sat and talked; his goings out and comings in, the character of his life, his personal appearance, his addresses to crowded congregations. I remember how he spoke of his intercourse with John and with the others who had seen the Lord; how he repeated their words from memory; and how the things that he had heard them say about the Lord, His miracles and His teaching, things that he had heard direct, from the eye-witnesses of the Word of Life, were proclaimed by Polycarp in complete harmony with Scripture. To these things I listened eagerly at that time, by the mercy of God shown to me, not committing them to writing but *learning them by heart*. By God's grace, I constantly and conscientiously ruminate on them, and I can bear witness before God that if any such suggestion had come to the ears of that blessed and apostolic presbyter he would have cried out and stopped his ears, exclaiming characteristically: 'Dear God, for what times Thou hast preserved me, that I should endure this!' [*Hist Eccl* 5.20]

It was not only the evangelists who were intent upon preserving an authentic record. Paul, the other major contributor to the New Testament draws attention to his own fidelity to received teaching:

---

[19] Although there were undoubtedly novelties in 'heretical' teaching, these were often justified by claiming secret lines of transmission. The principle of tradition was thus widely regarded.

I delivered to you as of first importance what I also received, that Christ died for our sins in accordance with the scriptures, that he was buried, that he was raised on the third day in accordance with the scriptures, and that he appeared to Cephas, then to the twelve. [1 Cor 15.3-5]

While he insists that his gospel is not man-made [Gal 1.11], nevertheless he reports that when he visited Jerusalem and laid before 'those who were of repute' [Gal 2.2] his teaching was verified. He had, of course, been trained in Pharisaic exactitude, 'extremely zealous ... for the traditions of [his] fathers' [Gal 1.13 cf. Phil 3.5; Acts 26.5], and so may be presumed careful also in his transmission of the Lord's teaching. This emerges when he writes to the Corinthians in response to 'the matters about which you wrote' [1 Cor 7.1]:

To the married I give charge, not I but the Lord ... To the rest I say, not the Lord ... [1 Cor 7.10, 12]

It is significant too that the earliest record of the Last Supper, found in Paul's writing, differs only in small details from accounts in the Synoptic Gospels:

For I received from the Lord what I also delivered to you, that the Lord Jesus on the night when he was betrayed took bread, and when he had given thanks, he broke it, and said, 'This is my body which is for you. Do this in remembrance of me.' In the same way also the cup, after supper, saying, 'This cup is the new covenant in my blood. Do this, as often as you drink it, in remembrance of me.' [1 Cor 11.23-25]

The vocabulary that Paul employs here suggests that these words are not his own or at least not his customary usage (e.g. 'body' in the verses above, with other instances later in the same letter). So his claim to have 'received from the Lord' does not exclude the agency of others in relaying these words to him from Christ himself as their source.

8. From Oral Testimony to Written Records

The Word made flesh

The veneration of sacred scripture should not cause the Christian to lose sight of the incarnation of God's Word in Jesus Christ. Although much of his ministry was occupied with preaching and teaching, he did not himself write a book: in fact, he often communicated God's truth more powerfully in his life and by his initiatives of love, for example, in healing the sick and in embracing those who were neglected or outcast. In his very being and in the depth of his relationships with those around him he was a witness to divine reality. Accounts of his time on earth are treasured by the Church in so far as they are faithful records of what took place, but words alone are inadequate to engage the reader (or listener) in the experience of encountering Christ:

> Above all the Gospel must be proclaimed by witness. Take a Christian or a handful of Christians who, in the midst of their own community, show their capacity for understanding and acceptance, their sharing of life and destiny with other people, their solidarity with the efforts of all for whatever is noble and good. Let us suppose that, in addition, they radiate in an altogether simple and unaffected way their faith in values that go beyond current values, and their hope in something that is not seen and that one would not dare to imagine. Through this wordless witness these Christians stir up irresistible questions in the hearts of those who see how they live: Why are they like this? Why do they live in this way? What or who is it that inspires them? Why are they in our midst? Such a witness is already a silent proclamation of the Good News and a very powerful and effective one. Here we have an initial act of evangelization. Nevertheless this always remains insufficient, because even the finest witness will prove ineffective in the long run if it is not explained ... *The Good News proclaimed by the witness of life sooner or later has to be proclaimed by the word of life* ... As we said recently to a group of lay people, "Modern man listens more willingly to witnesses than to teachers, and if he does listen to teachers, it is because they are witnesses." [Paul VI: *Evangelii Nuntiandi* 1975, 21-22, 41]

The Word of God does therefore need to be expressed in human words as well as in human lives. This at once presents a dilemma: how can earthly language convey the truths of heaven? The answer emerges in the same way that Christ's own person is discovered to be both human and divine. Jesus uses familiar words and traditional images to say new and challenging things, which may at times perplex, or disturb, or be at least only partially appreciated. Revelatory truth thus has depths of meaning which are not always immediately apparent. The deceptively simple language in which Jesus spoke was like seed falling on the ground: sometimes the soil was unreceptive or barren, but even when it was fertile a period of maturation was needed before its full potential could be realised. This perhaps helps to explain why the Fourth Gospel, written later than the three Synoptic Gospels, is stylistically so different: lengthier discourses which amplify Christ's teaching are more prominent than parables and pithy sayings, thereby inviting deeper reflection. The Church's liturgical use of Gospel readings suggests its own recognition of this truth; a year is spent with Matthew, then with Mark, finally with Luke, but at key times such as Lent and Easter attention turns to John's account. The retention of all four Gospels, each with their own emphases, may be seen in terms of Paul's spirit of becoming 'all things to all men' [1 Cor 9.22]. Their composition in Greek (rather than Aramaic) was itself a vital step in enabling Jesus' teaching to reach a much wider Mediterranean world, and their several ways of expressing the gospel 'inculturated' it in relation to the concerns of particular communities (or, in Luke's case, perhaps those of Theophilus). Jesus' mission injunction was after all to 'eat and drink what they provide' [Luke 10.7-8] – to be responsive to the local scene, not to impose pre-packaged ideas insensitively.

The Gospel evidence is that, even if Jesus' words were augmented in the oral tradition or by the evangelists themselves, his own imagery has not been lost. He spoke appropriately, in inculturated language, to the crowds who gathered round him – even if subsequently he often elucidated in more measured terms for the benefit of his disciples. As in the Bible's earlier wisdom writings, Jesus used metaphors of village life, of crops and plants, of birds and animals, of the lakeshore and the hills, as well as of religious people and places. Out of these emerged a particular focus on bread, wine, water and light, each of which was shown to carry a much deeper significance in meeting people's essential needs. While John's Gospel incorporates hardly any of the pithy sayings and stories found in the

Synoptic Gospels, it contains revealing discussions of these sacramental – but still earthy – symbols.

Teaching 'adapted to the occasion' (Papias)

What is particularly noticeable about Jesus' language – and the lessons he imparted – is its memorability. Learning by heart was far more prominent in the ancient world than it is today, and in the Jewish tradition pupils were expected to memorise both the scriptures and the teachings of the rabbis. Peter and John may have been considered 'uneducated common men' [Acts 4.13], but far from being simple peasants they were shrewd businessmen who had the benefit of lengthy association with an outstanding religious teacher. There were certainly also some Christians, 'believers who belonged to the party of the Pharisees', who remained watchful of any inauthentic developments [Acts 15.5].

Hence what is attributed to Jesus in the Gospels is likely to be faithful to what happened, *although expressed in terms that later and quite different audiences could grasp.* What mattered most was not simply what had been said and done, but what it truly meant. This necessarily called for a discerning appreciation of what had taken place: while oral transmission was always testimony (rather than mere reportage), this was also the thrust of the written record. Luke [1.1-4] and John [20.30-31], as we have seen, are both explicit about their careful selection of available material in order to convey what they considered essential to their purpose.[20] This may well have suggested some adjustments to the *ipsissima verba* of Jesus in order to allow them to make sense within the different cultural environment of the Graeco-Roman world. In particular, issues about food needed to engage with the practices of pagan temples; and those about marriage needed to

---

[20] Indeed, the beginning and ending of a writing often form an *inclusio* that reveals its main concern. For Matthew, this may be the revelation of Emmanuel – the One who offers the final assurance that he will be 'with you always, to the close of the age'. For John, it is the incarnation, recognised in the end even by Thomas as he touches his Lord and his God. For Mark, who describes the first and last days of Jesus' ministry, each preceded by a time of trial, it may be a case of 'in my beginning is my end' – a day that changed the world.

take into account that in Roman society a woman was permitted to initiate divorce, while also marriage was possible within closer kinships than in Jewish law. No such revision could, however, override God's fundamental purposes – here, the goodness of creation and the sanctity of marriage (see e.g. Mt 5.25ff; Mk 10.9).

In the arrangement of any Gospel, Primo Levi's observation (derived from his experience of Holocaust recollections) is worth bearing in mind:

> The *pattern* within which events are ordered is not always identifiable in a single unequivocal fashion.[21]

If, however, the evangelists select and arrange what they have sourced somewhat differently from each other, the results need not be understood as contesting for the truth about Jesus. Rather, by discovering his words and actions in different contexts, further insight is gained into their 'breadth and length and height and depth' [Eph 3.18]. Specific sayings, for example, may not necessarily have intrinsic links with any definite situations in Jesus' ministry;[22] by incorporating them differently the evangelists may well bring out different aspects of their meaning. Variations of expression too help to convey the implications of a saying or of an event, while chapter 2 of this book certainly suggested that, if Jesus himself and those who wrote about him often drew upon ideas and imagery found in

---

[21] Levi 22

[22] This enabled e.g. Matthew to group Jesus' teachings into five main collections, each concluding with the phrase 'When Jesus had finished these sayings'. Likewise Mark chapter 4 is a collection of several parables featuring 'seeds'. Luke chapter 15 narrates a sequence of three stories about the 'lost'. John has selected seven signs which help to structure his message, and introduces other linkages too e.g. Andrew brings people to Jesus on several occasions (his brother Simon, a lad, some Greeks).

And where Luke takes 'the lost sheep' to mean a marginalised person [Lk 15.1ff], it appears that Matthew thinks of 'little ones' as those who have strayed, or perhaps lapsed, in their discipleship [Mt 18.10ff]. Another contrast between these two evangelists is displayed in their birth narratives: Luke's poor shepherds are a counter to Matthew's much wealthier magi; a similar difference between relative poverty and untold riches is evident in their two versions of the parable of the talents. Such discrepancies surely reflect the social environments with which the writers are engaging, while illustrating their literary and theological competence.

the Old Testament, in so doing they transformed the language. Religious themes and symbolism exploited by the different evangelists came to be appreciated as profoundly fulfilled in Christ.

Yet this transformative process was not understood as confined to expressing or interpreting the ideology. The message was intended to change human lives. At the very beginning of Mark's Gospel there is the challenge of Jesus' opening proclamation:

> The time is fulfilled, and the kingdom of God is at hand; repent, and believe in the gospel. [Mark 1.15 cf. Matt 4.17]

The word 'repent' here is in Greek μετανοεῖτε, 'change your thinking'; so the call is for altered attitudes of heart and mind. In the first two gospels this is followed straightaway by the invitation to the fishermen to drop the net being cast at that moment into the sea, and to follow Jesus. Their response is immediate, and they turn expectantly, to be made 'fishers of men'. There is a close parallel to this story in the other two Gospels. In Luke 5.1-11, before becoming Jesus' disciples, the fishermen are urged to 'put out into the deep and let down your nets for a catch'; having spent the night doing so in vain, they heed his word and find 'a great shoal of fish'. In John 21.1-8 there is a similar situation in the days following Easter; now it is the risen Christ standing unrecognised on the shore who directs the disciples to the catch awaiting 'on the right side of the boat'. Each time a faithful response to Jesus' teaching reveals previously unknown dimensions of 'fishing': it is descriptive of a more rewarding (human) catch on dry land (Mark, Matthew) as well as in places that defy either conventional wisdom (Luke) or the habits of a lifetime (John). The experience is life-changing; the living Word of God changes the disciples' goals and their own relationship with the previously unknown (or partially known) Jesus.

Yet the evangelists are also realistic. If the encounter is dramatic, the ensuing transformation is often more gradual: the Word does not come to full fruition immediately. Mark draws attention to the disciples' learning curve, remarking on incidents that displayed their lack of understanding and even 'hardness of heart' [Mk 6.52]. Matthew is more respectful, but he too admits occasions of 'doubt' – or of 'little faith' – and this continues even after Jesus' resurrection [Mt 14.31; 28.17]. The crux was of course the path

96

of suffering that lay ahead for Jesus and potentially for his followers as well. In Luke's Gospel, despite much previous instruction, the disciples 'understood none of these things; this saying was hid from them, and they did not grasp what was said' [Lk 18.34]. It is John who perhaps appreciates most of all that, although their Easter experiences utterly changed the disciples' perspective and enabled them to interpret anew all that had preceded it, even these events were not wholly transparent. Those who came face to face with the evidence took time to comprehend it – as happened earlier in his Gospel when Jesus encountered first Nicodemus, then the woman of Samaria [Jn 20-21 cf. 3-4]. In fact, both Luke and John make it clear that true understanding emerges only after engagement with the Jewish scriptures:

> O foolish men, and slow of heart to believe all that the prophets have spoken! ... And beginning with Moses and all the prophets, he interpreted to them in all the scriptures the things concerning himself. [Lk 24.25, 27]
> Then he opened their minds to understand the scriptures. [Lk 24.45]
> The other disciple went in, and he saw and believed; for as yet they did not know the scripture, that he must rise from the dead. [Jn 20.8-9]

If therefore the written Gospels embody God's truth about Jesus, their authors do not claim that they stand independently of revelation already received.

The written records

So far as is known, no written records of the life of Jesus were compiled in the initial decades of the apostolic era. There may have been 'testimonies' comprising important scriptural texts, compiled for the benefit of travelling preachers. Perhaps too some of Jesus' sayings were collected together for the same purpose:

> The codex was quickly adopted by Christian scribes. Its predecessor was a wax-coated wooden writing tablet which could be used many times over. It is now increasingly clear that these note books were used widely at the time of Jesus. It is certainly possible, or even probable, that followers of Jesus made notes of his teaching and written reports of his actions long before the gospels were written. The terse nature of the Jesus traditions can be

accounted for both by the use of oral tradition and also by the use of notebooks.[23]

Yet, while the existence of notebooks or similar records is plausible, no copies have survived and the evidence remains hypothetical. Apart from Paul's letters, it is Mark's Gospel that is probably the earliest known Christian writing, most likely undertaken for the benefit of believers in Rome at a time when the prospect of suffering for their faith was very real i.e. during the Neronian persecution of the 60s CE. The alternative context of Galilee in the aftermath of the roughly contemporaneous Jewish revolt in Palestine has been suggested, since the emphasis upon 'taking up one's cross' would have been relevant there too in the face of Roman reprisals. Yet the translation of Aramaic phrases [Mk 3.17; 5.41; 7.11; 7.34; 10.46; 14.36; 15.22; 15.34] might then have been less necessary. Equally, the well-attested link with Peter (found not only in Papias, but also in 1 Peter, Irenaeus, and the late 2nd century *Anti-Marcionite Prologue* which specifies 'the regions of Italy' as the Gospel's place of origin) together with Jesus' declaration of all foods as *clean* [Mk 7.19] does not fit the Galilean setting so well.

The principal argument for the 'priority of Mark' arises from synoptic comparison of the Gospels of Matthew, Mark and Luke. This displays, not merely considerable similarities between the texts and their ordered arrangement (which might be attributed to some consistency in oral transmission), but sufficient verbal identity and detailed placing of parentheses to suggest literary dependence. If then one of these gospels was used in the compilation of the others, which one was it? Apart from the fact that in Luke's preface he explicitly refers to previous 'narratives' [Lk 1.1], the likeliest conclusion is that Mark's Gospel was used by both Matthew and Luke. The vast majority of his material is found in those other Gospels; Mark's is in any case much shorter (with a rougher style of Greek), and lacks their infancy stories as well as any resurrection appearances (the longer ending 16.9-20 is not found in all manuscripts, and appears to be a later addition). The belief held for centuries was that Mark had abbreviated the most popular of the gospels viz. Matthew's — but it is commonly

---

[23] Graham Stanton: *Gospel Truth?* (London 1995, 59)

accepted now that an expansion of Mark to include additional material is a more plausible development than the deliberate omission of valuable texts from Matthew. Much more recently the focus fell on the additions (230 verses, mainly sayings of Jesus) found in both of the other two Gospels, and for some time it was thought that these derived from a further written source ('Quelle' or Q for short) used by both Matthew and Luke. The Q hypothesis has, however, largely been superseded: the non-Markan overlap can be seen as resulting from Luke's use of Matthew's Gospel alongside Mark's together with common oral traditions. It is also generally accepted now that if John's Gospel differs from the other three in various details (such as his timing of the Last Supper *before* the feast of the Passover) this may well reflect a different oral source of historical value.

Although other 'gospels' have come to light, including the *Gospel of Peter*, the *Gospel of Thomas* and latterly the *'Secret Gospel' of Mark*, none of these can command the same extensive manuscript support and patristic citation as the four canonical Gospels. Some of these (although now for the most part lost) were still in circulation in the late 4th century as noted by Ambrose:

> One hears tell of another gospel, supposedly written by the twelve apostles. Basilides was bold enough to write one, called 'the Gospel according to Basilides'. They also say that Thomas wrote a gospel. I myself have come across one attributed to Matthias. We read them merely in order that others might not read them. We have read them so as not to ignore them. We have read them not with a view to retaining them but in order to reject them. We wanted to learn what precisely was the quality of work that inflated the pride of these fantastical and self-important people. [*Comm S Luk* 1.2]

There is little likelihood of much being added from these apocryphal sources to the stock of genuine traditions about the life of Jesus and his teaching, although a few isolated sayings may have been preserved, such as:

> Whoever is near me, is near the fire; whoever is far from me, is far from the kingdom. [*Gospel of Thomas* 30, 82]

There is a school of thought that the author of the Fourth Gospel knew of this *Gospel of Thomas* and specifically challenged its teaching about 'the inner light'. However, its dating is very uncertain.

The *Infancy Gospel of Thomas* is a separate text, which illustrates how a later generation of often over-zealous (and sometimes heretical) Christians sought to fill gaps in the preserved tradition about Jesus. Various *Apocryphal Acts* did the same for the later lives of some of the apostles. The focus in the infancy gospel is upon the childhood of Jesus, who is no ordinary boy but one endowed with divine power. His readiness to perform miracles, including the infliction of instant death upon a playmate who crossed his path, illustrates a skewed faith in whoever propagated the story: Jesus as depicted here has more in common with a capricious Greek or Roman god than with the One who gave his life for others.

Perhaps the only point of interest in the mere 20 extant lines of the *Secret Gospel of Mark* is the reference to the almost naked youth who is taught 'the mystery of the kingdom of God' in an all-night session with the risen Jesus. It thus appears to identify the author of Mark's Gospel with the young man who makes a mysterious appearance after Jesus' arrest and follows him 'with nothing but a linen cloth about his body; and they seized him, but he left the linen cloth and ran away naked' [Mk 14.51-52]. The same identification has often been (more reliably) inferred from the canonical text of Mark.

The corroboration of Christian lives

If the inference above is correct, by mentioning his personal involvement here as a disciple who 'left everything' (to quote Peter's words from Mark 10.28) Mark may be reminding the reader of his own credentials. If this earliest Gospel is not directly the work of an apostle – a criticism some also levelled at Luke's Gospel in the later 2nd century when the Church was assessing the authenticity of various early writings – it would thus appear to claim that its author was nevertheless an eyewitness, one who followed closely in the footsteps of the Twelve and indeed of the Lord himself.

A similar self-reference is found in the Fourth Gospel:

This is the disciple who is bearing witness to these things, and who has written these things. [Jn 21.24]

The identity of this Beloved Disciple remains uncertain, but his credentials certainly place him close to Jesus at critical moments: at the Last Supper, at the foot of the Cross, in the empty tomb [Jn 13.23; 19.26; 20.2-9]. The implication of the closing verses of chapter 21 is that he will remain faithful until his death, whenever that comes.

Other writers of New Testament books show a similar awareness that it is not words alone that carry authority but their expression too in lives that testify to their truth. For example, as Paul saw it, the gospel is not a new 'law' ordering human affairs in a radically different way, even if that is one of its consequences: it is life 'in Christ'. He can therefore summarise it, not in any moral code or utopian vision, but as the 'imitation' of Christ:

Be imitators of me, as I am of Christ. [1 Cor 11.1]

This surely echoes the Dominical saying found in John's Gospel:

I have given you an example, that you also should do as I have done to you. [John 13.15]

When Paul was accused of being an 'inferior' apostle by Christians in Corinth, his appeal was to 'the things that show my weakness'; he explained that, as with Christ, 'When I am weak, then I am strong' [2 Cor 11.30; 12.10]. Not least were his physical sufferings, so that he claimed to carry even in his body 'the death of Jesus' in order for the life of Jesus to be visibly manifested [2 Cor 4.10–11]. His final appeal to any Galatians who might still dispute his teaching was the same:

Henceforth let no man trouble me; for I bear on my body the marks of Jesus. [Gal 6.17]

When Luke came to write, not only did he script himself unostentatiously via the well-known 'we' passages into the text of Acts [20.5 – 21.26] as a fellow witness and companion of Paul, but again and again demonstrates how the life, death and resurrection of Jesus were exemplified in the apostolic Church. There are many deliberate parallels between Luke's

Gospel and the book of Acts: these cross-references provide a double check on the truth of what is recorded, which in legal terms is of considerable importance.

The following are worth noting:

- Both volumes begin in Jerusalem, where a fresh dispensation of the Holy Spirit is granted to those devoutly waiting upon God.

- There is a testing time of forty days, both for Jesus and for his disciples.

- Jesus prepares for the descent of the Spirit in prayer, as do the apostles. On both occasions there are visionary happenings.

- The apostles continue as a united body, preaching and healing as Jesus did. Perhaps their frequent presence in the temple is a reminder that this is where Jesus found himself – in his Father's house [Lk 2.49]. Paul encounters him there too [Acts 22.17].

- In obedience to Jesus' instruction to the Twelve to carry no money on their missionary rounds, Peter and John are depicted in Acts as having neither silver nor gold [Acts 3.6].

- 'What shall we do?' is the question asked, first of John the Baptist, then of Peter and the apostles.

- The gospel imagery of the fishing net is renewed in Peter's vision of the all-inclusive sheet.

- There is opposition, including detention and questioning, by the authorities. The Sadducees reject both Jesus' and Paul's belief in the resurrection. Each faces the triple combination of the Sanhedrin, the Roman governor and the ruling Herod, as well as a hostile crowd – yet each is three times declared innocent.

- When Stephen is stoned to death he echoes the dying words of Jesus about forgiveness, and likewise commends his spirit.

- When the apostles are imprisoned, they are miraculously released at night [Acts 5.19], as is Peter on a further occasion – experiences akin to Jesus' rising from his tomb, with Peter's release being recorded as taking place immediately after Passover [Acts 12.1–11].

- The encounter of Philip with the Ethiopian bears several resemblances to the two disciples' walk with Jesus to Emmaus: the exegesis of scripture, the 'sacramental' climax, the sudden vanishing of 'the host'.

- Jesus' commission, first to the Twelve and then to the seventy, carries the instruction to 'shake off the dust from your feet' in places where the message has been rejected: this is precisely Paul and Barnabas' action on leaving Pisidian Antioch [Acts 13.51].

In fact, these incidents are not recorded simply as an 'historical' record, but serve as a paradigm from which the Church in later generations can take heart. Fulfilment of Jewish hopes and scriptural prophecies was of wide importance in the early church, but so too were Jesus' predictions and parabolic actions which carried their own promise of future realisation. The very outline of Acts has been shaped by Luke to demonstrate how Jesus' prediction made just before Pentecost was steadily being implemented:

> You shall be my witnesses in Jerusalem and in all Judea and Sama'ria and to the end of the earth [Acts 1.8].

Luke also reflects in his second volume how 'the secrets of the kingdom of God' revealed in the parable of the sower [Lk 8.4–15] have marked both the setbacks and the steady advance of the Church's mission:

> Those who received [Peter's] word were baptized, and there were added that day [Pentecost] about three thousand souls. [Acts 2.41]

Use of the Gospel phrase 'receiving the word' is more than coincidental, given that Luke includes phrases such as 'the word of God grew' no less than four further times in Acts [6.7; 12.24; 13.48; 19.20]. Other passages [e.g. 5.14; 9.31; 16.5] note how numbers continued to multiply; arguably, Luke anticipates a hundredfold growth [Lk 8.4] in 'the company of persons ... in all about a hundred and twenty' who were assembled on the day of Pentecost [Acts 2.13], and sees them gradually adding up (after the initial 3000, 5000 are mentioned next – but the lure of false accounting is rejected by Paul when the tribune tasks him about a further 4000!). Interspersed with these verses are incidents that correspond to interruptions and failures in the seed's growth:

- *'The devil comes and takes away the word'* [Lk 8.12], as when 'Satan filled [Ananias'] heart to lie to the Holy Spirit' [Acts 5.3].

- *'They believe for a while and in time of temptation fall away'* [Lk 8.13], as when 'many Jews and converts to Judaism followed Paul and Barnabas' – but on the next sabbath, when 'almost the whole city gathered together to hear the word of God, they were filled with jealousy, and contradicted what was spoken by Paul, and reviled him' [Acts 13.43–45].
- *'They are those who hear, but as they go on their way they are choked by the cares and riches and pleasures of life, and their fruit does not mature'* [Lk 8.14], as when Demetrius addressed his fellow craftsmen in Ephesus and warned them of how 'this Paul has persuaded and turned away a considerable company of people', endangering their wealth and their business [Acts 19.25–27].

Other predictions, from Jesus' teaching on the end-times [Lk 21.5–36], are also shown to have taken place:

- *There will be famines* [Lk 21.11], and indeed Agabus also predicted one, which 'took place in the days of Claudius' [Acts 11.28].
- *Believers will be delivered up* to synagogues and prisons [Lk 21.12], of which several occurrences are mentioned later [Acts 4.3 etc].
- *Testimony before kings and governors* [Lk 21.12] is given by Paul before Felix and his successor Festus [Acts 24.33; 25.7], subsequently before king Agrippa [Acts 25.23] and in anticipation before Caesar himself [Acts 25.12].
- *Some will be put to death* [Lk 21.16], of whom the first was Stephen [Acts 7.60] soon to be followed by James, the brother of John [Acts 12.2].
- *Jerusalem will be trodden down* [Lk 21.24]: this further sign is *not* recorded in the book of Acts, although Luke is probably writing some years after 70 CE when this occurred. His narrative ended with Paul under house arrest in Rome.

The message is clear: Jesus' teaching in word and deed is conveyed not only in the authentic gospel records, but in the continuing witness of faithful Christians. The story can be studied in manuscripts that set down all that happened, but it can equally well be seen happening in the life of the contemporary Church.

9. The Emergence of Christian Scripture

The dissemination of Christian writings

It inevitably took time for specifically Christian texts (such as Paul's letters or the newly written Gospels) to supplement, and eventually to overtake in importance, the reading of Hebrew scripture in Christian worship. Such writings needed first to be copied and disseminated, and even then their usage might remain far from universal: some churches might lack the text, others might prefer alternatives – or doubt its authenticity, especially if, as happened to John's Gospel, it became the preserve of unorthodox tendencies such as Gnosticism. It was the wide acceptance and liturgical use of a Christian writing that effectively raised it to the status of scripture. Some inconsistencies of usage were probably unavoidable, but when disagreements raised serious challenges to the tradition of faith or to church authority it became necessary to clarify the criteria for acceptability.

It is by no means always clear how rapidly or how widely the earliest writings became known beyond their place of origin, since their apparent use by others may have drawn similar material from commonly accepted teaching rather than from a particular text; dominical sayings especially are likely to have been retained within the collective memory of the Church. In the *Epistle of Barnabas* – from the late 1st century or early 2nd century – there is a stream of quotations from the Old Testament (especially the Pentateuch, Isaiah, Jeremiah, Zechariah and the Psalms) and just two plausible references to written gospels viz. Matthew 20.16 and Mark 2.17, of which the former is introduced explicitly by the words 'it is written' [*Ep Barn* 4.14]. Another writing of similar date, the *Didache*, has the saying, 'Every sin shall be forgiven, but this sin shall not be forgiven' [*Did* 11], which may be a gospel reminiscence [Mt 12.31] or may have been familiar to the author from oral tradition. Elsewhere, however, there is an unequivocal reference to a written gospel:

> Reprove one another, but peaceably and not in hot blood, as you are told in the gospel ... In your prayers, your almsgiving, and everything you do, be guided by what you read in the gospel of our Lord. [Did 15]

Clement of Rome, writing to the Corinthians at this time, reminds them of 'what the Lord Jesus Christ said in one of his lessons on mildness and forbearance'[*1 Clem* 13], in phrases which are partially echoed in the gospels of Matthew and Luke– but could well have been known independently of them both.

A decade or two later, Ignatius of Antioch wrote a series of letters on his journey to Rome to face martyrdom. The heart of his faith is detailed as follows:

> I am clinging for refuge to the Gospel message as though to the incarnate Christ, and to the Apostles as the collective ministry of the Church. Not, indeed, that the Prophets do not have a place in our hearts as well ... For me, the sacrosanct records are [Jesus'] cross and death and resurrection, and the faith that comes through him. [*Ep Philadelphians* 5, 8]

It is possible that, just as the term 'Prophets' is a reference to scripture, so also either or both of the terms 'Gospel message' and 'Apostles' have a textual meaning, but this is far from certain. It may be significant that Ignatius seems here to share the Pauline ('sacrosanct') focus upon Jesus' death and resurrection, rather than upon his teaching – perhaps in contrast to the way that Clement concludes his citation of Jesus' sayings with the hope that his readers' 'resolve to live in obedience to his sacred words' will be thereby strengthened. A number of parallels have, however, been detected in Ignatius' letters to verses found in Matthew [3.15; 10.16; 18.19-20; 19.12] and even more similarities to those in the Fourth Gospel [1.1; 3.8; 4.10; 6.33; 7.42; 8.28-29; 12.31 etc.]. Yet it remains Paul's influence (especially 1 Cor 15.8-10) that seems predominant. When Polycarp of Smyrna wrote, probably not much later, to the church in Philippi, parallels with a wide range of New Testament writings (including Matthew, Acts, 1 Corinthians, Galatians, Ephesians, Philippians, 2 Thessalonians, 1 & 2 Timothy, Hebrews, 1 Peter and 1 John) are abundant, although once again they seldom appear to be direct quotations. By contrast, *The Shepherd of Hermas*, another early work, exhibits little awareness of writings other than Matthew, Ephesians and (especially) the letter of James.

The picture gleaned from the late 1st and early 2nd centuries is therefore one of increasing familiarity with texts that later became canonical. The evidence suggests that Paul's letters were particularly well known, and that Matthew's Gospel had also gained a wider circulation. The former offered more of a theological focus upon the meaning of Christ's life and death, while the latter relayed his specific teachings. While the sense of unity between these different aspects is not always clear in the early Church, it is certainly true that Jesus' own words were accorded the greatest respect. It was the acknowledgement that the written Gospels (which were not initially attributed to particular authors) were faithful guardians of these sayings that eventually led to their acceptance as 'scripture'. This was perhaps an inevitable development: as time progressed, an oral tradition which was susceptible to inauthentic additions might begin to seem a less secure foundation for Christian belief than well-attested written records. During the course of the 2nd century different sects emerged within the Church, some of whom (e.g. the Valentinians) became renowned for their idiosyncratic teachings, at times claiming the support of a 'secret' line of oral transmission. This does not mean that the Gospels now gaining widespread acceptance were wholly immune from textual variation (as is evident from the earliest fragmentary deposits), but the disparities arising are usually matters of detail rather than substance – as with those found in ancient copies of the Hebrew scriptures. Often, indeed, these arose through scribal mistakes, such as inverting, omitting or confusing letters, rather than through attempted improvements or corrections. It is only occasionally that 'dogmatic' interests seem to have been at work e.g. manuscripts differ about the inclusion of the word of forgiveness from the Cross [Lk 23.34], perhaps reflecting contemporary attitudes to local Jewish communities.

By the mid 2nd century many of the writings that now comprise the New Testament were well known, and there were others, such as *The Shepherd of Hermas*, which were also read in church assemblies. An initial collection of some of Paul's letters is implied even in his lifetime:

> When this letter has been read among you, have it read also in the church of the Laodiceans; and see that you read also the letter from Laodicea. [Col 4.16]

2 Peter, perhaps the latest of the NT writings, refers to 'all his letters' [2 Pet 3.16]; and the habit of collecting cherished Christian documents is evident also in Polycarp's letter to the Philippians:

I am sending you Ignatius' letters, as you requested; the ones he wrote to us, and some others that we had in our possession.

Some decades later Marcion caused controversy in Rome by proposing in his work *Antitheses* that the entire Old Testament (whose God of 'justice' appeared to him to be irreconcilable with the Christian God of 'goodness') should be abandoned along with any allegorical forms of interpretation, and that the norm of Christian teaching should be considered as the ten Pauline letters together with Luke's Gospel – so long as they were purged of what he termed corrupt Jewish interpolations. Marcion's omissions included the reference in Galatians to Abraham, plus the Lukan genealogy linking Jesus with patriarchal figures. In fact, his 'docetic' understanding – that Jesus only appeared to be human – caused him to delete most of the birth and resurrection stories as well. Not long afterwards, Tatian, who would have been familiar with these ideas from his years in Rome, was similarly selective in his reduction of the four Gospels to a single composite life of Christ, the *Diatessaron*, which was then used as the standard 'gospel' for several centuries in Syriac-speaking churches.

These individual initiatives, although unacceptable to majority opinion, undoubtedly accelerated the process whereby the Church clarified its own mind about which writings were to be regarded as upholding the authentic tradition of faith. Reacting against Marcion, the Jewish scriptures were seen as a valuable witness to Christ – indeed, in Justin's response to Marcion (his *Dialogue with Trypho*) he reported that it was these very scriptures which had prompted him to become a Christian. Tertullian too argued that it was the fulfilment of its prophecies that allowed the Old Testament to be treated as a Christian document. By his time there was no doubt that conformity with the gospel accounts had become the criterion for assessing the status of these existing scriptures, which was similar (but not identical) to Marcion's stance. Further, all four Gospels, now in general use, were seen to be indispensable (and could conveniently be contained together within a single codex, which until the 4th century lacked the capacity to include other canonical writings as well). Irenaeus of Lyons likened them to the four winds of heaven, to the four living creatures found in the Apocalypse, and to the four biblical covenants made by God with humankind (in the persons of Adam, Noah, Abraham and Moses), thus claiming divine sanction for their plurality [*Adv Haer* 3.11.8]. They were not, however, always listed in the order that is familiar today – altogether, eight different gospel sequences are found in the manuscripts, although in none of them is Luke listed first. Marcion's linkage of the Pauline letters with the gospel record was in fact a positive recognition of their interdependence, and his clear preference for distinctively Christian writings, of which there was now an abundant supply, was a step towards the separation of the Old and the New Testament (a term first found in Tertullian, a North African Christian). By the end of the 2nd century the Pastoral Letters were also generally counted within the Pauline corpus in the Eastern (but not yet the Western) Church, together with the letter to the Hebrews – whose inclusion was sometimes defended on the grounds that it brought the number of Paul's letters up to the 'sacred' number of fourteen (i.e. twice seven).

Criteria for 'canonical' status

The reluctance in Rome to recognise Hebrews as on a par with other letters arose from well-founded doubts about its Pauline authorship. This hesitation was readily overcome with the two Gospels not named after an apostle: Peter's memoirs were considered to lie behind Mark's Gospel (and it was surely this factor which promoted retention of the work, considering that its contents were largely to be found within the other Synoptics), while Luke was associated with Paul. The acceptance of non-apostolic writings suggests that Mark and Luke were indeed the actual authors. An important 8th century Latin codex was discovered in 1740 by the Italian scholar Muratori, within which the barely decipherable *Muratorian Fragment* is usually held to date back to the late 2nd century. It throws considerable light on the Christian documents considered as authoritative at that time by the church in Rome. The first 34 lines read as follows (beginning presumably with Mark):

> ... at which however he was present, and so he set it down. The third book
> of the Gospel, according to Luke. This physician Luke after the ascension of
> Christ, when Paul had taken him with him as a legal expert, composed it in

his own name in accordance with Paul's thinking. He himself, however, did not see the Lord in the flesh and therefore, as far as he was able to follow events, he began to tell the story from the nativity of John. The fourth of the Gospels, that of John, one of the disciples. When his fellow-disciples and bishops encouraged him, John said, 'Fast with me from today for three days, and whatever may be revealed to each one, let us relate it to one another.' The same night it was revealed to Andrew, one of the apostles, that while all were to revise it, John in his own name should write down everything. Thus, though different beginnings are taught in the various gospel books, yet that makes no difference to the faith of believers, since by the one primary Spirit, everything is declared in all concerning his nativity, his passion, his resurrection, his life with his disciples, and concerning his two comings, the first in humility when he was despised, which is past, the second, glorious in royal power, which is still in the future. It is no wonder, then, that John should so constantly mention these particular points in his letters, saying about himself, 'What we have seen with our eyes and heard with our ears and our hands have handled, these we have written.' For in this way he claims to be not only an eyewitness and hearer, but also a writer in order of all the wonderful deeds of the Lord.

It is particularly noteworthy that John's Gospel is presented as one that was approved by 'all' the apostles, and that John's letters are implicitly commended as well. John's writings were at that time viewed with some suspicion because of their appeal to Gnostic teachers, so the Muratorian text is giving reassurance about their acceptability within the mainstream Church. Certainly its differences from the Synoptic writings prompted pause for thought, with Clement of Alexandria around this time referring to three 'earthy' Gospels (the Synoptics) and to John's as the 'spiritual' Gospel. The text quoted here insists that such variations make 'no difference to the faith of believers' since the one Spirit informs them all. Such a defence suggests that objections continued to be made, both within the Church and by pagan critics. A hundred years later, Porphyry wrote his attack *Against the Christians*, focusing especially on 'contradictions and inconsistencies' in the scriptures. Indeed he further claimed:

It is common knowledge that Christians brazenly alter their sacred writings to make them conform to their theological whims.

Certainly any critical edition of the Greek New Testament will reveal quite a number of discrepancies in the available manuscripts. Some are surely scribal errors, others may be attempts to correct those errors, and a few perhaps given for clarification or to express specific theological nuances; but their collective testimony is broadly consistent – in line with the conclusion offered by the *Muratorian Fragment* about the overall harmony of the New Testament. It is worth recalling that the charge of textual emendation was also levied against the Jews by Christians: Justin Martyr (see above, page 31) claimed that the words 'from the tree' had been omitted in Psalm 96.10 to avoid their prophetic reference to the Cross.

The importance attached by Christians to their scriptures became well known throughout the Roman world; 'the churches of the Galileans' were characterised as places where they 'engage in interpretation of Matthew and Luke' [Julian: *Ep.* 61c]. Hence their opponents sought to undermine their faith, if not by deriding the reliability of these scriptures, then ultimately by confiscating them – as subsequent emperors attempted. In the 4th century, when persecution ceased, it was still important to be reminded of the scriptural heritage – as, for example, in the catechesis offered by Cyril of Jerusalem:

> The faith which the Church hands down to you has all the authority of the scriptures behind it. [*Cat* 5.12]

If 'through lack of education' or 'by want of leisure' any catechumens were unable to read the scriptures for themselves, they should be assured that the Church's creeds provided an authentic summary of their teaching.

Apostolic authorship was, however, insufficient in itself to establish fidelity to the apostolic tradition. Pseudonymous writings, including gospels and letters, were in circulation during the 2nd century or even earlier. Origen, for example, claimed knowledge of a *Gospel according to Matthias* as well as a *Gospel of Peter*, while Clement of Alexandria knew of a slightly earlier document entitled *The Preaching of Peter*. What mattered more than authorship, though, was the orthodoxy of the contents. Here the *Muratorian Fragment* insisted that 'gall cannot be mixed with honey', and singled out as unacceptable any writings that conveyed the ideas of Valentinus, of Marcion, and of the lately influential apocalyptic teacher

Montanus (who believed that the new Jerusalem was about to descend from heaven upon a region of Phrygia).

Around the same time Christian theologians began to offer summaries of what came to be called 'the rule (or canon) of faith'. Irenaeus urged that 'the substance of the tradition' was to be found identically across the Church, even though it is 'scattered throughout the whole world' [*Adv Haer* 1.10.1-2]. It might find different expressions (and in fact Irenaeus gave various expositions of the threefold baptismal creed as well as of the basic 'kerygma' about Christ), but in essence these conveyed the same truths. Tertullian too (despite eventually being drawn into Montanism himself) spelt out the key truths shared by Christians everywhere, which he said were 'incapable of alteration and reform' [*De Virg* 1]. Both writers contrasted this consistent rule of faith with the often mutually incompatible teachings of the heretics.

For the compiler of the *Muratorian Fragment*, the safest course was to find the apostolic tradition precisely in writings of the apostolic age. Hence, although *The Shepherd of Hermas* was widely accepted within the Church (and subsequently was partially included in the 4th century Codex Sinaiticus), the *Fragment* played down its status on the grounds that it had been composed 'quite recently ... after the time of the apostles'. For Irenaeus, the early dating of a text was less significant than the derivation of its teachings from the apostles themselves; here he was aware that the tradition of faith was guarded by their successors:

> We are in a position to reckon up those who were by the apostles instituted bishops in the Churches, and the succession of these men to our own times; those who neither taught nor knew of anything like what these [heretics] rave about ... Since, however, it would be very tedious ... to reckon up the successions of all the Churches, we put to confusion all those who ... assemble in unauthorized meetings by indicating the tradition of the very great, the very ancient, and universally known Church founded and organized at Rome by the two most glorious apostles, Peter and Paul ... For it is a matter of necessity that every Church should agree with this Church, on account of its pre-eminent authority ... inasmuch as the apostolic tradition has been preserved continuously by those [faithful] who exist everywhere.

While Irenaeus saw Rome as the principal guardian of Christian teaching, he affirmed too that other ancient churches upheld the same witness. Polycarp, for example, 'was not only instructed by apostles, and conversed with many who had seen Christ, but was also, by apostles in Asia, appointed bishop of the Church in Smyrna':

> He always taught the things which he had learned from the apostles, and which the Church has handed down, and which alone are true. To these things all the Asiatic Churches testify, as do also those men who have succeeded Polycarp down to the present time,—a man who was of much greater weight, and a more steadfast witness of truth, than Valentinus, and Marcion, and the rest of the heretics ... Should we not have recourse to the most ancient churches with which the apostles held constant intercourse, and learn from them what is certain? [*Adv Haer* 3.3-4]

The long-established connection of any writing with one of the main centres of Christian faith, along with its continued use in church worship (as mentioned by Justin in his *First Apology*), would thus be a strong recommendation for the authenticity of its teaching. The principle was summarised by Augustine in the late 4th century, at a time when lists of canonical books were being drawn up:

> [The reader] should follow the authority of the greater number of catholic Churches, among which are those which have deserved to have apostolic seats and to receive epistles ... He will prefer those accepted by all catholic Churches to those which some do not accept. Among those which are not accepted by all, he should prefer those which are accepted by the largest number of important Churches to those held by a few minor churches of less authority. [*De Doct Christ* 2.12]

It was, of course, these 'important' churches which would in any case have held a more complete library of Christian writings; those who lacked their resources might understandably wish to use their own stock of writings, even if some of these were regarded as suspect elsewhere.

It appears from Augustine's advice that, while the idea of limiting the New Testament (as it may now be termed) to books of apostolic authenticity was generally agreed, the actual implementation of a universally recognised canon was probably unattainable. The church historian Eusebius offers some evidence about developments from the early 3rd century onwards. He mentions that Serapion of Antioch knew of writings 'falsely attributed' to Peter and the other apostles, and had particular occasion to reject the so-called *Gospel of Peter*. Turning to his contemporary, Clement of Alexandria, he notes his use of testimonies from the *disputed* writings, including Hebrews, Jude and Barnabas, in addition to those that he terms the *acknowledged* writings. He cites Origen's acceptance of 'the traditional view of the four Gospels which alone are undeniably authentic in the Church of God', along with his acknowledgement of Revelation as the work of John, and of Hebrews as 'quite equal to the apostle's [i.e. Paul's] acknowledged writings' – even if the phraseology and construction are by one of Paul's disciples. Elsewhere Origen also referred to Barnabas as 'a catholic letter', but seems to have had hesitations about James and Jude. Eusebius' own classification of writings is as follows:

It is proper to sum up the writings of the New Testament which have been already mentioned. First then must be put the holy quartet of the gospels; followed by the Acts of the Apostles. After this must be reckoned the epistles of Paul [including Hebrews which is mentioned nowhere else], and after them the epistle called 1 John, likewise the epistle of Peter. After them is to be placed, if it really seem proper, the Apocalypse of John, concerning which we shall give the different opinions at the proper time. These then belong among the accepted writings. Among the disputed writings, yet recognised by many, are the epistles known as James, Jude, and 2 Peter, and those called 2 and 3 John, the work either of the evangelist or of someone else with the same name. Among the rejected writings must be reckoned the Acts of Paul, the so-called Shepherd, and the Apocalypse of Peter, also the alleged epistle of Barnabas, and the so-called Teachings of the Apostles; and besides, as I said, the Apocalypse of John, which some, as I said, reject, but which others class with the accepted books. And among these some have placed the Gospel according to the Hebrews, a book which has a special appeal for those of the Hebrews who have accepted Christ. All these may be reckoned among the disputed books. But we have nevertheless felt compelled to give a catalogue of these also, distinguishing those works which according to church tradition are true and genuine and commonly accepted from those others which, although not canonical but disputed, yet familiar to most ecclesiastical writers. [*Hist Eccl* 3.25]

It seems likely that Eusebius' *History* was available prior to the landmark Council of Nicaea in 325 CE, convened by the emperor Constantine to resolves disputes surrounding the Arian controversy. Shortly before it happened he placed Porphyry's attack on Christians on an Index of banned books – and soon afterwards added those of Arius. He then wrote to Eusebius instructing him to arrange for 'fifty copies of the sacred scriptures' to be made – in Caesarea, where he was bishop and where a tradition of scriptural and scribal expertise had been maintained since the days of Origen. Although these new codices were intended for the growing number of churches in Constantinople itself, the recently created capital city, the actual selection of the writings to be included – Eusebius' own preferences – would undoubtedly have set an important precedent for churches elsewhere.

Another significant milestone in defining the Church's canon of scripture has long been identified as Athanasius' *Easter Letter* of 367 CE to the clergy and the monasteries under his jurisdiction. In a context of fiercely contested theological views, he sought to clarify the boundaries of scriptural authority, and listed the books of both Old and New Testaments; the latter are in the order known today, apart from the Catholic Epistles being placed immediately after Acts. He added:

> There are also other books besides these, which have not indeed been put in the canon, but have been appointed by the Fathers as reading-matter for those who have just come forward and wish to be instructed in the doctrine of piety: the Wisdom of Solomon, the Wisdom of Sirach, Esther, Judith, Tobias, the so-called Teaching [Didache] of the Apostles, and the Shepherd. And although, beloved, the former are in the canon and the latter serve as reading matter, yet mention is nowhere made of the apocrypha; rather they are a fabrication of the heretics, who write them down when it pleases them and generously assign to them an early date of composition in order that they may be able to draw upon them as supposedly ancient writings and have in them occasion to deceive the guileless.

Athanasius' canon gained gradual acceptance; when Jerome made his Latin translation, the Vulgate, he acquiesced with the general practice of his day, which now followed Athanasius. Jerome's commission dated from 383 CE, and in the succeeding decade the 3rd Synod of Carthage actually listed

115

these 27 books as 'canonical scriptures'. Yet there were those such as the Syrian, or Nestorian, or Coptic churches who to this day have retained their own variations: thus, Revelation is not accepted in the Syrian church, whereas it is found in the Coptic church with the addition of *1 and 2 Clement*. Other leading contenders for canonicity, *Barnabas* and *The Shepherd of Hermas*, did not readily fall out of use: Jerome described *Barnabas* as 'almost a New Testament book' [*De Vir* 3.6], while the *Shepherd* was still included in the much later 9th century *Codex Sangermanensis*. It should also be remembered that, even when the NT canon had been agreed, this did not mean that the text itself had been carefully examined and finalised (nor that the included writings were invariably in the same order). The task of scrutinising the many manuscripts, fragmentary remains, citations and translations of the New Testament remains an ongoing challenge.

The canonical principle

The evolution of the New Testament as a collection of widely accepted canonical writings was a lengthy process: over two hundred years elapsed between Marcion's proposals of the mid 2nd century and Athanasius' Easter letter. It must be remembered, however, that during this period there was serious persecution of the Church, in which the initial move was often to seize church property – especially the books that the authorities realised were so precious to Christian communities. This happened in the Decian persecution of the 250s CE and again under Diocletian fifty years later. It is hardly surprising that Eusebius' account of scriptural usage falls silent after the time of Origen. Yet when the Peace of Constantine gave public recognition to the Church in the early 4th century, the issue that needed urgent resolution before widespread agreement could be reached over the NT canon was the raging doctrinal dispute over the teachings of Arius and his followers. The purpose of approving scriptural texts was to give public articulation to the apostolic faith; otherwise, if the latter was being challenged, there was an inadequate basis for a decisive response. Despite Irenaeus' readiness to defer to the apostolic authority of Rome, the early Church was far less centralised than it is today; it is perhaps surprising to a modern generation of Catholic Christians that there was no encyclical from the bishop of Rome to resolve the considerable uncertainty about the various 'disputed' texts, and that it was initiatives from Caesarea and Alexandria that seem to have brought eventual accord.

Subsequent church history demonstrates that even then doubts and disagreements remained – and are surely still alive today. The inclusion of Revelation within the canon has from time to time been challenged, and has certainly given rise to very mistaken interpretations:

> An elderly man was recently observed on the sunny seafront of a well-known resort [*so a local reporter noted*] hosting an assemblage of placards whose main theme was 'eternity'. He explained to passers-by that God was about to destroy two-thirds of humankind (including all of America's enemies) and reward the remaining one-third of true believers (numbering among others – somewhat curiously – the entire population of Israel).

His assertions were evidently based on select quotations from the book of Revelation and to a lesser extent from apocalyptic verses in Matthew's Gospel. Nevertheless, such common abuse of biblical texts does not warrant any pruning of the canon, since it is but a crude example of what may happen when the Church's scriptures enter the public domain.[24] Ancient writings in unfamiliar genres, while still able to convey uplifting messages of faith when properly understood, are otherwise prone to being distorted. Their true meaning – and hence the justification for their remaining within the New Testament – is, as ever, to testify to apostolic teaching, which requires reference to the rest of the canon and indeed to the living Church that continues to witness in that same tradition.

If any doubts linger concerning the consensus achieved in the late 4th century, they may perhaps concern the inclusion of Jude more than any other writing. It is seldom read in the liturgy, and seems to add little to

---

[24] It remains an essential task to foster a balanced (i.e. canonical) appreciation of the scriptures revered by different faith traditions. The selective use of texts has certainly been used to justify extreme positions. Thus, anti-Semitism – which has a long history in the Christian Church – can appeal to verses such as John 8.44 ('You are of your father the devil') or 1 Thessalonians 1.15 ('The Jews … killed both the Lord Jesus and the prophets, and drove us out, and displease God') in ignorance of their specific context and of other New Testament passages presenting quite different messages.

what is already found in the New Testament elsewhere; its main focus is upon the perversion of the gospel [v4], using very oblique language [vv5-16]. But perhaps the final verses which speak of love and mercy [vv20-23], as well as the magnificent doxology [vv24-25], are redeeming features that still suggest the proper spirit of forbearance in the face of opposition.

As it has been handed down to the Church today, the New Testament is not the tidiest of works. There are significant differences between the Gospels, contrasting evaluations of the Jewish law, varying stances about the expected Parousia of Christ, and so on. Yet sometimes its very ambiguities can be a source of strength; by offering a broad theological base, the Church can itself accommodate a wider constituency of faith. Provided there is agreement in essentials, other issues may be understood as *adiaphora* – 'indifferent' matters where communities of Christians rooted in diverse cultures or contending with life in particular contexts can adapt what is still the apostolic faith to changed circumstances. Historically the Church's scriptural texts served not only to distinguish Christianity from other cults, but also enabled it through scriptural commentary to engage with issues of the day, to communicate across a wide social and geographical spectrum, and – by reflecting upon the vital testimony within these writings – to develop a whole new 'philosophy' (or world-view). And while scripture could not of itself resolve every question, even when its apparent inconsistencies were overcome, its rejection, as Ambrose of Milan declared, was 'a likely cause of heresy' [*De Fide* 4.11].

The essential point is that the canonical scriptures of the New Testament remain a collective witness to the faith declared once and for all by the apostles. The truth they express lies beyond the various texts, which need to be understood as complementary rather than in opposition. It is not only a faith of long ago, but the living faith of the Church today, which is still discovering the riches of Christ for itself.

10. Ongoing Formation of Faith

The growth of Christian literature

The core of the Christian message – the 'good news' of the gospel – was of course communicated in a variety of ways. The message, recalling the life, death and resurrection of Jesus, was taught and preached, and was expressed in a variety of written genres as well as in popular oral transmission. It was also embodied in rituals and in the practice of the faith, not least in the exercise of charity and of healing activities. What the apostles and the company of believers passed on 'comprises everything that serves to make the People of God live their lives in holiness and increase their faith'.[25] This is evidently a living tradition, which continues to develop (under the promised guidance of the Holy Spirit) in response to the changing situations and differing contexts in which Christians find themselves.

The familiar texts of the New Testament are, as we have seen, by no means the only early Christian writings. When they were first collected together in codices others were sometimes included as well. Even where there are no extant manuscripts, however fragmentary, the proliferation of these writings is known from patristic authors who cite them, sometimes approvingly but, when necessary, attempting to counter any mistaken or even heretical views. From the mid 2nd century there was certainly an explosion of Christian literature, which may not have gained liturgical usage, but was nevertheless intended to clarify Christian belief and to counter objections to it (the aim of the so-called apologists) or to propagate distinctive interpretations of the Gospel within the growing number of sects: for example, there was a considerable Gnostic literature in which the dualism between 'matter' and 'spirit' in effect denies the reality of Christ's incarnation.

It is clear too that both the newly minted 'gospel' genre and that of the book of Acts prompted writers in this later period to imitate their achievements, and to expand the material found in the (by now) recognised

---

[25] *Dei Verbum* 8 (Vatican II)

scriptural deposit: other teachings of Jesus might feature, as well as missing episodes from his life or those of the apostles who followed him. Some of these extra sayings and stories may have been gleaned from the *agrapha* heritage passed on orally in church circles, while others may have more the character of imaginative or fictional reconstruction, influenced by sectarian views. Particular scrutiny will be given here to the accounts of some of the leading apostles that are found in the *Apocryphal Acts*, which may well have been intended to promote deeper commitment to the faith by offering heroic role models, initially at least to that narrower class of Christians who were literate. Like others, they may have been brought to belief by observing the remarkable impact of the Gospel – in healings or other miracles, in the change brought about in people's lives, in the distinctive pastoral care and compassion of church communities – but needed now to develop their own dedication to God. It is important to appreciate that, despite the occurrence of the miraculous in these *Acta*, there is an underlying emphasis upon the need for faith to be consolidated with sound teaching. This is also a strong New Testament theme, and in using the book of Acts as their literary model the *Acta* generally remain true to its focus (and that of the Gospels) on hearing and responding to God's word.

A brief resumé of some New Testament narratives will illustrate this point. Miracles such as exorcisms and healings are more prominent in the Gospels and in the book of Acts than is sometimes realised. Yet predominantly they were seen by the early Church as initiating a process in which faith would subsequently develop. Their aftermath in Mark's Gospel, for example, is typically an injunction to `secrecy' followed by the learning experience necessary both to understand and to share Jesus' mission. The gradual healing of the blind man of Bethsaida (whence Philip, Peter and Andrew all originated, according to John) typifies this process. There is also an accent upon the disciples receiving private as well as public instruction, along with special revelation reserved to an inner group (most notably on the occasion of the transfiguration). When Matthew (arguably written for a relatively affluent urban church) adapts Mark's Gospel it is noticeable that he stiffens it with teaching content, while elsewhere [e.g. Mt 11.16-19] he heightens the lack of popular response to Jesus. As in Mark, the demand for a 'sign' is firmly rejected [Mt 11.38-42], although in a deeper sense, signs are discernible to the eye of faith. Indeed, it is as 'signs' that a limited selection of miracles is presented in John's Gospel, to which there are a variety of responses: outright rejection – muted acceptance – a temporary welcome for Jesus' wonder working – belief in his teaching – commitment in spite of misunderstandings – paradigmatic discipleship – defection.[26] These (fluid) categories might well be applied also to reactions found in later epochs of the Church.

Whereas these Gospels are addressed to particular Christian communities, Luke's Gospel and its sequel the book of Acts are both apparently written for an individual, 'most excellent Theophilus'. Jesus is presented as a Spirit-filled healer, who casts out demons and ministers to the poor and needy. There is resistance to his message 'in his own country' and among some religious leaders, but the general reaction is one of amazement and awe. Some conversions follow his miracles, including that of a centurion with whom Theophilus might well have identified as a fellow Gentile: 'Not even in Israel have I found such faith'. Jesus' death is here a clear miscarriage of justice since both Pilate and Herod find him guiltless, as does the penitent thief hanging by his side. Such suffering is foretold in scripture, where God's purposes are to be found: the miracle of the resurrection affords therefore a paradigmatic learning experience [Lk 24.25-27, 45-47].

The story of the expanding church in Acts is then the story of Jesus writ large. The apostles are endowed with the Spirit to perform the same works on a much wider front. Representatives of the whole world are in Jerusalem to witness the outpouring of Pentecost, which is above all a miracle of God's spoken word. Although healings and exorcisms take place, they are not actually the prime catalyst for conversion. Rather they arouse wonder and a readiness to listen to the apostle's words; or, as Paul expresses it [2 Cor 12.12] they authenticate his apostolic status. Luke emphasises frequently that it is the preaching of the word which leads many to believe and to be baptised. Only two exceptions to this pattern occur – the stories about Peter in Acts in which mass conversions follow a healing in Lydda and a resurrection in Joppa. Luke does make clear, however, that Peter stayed on afterwards 'for many days' to instruct these new believers. In Paul's ministry, although Sergius Paulus, proconsul of Cyrus, is persuaded by the

---

[26] R. Alan Culpepper: *Anatomy of the Fourth Gospel* (Philadelphia 1983, 146-148)

sudden blinding of Elymas the magician, this is only a confirmation of the message he has already heard. Likewise the spectacular challenge to the seven sons of Sceva is set in the context of Paul's teaching programme in Ephesus, and this again confirms his credentials as an agent of the one true God [Acts 19].

In general, therefore, 'healings' are seen by Luke as expressions of Christian compassion, but not as an essential tool of mission. Nevertheless, their inclusion may have paved the way for more exotic accounts in the *Apocryphal Acts*. Perhaps the most significant difference between these writings and the book of Acts lies in Luke's emphasis upon the apostles as a *unified body* of witnesses, which is hardly evident in the later stories of their *individual* exploits. Thus, Acts 9.32-11.18 is not written to glorify Peter, but to prepare the ground for Paul's future ministry among Gentiles – showing as it does the precedent of Cornelius' acceptance, first by Peter and then by the church in Jerusalem.

The process of church growth and Christian formation

After the close of the Pauline era there was so far as is known almost no specifically missionary activity. Yet the Christian community went on expanding through networks of family, friends, and business contacts, through migrancy and the scattering effect of persecution, through the moral example of faithful believers and also through its growing corpus of literature. The most potent single cause of Christian success was probably the practical application of charity i.e. caring for the destitute, for widows and orphans; visiting those in prison; providing burial for the poor and hospitality to travellers. Because of this, Christianity generally made greater impact upon the poorer classes than upon those who were richer (and often resistant to its culturally subversive character).

When Eusebius describes evangelism in the province of Asia around the start of the 2nd century CE he remarks on the 'miraculous powers' at work, 'so that at the first hearing whole crowds in a body embraced with whole-hearted eagerness the worship of the universal Creator' [*Hist Eccl* 3.37]. There is, however, little supporting evidence, apart from a more general upsurge of belief in miracle-working during previous decades. The only name proffered by Eusebius is that of Quadratus, but his exploits are not detailed [*Hist Eccl* 4.3.2]. There is just one identifiable evangelist in the whole of the 2nd century CE, namely, Polycarp, preaching in and around Smyrna. Thus, 'after St Paul, the church had no mission, it made no organised or official approach to unbelievers; rather it left everything to the individual'.[27] Yet the Christian Church saw steady growth, to a lesser extent among the middle classes, but mainly (as admitted by Origen) among the lower orders who gathered in private houses or rented accommodation [*Contra Cels* 3.55]. Even in the mid 3rd century, according to one of the *Pseudo-Clementine Letters to Virgins*, Christian teachers were to be found exclusively among the households of believers.

Several different routes to conversion may be noted. A few intellectuals, such as Justin and Tatian, were attracted philosophically to the Christian faith – but Celsus, who despised the rational credentials of Christianity, would have considered them exceptional [*Contra Cels* 3.44]. Origen was proud of the few 'who converted through the exercise of reason and the reading of the scriptures'.[28] In another of the *Pseudo-Clementine* writings from around 200 CE, there is a fictional account of the young pagan Clement who agonised about the fate of the soul after death until he met St Peter and became a Christian [*Recogn* 1.1]. Justin, however, seems to reckon the impact of exorcisms rather than apologetics as a more effective measure:

> For numberless demoniacs throughout the whole world, and in your city, many of our Christian men have exorcised them in the name of Jesus Christ, who was crucified under Pontius Pilate; they have healed and do heal them, rendering the possessing devils helpless and driving them out of the men, though they could not be cured by all the other exorcists, or by those who used incantations and drugs. [*2 Apol* 6]

Tertullian also confirms this phenomenon:

---

[27] Ramsay MacMullen: *Christianizing the Roman Empire AD 100-400* (New Haven & London 1984, 34)

[28] Eugene V. Gallagher: *Conversion and Salvation in the Apocryphal Acts of the Apostles* (Second Century JECS 8.1, 1991, 27)

Why, all the authority and power we have over [the demons] is from our naming the name of Christ, and recalling to their memory the woes with which God threatens them at the hands of Christ as Judge, and which they expect one day to overtake them... It has not been an unusual thing, accordingly, for these testimonies to convert men to Christianity. [*Apol* 23]

The clerk of [an advocate] who was liable to be thrown upon the ground by an evil spirit, was set free from his affliction; as was also the relative of another, and the little boy of a third. How many men of rank (to say nothing of common people) have been delivered from devils, and healed of diseases! Even Severus himself, the father of Antonine, was graciously mindful of the Christians; for he sought out the Christian Proculus, surnamed Torpacion, the steward of Euhodias, and in gratitude for his having once cured him by anointing, he kept him in his palace till the day of his death. [*Ad Scap* 4]

Rather more cautiously Theophilus, writing in the 180s, remarks that exorcisms work 'sometimes', and even the sceptical Celsus admits that exorcisms and healings have taken place. The outcome, according to Irenaeus, may well have been a conversion to Christian faith:

Some do certainly and truly drive out devils, so that those who have thus been cleansed from evil spirits frequently both believe [in Christ], and join themselves to the Church. [*Adv Haer* 2.32.4]

What evidently induced other unbelievers to convert was the overwhelming thought of 'judgment fires'. Justin mentions this too:

For [the words of Christ] possess a terrible power in themselves, and are sufficient to inspire those who turn aside from the path of rectitude with awe. [*Dial* 8.2]

Luke had much earlier made the same observation in the book of Acts, when Paul was on trial before Felix:

And as he argued about justice and self-control and future judgment, Felix was alarmed and said, 'Go away for the present'. [Acts 24.25]

No doubt other Christians testified likewise when they too were being tried; while the church did not encourage martyrdom, there were nevertheless some (numbered perhaps in hundreds) who steadfastly confessed their faith before hostile accusers and by so doing sometimes began to turn their hearts and minds. Perpetua, executed in Carthage in 203, records such an outcome:

> Pudens the adjutant in whose charge the prison was ... also began to magnify us because he understood that there was much grace in us ... [and] now believed. [*Passio S Perp* 9.1; 16.4]

Tertullian famously considered that this happened on a larger scale:

> The oftener we are mown down by you, the more in number we grow; the blood of Christians is seed... For who that contemplates it, is not excited to inquire what is at the bottom of it? who, after inquiry, does not embrace our doctrines? and when he has embraced them, desires not to suffer that he may become partaker of the fulness of God's grace, that he may obtain from God complete forgiveness, by giving in exchange his blood? [*Apol* 50]

For whatever reasons 'Christians spread and increased: no other cult in the Empire grew at anything like the same speed' – although their numbers were not as great as sometimes conjectured. Lane Fox points out that 'inscriptions, pagan histories, texts and papyri make next to no reference to Christians before 250', while 'if Christians really were so numerous, we could also expect some evidence of meeting places which could hold so many worshippers'. His assessment is that 'whereas pagan cults won adherents, Christianity aimed, and contrived, to win converts. It won them by conviction and persuasion, long and detailed sequels to the initial proof that faith could work... The *ideas* appealed... it was not just because of some past miracle that simple Christians were prepared to die agonizingly for their religion'[29].

Rigorous instruction prior to baptism was certainly practised in the early 3rd century. According to Hipplolytus:

> Catechumens will hear the word for three years. Yet if someone is earnest and perseveres well in the matter, it is not the time that is judged, but the conduct [*Ap Trad* 17]

---

[29] Robin Lane Fox: *Pagans and Christians* (Harmondsworth 1988, 269, 271, 330)

Origen contrasted how Christian communities, unlike philosophical schools open to all, would 'pick and choose', thoroughly testing potential new members [*Contra Cels* 3.51]. Hence this conclusion:

> Historically, it is less significant that Christianity could bring in a diversity of persons for a diversity of initial reasons than that it could retain them while imposing these long apprenticeships. The years of instruction and preparation became, in their turn, one of the faith's particular appeals. People felt that they were exploring a deep mystery, step by step.[30]

Instruction was of course not just for neophytes. Christian parents were always expected to educate their children 'in the fear of the Lord' [*Didache* 4.9]. Polycarp urged that they should be trained in the 'knowledge' of the Lord, and the apologist Theophilus of Antioch wrote to Autolycus that such wisdom must increase 'in an orderly progress' [2.25], implying an ongoing process of formation – in the terminology of both 1 Corinthians [3.2] and the Letter to the Hebrews [5.13], a diet proceeding from 'milk' to 'solid food'. The emphasis was apparently more upon moral and spiritual virtues than upon doctrinal content. In the Didache the essential difference was between 'the way of life' and 'the way of death', while Clement of Rome drew particular attention to the hope of resurrection:

> The Master continually shows to us the resurrection that shall be hereafter. [*1 Clem* 24.1]

Thus, the Church's initial emphasis on the teaching of the word was certainly maintained over the years; this is the appropriate context in which to consider further the *Apocryphal Acts*.

The *Apocryphal Acts*

It is likely that most of the major *Apocryphal Acts* were written before the end of the 2nd century, although additions and alterations (particularly to the text of the *Acts of Paul*) may have continued long afterwards. It is generally held that these *Acta* were for the edification of church members:

---

[30] Lane Fox 317

Writings originally directed or later offered from within the church to an audience beyond did not include, of course, any pages that are now canonical or, for that matter, apocryphal; for those pages were rather for *internal consumption*. At best, the occasional outsider who investigated them was an enemy, like Celsus or Porphyry... And there was little enough reading of any sort, anyway. Three quarters or more of the population were illiterate.[31]

Further, 'although the legendary acts of apostles laid great weight on the signs and wonders which their heroes worked, they were not historical texts, nor were they written to win pagan converts: they aimed to impress Christian readers and spread the views of a minority of fellow Christians through vivid fiction'.[32] These *Acta* were not generally addressed to the mass of the churches' membership – the humbler free classes – but tended to place the apostles in the highest provincial society, for good measure dropping well-chosen names. This is reminiscent of the book of Acts, dedicated to one who was 'most excellent' which in contemporary usage indicated a person of rank, suggesting that Theophilus might be 'the cover name for a highly placed figure in Roman circles'.[33] Here the *Acts of Andrew* features the wealthy Aegeates and his wife Maximilla ; in the *Acts of John*, one of the first encountered is Tycomedes, the commander-in-chief of the Ephesians, a rich man who seeks help for his wife Cleopatra; Thecla, heroine of the *Acts of Paul*, is soon discovered to be sought after by Thamyris, 'chief man' of the city of Iconium; the *Acts of Peter* describes how Peter came to Rome on account of Simon Magus, who is found staying 'at the house of the senator Marcellus whom he had won over by his magic', while later a woman called Eubola is mentioned, 'highly esteemed in this world, possessing much gold and valuable pearls':

And on Sunday Peter spoke to the brethren and encouraged them in the faith of Christ. And many senators and knights and wealthy women and matrons were present, and they were strengthened in the faith. There was also present a very rich woman, named Chryse, because all her vessels were

---

[31] MacMullen 20-21

[32] Lane Fox 329

[33] Lane Fox 430

of gold. [*APt* 30 - in fact, more upper class women feature in *APt* than in the other *Acta*]

Finally, mention may be made of how in the *Acts of Thomas* the apostle engages in India first with king Gundaphorus, then with king Misdaeus. There are therefore remarkable similarities to be observed between references in the *Acta* and in the book of Acts, which – quite apart from its opening inscription – features the illustrious names of Sergius Paulus in Cyprus and Publius in Malta. One may conclude that the *Acta* too seem to target the well-connected (especially their womenfolk, including widows and virgins).

Since at the time they were written there was a growing regard for authority in the church, it is understandable that the desired teaching is linked to the more *prominent* of the apostles. No doubt too the legends – particularly about Andrew, John and Thomas – were encouraged by their meagre mention in the canonical Acts, in the same way that infancy stories about Jesus met a demand for missing information. They may be termed perfectionist texts, 'propelled by the interests of over-achievers', as well as 'moralizing [novels] calculated to provide instruction in Christian piety'.[34] Their 'popular' character is evident in the displays of supernatural power used by each apostle (in the many healings, in exorcisms, in the raising of the dead, in Peter's superior powers against Simon Magus and in John's destruction of the temple of Artemis). Yet while these displays are more prominent than in the book of Acts, they are not always as effective as the apostles' many exhortations and speeches in changing lives: further instruction is often portrayed as necessary for converts to be fully confirmed in their new faith [e.g. *AAnd* 8-10, *AJn* 57, *APt* 13]. The apostles are thus not seen as *theioi andres* (divine men) in the fully pagan sense, since their activity is not designed to authenticate their own personalities or abilities but to promote true belief. Peter, for example, is recognized as 'servant of the ineffable living God' [*APt* 9], while at John's death the people cry out 'he whom John worships is the one true God' [*Virtutes Johannis* VIII]. Miracles in the *Acta* thus not only sway the hearts of unbelievers, but

---

[34] David E. Smith: *The Canonical Function of Acts* (Collegeville 2002, 112)

also provoke a readiness to hear the apostles' teaching, giving added credibility to the no less dramatic power of their divinely charged words.

Some examples of the latter may be noted, beginning with the *Acts of Andrew*:

> She entered and found the apostle speaking with his fellow inmates, whom he had already strengthened by encouraging them to believe in the Lord...
> Most blessed Andrew...the words which came from you are like fiery javelins impaling me...
> Maximilla was not present... for when she heard the words that applied to her and in some way was changed by them, she became what the words themselves had signified.
> When the crowds heard Andrew's speech, they were won over by him, so to say, and did not leave the spot...
> When they observed his nobility, the adamance of his thought, the sheer abundance of his words, the value of his xhortation, the stability of his soul, the prudence of his spirit, the firmness of his mind, and the precision of his reasoning, they were furious with Aegeates... [AAnd 28, 44, 46, 59, 65]

The *Acts of Paul* corroborate the same theme:

> Thecla...listened day and night to the discourse of virginity, as proclaimed by Paul. And she did not look away from the window, but was led on by faith, rejoicing exceedingly...
> And Thecla went in with her and rested eight days, instructing her in the word of God, so that many of the maidservants believed...
> When Paul saw them he rejoiced and rented a barn outside Rome where he and the brethren taught the word of truth. He became famous and many souls were added to the Lord...
> But Paul was not silent and communicated the word to Longus the prefect and Cestus the centurion...when [they] continued to ask about salvation he said to them..."Titus and Luke will give you the seal in the Lord"... [AP13.7, 3.37, 11.1, 11.3-5]

Likewise, there are references in the *Acts of Thomas*:

> And when the young people heard this, they believed the Lord and gave themselves over to him and refrained from   filthy lust...
> When the multitude of those assembled heard these things, they wept...

The whole people therefore believed and presented obedient souls to the living God and Christ Jesus... [AT 13, 38, 59]

The focus in the *Acts of Peter* is, however, generally more upon Peter's spiritual contest with Simon Magus. Since Simon 'deceived with flattering words... and spoke of piety with his lips alone whereas he is wholly impious', the apostle himself is advised to defeat him with 'signs and wonders'; it is by his deeds in these particular circumstances, and not with words, that Peter will 'convert many' [APt 16-17]. Yet tribute is also paid to the power of Peter's words:

> When Peter had spoken with great sorrow of soul many more believers were added to the congregation... [APt 9]

Mission addresses are scarcer in the *Acts of John*, where the apostle's words often precede a miracle or are cast in the form of prayer; but when an old man is brought back to life it is made clear that this is nothing without further spiritual conversion:

> And now, man of the living God, you have called me back: to what purpose?" John replied, "If you rise up to the same life, you would be better to remain dead. But rise up to a better!" And he... preached to him of the mercy of God, so that before he came into the gate the old man believed. [AJn 52]

What is depicted in the canonical Acts and in the *Acta* is the inexorable advance of the Christian mission. Its success, however, is seen more variously; not only in the winning of more unbelievers, but, as some of the above quotations aptly illustrate, in *the transformation of the converts' behaviour*. 'The [conversion] stories often give evidence of being carefully composed in order to express how conversion should be understood, how it actually happens, how it is motivated, and what its proper results are.'[35] In particular, virginity is much prized, and sexual lapses (especially relationships with unbelievers) are a serious threat to spiritual well-being:

> Blessed are those who have kept the flesh chaste, for they shall become a temple of God; blessed are the continent, for God shall speak with them;

---

[35] Gallagher 17

blessed are those who have kept aloof from the world, for they shall be pleasing,to God; blessed are those who have wives as not having them, for they shall experience God. [AP13.5]

However, there can also be some moderation of more extreme demands:

You should not have destroyed your private parts ... For your organs are not hurtful to man, but it is the hidden sources by which every shameful inclination is stirred and becomes manifest. [AJn 54]

And although the focus is mainly upon individual salvation, an important communal dimension is retained in the *Acta*. There are references to the Eucharist, and to the duty of Christian care for slaves and for the poor:

The story of Thomas tells how the apostle takes large sums of money from the king [Gundaphorusi in order to build for him a magnificent palace - only to spend it all on the poor and afflicted. [36]

The twist of the story is that a palace in heaven is then revealed as the king's reward, so the general tenor of the *Acta* is maintained in its fundamental reversal of human values. This contrasts starkly with contemporary popular romances. Indeed, it is clear that Christians live in a society that is hostile to the gospel:

We have learned not to recompense evil for evil, but we have learned to love our enemies and to pray for those who persecute us. [APt 28]

The imitation of the apostles in martyrdom is therefore highly prized. Significantly each of the *Apocryphal Acts* ends with the apostle's death, the gateway to true life after the suffering of this world. So the cross is 'pure, radiant, full of life and light' for the apostle Andrew, 'weary for so long' [AAnd 54 – cf. APt 37 where the real cross is not 'visible']. In the *Acts of John* this idea is taken far beyond the bounds of orthodoxy – although the particular passage may have been a later addition [AJn 98-101]. Spiritual death and spiritual resurrection lies at the heart of the *Acta*'s message: nearly half the conversion stories portray a raising up from the dead or the

---

[36] Wayne A. Meeks: *The origins of Christian morality: the first two centuries* (New Haven & London 1993, 55)

apparently dead. These reinforce the central imperative of dying – particularly to sex, error, unbelief and idolatry – in order to live, which is the attainment of true belief. A strong tendency to dualism may clearly be observed at work, developing an opposition between the flesh and the spirit – although curiously the *Acts of Thomas* concludes with miracles worked by apostle's relics [*AT* 170].

Success for the writers of the *Apocryphal Acts* meant winning and training recruits for an uncompromising lifestyle, those who were prepared to die to the world in radical Christian commitment. Many features of this lifestyle are arguably drawn from teaching found in the canonical tradition, but its vivid portrayal in the *Acta* in the actions of the apostles powerfully reinforced the message that the readers too could overcome the challenges confronting them. The emphasis was upon disciplined instruction: the fictional accounts of truth competing triumphantly with pagan idolatry or depraved morality would lead these neophytes into profounder realms – at which point, so the *Acts of Andrew* suggest, philosophy might become their surer guide.

Yet here one might begin to sail into uncharted waters, with the risk of parting company from the Church's gospel foundations. Or, to express it differently, there is a possibility that reason might begin to overtake revelation, and that Hellenistic subtleties might blunt starker Semitic expressions of the truth. Several centuries later, a prophet emerged from the desert to call believers 'back to basics', as he saw it. Like Jesus (who taught in parables) he preferred to illustrate his message with vivid narrative: the tendency of the Church to over-philosophise was not for him. He did not, however, necessarily foresee that the story of his own life and works (the *hadith*) would later become as influential in interpreting the Qur'an as the 'apocryphal' writings were for some Christians in the discernment of their biblical faith.

PART 3

Responding to the Qur'an

*One of the oldest surviving fragments of the Qur'an
discovered in 1972 in the Great Mosque of Sana, Yemen.
It is a palimpsest, displaying a previous version
(perhaps dating from within 20 years of Muhammad's death)
underneath the later text of around 705 CE.*

11. Encountering the Qur'an

First impressions

Anyone unfamiliar with sacred writings other than the Bible is likely to experience a degree of culture shock on opening the pages of the Qur'an. Whereas the Bible is a library of diverse texts that emerged over a long period of history, written – and often reworked – in a variety of genres, and eventually 'canonised' after much debate, the Qur'an is composed of 114 *suras* revealed to one prophet alone over a couple of decades in the early 7th century. With roughly 6000 verses it is about one-fifth of the length of the Bible; perhaps surprisingly, a number of biblical names are mentioned more often than Muhammad himself. Although the *suras* differ in length, nearly every one of them has the character of a sermon offering impassioned variations on much the same theme, often using the same – or at least very similar – illustrations and arguments e.g. the experiences of earlier prophets such as Moses. Thomas Carlyle, who included the prophet Muhammad in his lectures, *On Heroes, Hero Worship, and the Heroic in History* (London 1841), perhaps speaks for many non-Muslims who have sat down with the Qur'an:

> I must say, it is as toilsome reading as I ever undertook. A wearisome confused jumble, crude, incondite; endless   iterations,   long-windedness, entanglement ... Nothing but a sense of duty could carry any European through the Koran. [Carlyle 57]

However, unlike those whose patience has thereby been exhausted, Carlyle recognised that for all its 'wearisome' style -there was something genuinely powerful and moving that spoke to him – and could appreciate that in Arabic its poetic style might well be even more uplifting :

> It is true we have it under disadvantages: the Arabs see more method in it than we. Mahomet's followers found the Koran lying all in fractions, as it had been written down at first promulgation; much of it, they say, on shoulder-blades of mutton, flung pell-mell into a chest: and they published it, without any discoverable order as to time or otherwise;—merely trying, as would seem, and this not very strictly, to put the longest chapters first ...

Read in its historical sequence it perhaps would not be so bad. Much of it, too, they say, is rhythmic; a kind of wild chanting song, in the original [Arabic] ... Yet I should say, it was not unintelligible how the Arabs might so love it ... If a book come from the heart, it will contrive to reach other hearts. [Carlyle 57-58]

The overwhelming evidence today is that the text does indeed speak directly to the hearts of devout Muslims.

If there was one theme that Muhammad wanted to hammer home, it was his insistence upon Allah as the one true God; necessarily this led to his fierce condemnation of the much prevalent idolatries of his day. Allah was no god of recent invention, but the One who had spoken from the dawn of history to all true believers. Thus, Islam ('submission') is the essential religion of all humankind, as manifested earlier in the teachings of the biblical prophets. Jesus has an honoured place among them, but he has no divine status in Muhammad's view – understandable if his perception of Christian faith as tritheism was the popular form in which he encountered it. He was prepared to recognise the People of the Book as monotheists like himself, but only the faithful among them.

It is also apparent on reading the Qur'an that the abundant biblical references seldom correspond closely to those found in the canonical Bible; indeed, there are hardly any (undisputed) quotations other than those included explicitly in *suras* 5 and 21:

In the Torah We prescribed for them a life for a life, an eye for an eye, a nose for a nose, an ear for an ear, a tooth for a tooth, an equal wound for a wound: *if anyone forgoes this out of charity, it will serve as an atonement for his bad deeds.* [Q5.45 cf. Exod 21.23-25; Lev 24.19-20; Deut 19.21]
We wrote in the Psalms, as We did in Scripture; 'My righteous servants will inherit the earth.' [Q 21.105 cf. Ps 37.29]

Although critical scholarship would detect numerous apocryphal embellishments elsewhere, probably received through oral tradition, the Qur'an – as handed down by direct revelation – would claim to be the authentic version, implying that differences found in the biblical text must be the result of Jewish or Christian 'misunderstanding'. Carlyle elaborates:

135

The [Koran] is made up of mere tradition, and as it were vehement enthusiastic extempore preaching. He returns forever to the old stories of the Prophets as they went current in the Arab memory: how Prophet after Prophet, the Prophet Abraham, the Prophet Hud, the Prophet Moses, Christian and other real and fabulous Prophets, had come to this Tribe and to that, warning men of their sin; and been received by them even as he Mahomet was,—which is a great solace to him. These things he repeats ten, perhaps twenty times; again and ever again ... This is the great staple of the Koran. But curiously, through all this, comes ever and anon some glance as of the real thinker and seer ... with a certain directness and rugged vigour, he brings home still, to our heart, the thing his own heart has been opened to. [Carlyle 59]

It may be that what resonates as spiritually authentic is more often found in the earlier, rather than the later, *suras*. Muhammad was initially rejected by many in Mecca after his revelations began in 610 CE; then in the year 622 CE, when he was about 40 years old, he was invited to follow some of his supporters north to the town of Yathrib, subsequently known as Medina (a name which some later related to 'Midian'). This *hjira* has been taken ever since as the starting point of the Muslim era, from which their calendar is dated. Traditionally the *suras* are divided stylistically into those of Meccan origin and those pronounced in Medina, but in fact not all can be so neatly classified. Some certainly make reference to contemporary locations or events, enabling them to be dated fairly accurately. Particular examples are those *suras* that mention significant battles:

God has helped you on many battlefields, even on the day of the Battle of Hunayn [Q 9.25]
The Byzantines have been defeated [by the Persians] in nearest land. They will reverse their defeat with victory in a few years' time. [Q 30.2-3]

There is also an enigmatic allusion in *sura* 18.83-102 to a person named Dhu 'l-Qarnayn, plausibly explained as Alexander the Great taking the guise of Muhammad's contemporary Heraclius, the Byzantine ruler who saved his empire from defeat at the hands of the Persians in 627-8 CE:

The [qur'anic] reference to contemporary wars reflects the notion, widely held around this time, that the violence and strife of this period were indeed an indicator of the rapidly approaching end of the world.[37]

Many other *suras*, however, are of more general application (and may even have been modified over a period of time): those that offer detailed guidance on family or social matters usually seem to reflect the legislative and defensive needs of Medina. It is now recognised that stories which aim to supply particular contexts for the *suras* are often unreliable i.e. have the character of *post eventum* reconstructions, like some of the biblical apocrypha.

Whereas in Mecca Muhammad appears as a prophet in the biblical mould, frequently attacked by those he describes as 'disbelievers' – who say of his oracles, 'these are nothing but ancient fables' [Q 6.25] – his personal status was very different in Medina where he became an increasingly important political leader. One or two *suras* indicate the pressure he came under there at times, and read as a plea for some personal privacy:

> Believers, do not enter the Prophet's apartments for a meal unless you are given permission to do so; do not linger until it is ready. When you are invited, go in; then, when you have taken your meal, leave. Do not stay on and talk, for that would offend the Prophet, though he would shrink from asking you to leave. [Q 33.53]

Despite his increasing responsibilities and status, his life-style seems to have remained simple.

In the decades – and indeed centuries – following his death the *hadith* started to grow. This collection recounts stories about him, including his various sayings and instructions. Given that the Qur'an itself has only a limited legal content (fewer than five hundred verses) which is often expressed in general principles, it became increasingly important for Islamic legislators to supplement it from Muhammad's own example and teaching. This material ('the custom of the prophet' or *sunna*) was a useful resource

---

[37] Kevin van Bladel: *The Alexander Legend in the Qur'an* (TQHC 2008, 195)

too for qur'anic interpretation and commentary. It was legitimised by *sura* 33:

> The Messenger of God is an excellent model for those of you who put your hope in God and the Last Day and remember Him often. [Q 33.21]

Indeed, the Qur'an also upholds Muhammad as an infallible arbiter;

> By your Lord, they will not be true believers until they let you decide between them in all matters of dispute, and find no resistance in their souls to your decisions, accepting them totally. [Q 4.65]

However, *sura* 5 makes clear that Jews and Christians continued to have adequate legal instruction in their own scriptures:

> Why do they come to you for judgement when they have the Torah with God's judgement ... those who not judge according to what God has sent down are rejecting [God's teaching]. [Q 5.43-44]
>
> We gave (Jesus) the Gospel with guidance, light, and confirmation of the Torah already revealed – a guide and lesson for those who take heed of God. So let the followers of the Gospel judge according to what God has sent down in it. [Q 5.46-47]

Although the development of *hadith* is reminiscent of Jewish or Christian apocryphal writings, the key difference is that each contribution is supported by its own chain of authorities through which the report has come down. One of the best regarded compilations of *hadith* dates from the early 9th century, and is known as Sahih Al-Bukhari after the Persian scholar who devoted many years to this work. Its opening recounts the initial revelation to Muhammad:

> The Messenger of God, peace and blessings of God be upon him, returned with the message, his heart trembling ... He spoke to Khadija, daughter of Khuwailid, and said, 'I fear for myself.' Thereupon Khadijah said, 'No, by God, He will never bring you to disgrace: for you support the bonds of relationship and bear the burdens of the weak and give to the destituteand honour the guest and help those in real distress.'

In Carlyle's summary of various 'recollections' represented in the *hadith*, Muhammad's personal restraint is particularly prominent:

Mahomet himself, after all that can be said about him, was not a sensual man. We shall err widely if we consider this man as a common voluptuary, intent mainly on base enjoyments, - nay on enjoyments of any kind. His household was of the frugalest; his common diet barley-bread and water: sometimes for months there was not a fire once lighted on his hearth. They record with just pride that he would mend his own shoes, patch his own cloak. A poor, hard-toiling, ill-provided man; careless of what vulgar men toil for. Not a bad man, I should say; something better in him than hunger of any sort,—or these wild Arab men, fighting and jostling three-and-twenty years at his hand, in close contact with him always, would not have reverenced him so! ... His last words are a prayer; broken ejaculations of a heart struggling up, in trembling hope, towards its Maker. We cannot say that his religion made him worse; it made him better; good, not bad. [Carlyle 62-63]

We may, however, wish to challenge Carlyle on the question of Muhammad's 'sensuality': did he not allow his followers to marry up to four women, as he proceeded to do himself? This permission is indeed found in *sura* 4, yet it is circumscribed by the need for their equitable treatment [Q 4.4] which is subsequently considered unlikely:

You will never be able to treat your wives with equal fairness, however much you may desire to do so. [Q 4.129]

It can be argued that there was a specific context that gave rise to Muhammad's accommodating attitude viz. the situation of women who had been orphaned, and a growing shortage of eligible men as a result of fighting. His own marriages were indeed probably arranged in pursuit of political alliances – but his wives are warned:

Prophet, say to your wives, 'If your desire is for present life and its finery, then come, I will make provision for you and release you with kindness.' [Q 33.28]

Qur'anic ambiguities

This is but one illustration of the difficulty of establishing an unambiguous message from at least some of the Qur'an's teachings, which self-confessedly admits its own complexity:

139

Some of its verses are definite in meaning – these are the cornerstone of the Scripture – and others are ambiguous. The perverse at heart eagerly pursue the ambiguities in their attempt to make trouble and to pin down a specific meaning of their own: only God knows the true meaning. [Q 3.7]

Various problems of interpretation arise:

- The text itself was sometimes known in more than one version: a cache of the earliest extant manuscripts coming to light in 1972 in the Great Mosque of San'a', Yemen arguably indicates discrepancies with later approved versions. At first (like the pre-Masoretic text of the Hebrew scriptures) it lacked any adequate vowel indications, while the absence of diacritical points sometimes resulted in an ambiguity about consonants. If the written text was used as a kind of aide-memoire for what was already known by heart, this mattered little; but it became of increasing concern when accurate liturgical recitation of the Qur'an was required.

- As with any manuscript tradition, the possibility of scribal errors cannot be ruled out. Thus, one of the early Caliphs, 'Ali ibn Abi Talib (died 661 CE), is reported to have preferred the reading *tal'in* (cluster of dates) to *talhin* (bananas) in *sura* 56.29 on the grounds that 'dates' are mentioned elsewhere in the Qur'an, corresponding to the environment in which it was received. Other 7th century Caliphs – both Umar (died 644 CE) and 'Aisha (died 678 CE) – claimed to have 'remembered' particular verses that had been omitted at some stage from the text.

- The Qur'an's very style is often allusive – readers, even those well versed in Arabic, disagree among themselves (and evidently did so in early days as well) about the meaning of certain words or the weight to be attached to a whole verse or two. The term *ijaz* ('inimitability') has been used to designate instances of particular concision, which for a Muslim point to the text's sublime origin.

- *Suras* can offer different teachings according to the circumstances:

> Since qur'anic prescriptions were often mutually contradictory, pioneers of Islamic jurisprudence had to exercise considerable ingenuity. Thus, they introduced the theory of abrogation (*naskh*),

140

according to which earlier legal norms were superseded by later regulations. [*CCTQ* 217]

In fact, the principle of abrogation is there in the Qur'an itself:

Any revelation We cause to be superseded or forgotten, We replace with something better or similar. [Q 2.106]
We shall teach you and you will not forget, unless God wishes. [Q 87.6]

This certainly brought criticism down upon Muhammad's head:

When We substitute one revelation for another – and God knows best what He reveals – they say, 'You are just making it up,' but most of them have no knowledge. Say that the Holy Spirit [i.e. Gabriel] has brought the Revelation with the Truth step by step from your Lord. [Q 16.101-2]

The idea of 'progressive revelation' is of course familiar to biblical students, while 'development of doctrine' under the guidance of the Holy Spirit, leading Christ's followers into fullness of the truth, is both a historical reality and a defensible theological principle. Even within the pages of the New Testament it is possible to trace some evolution in Paul's thought, or amongst the four Gospels. Again, the commonly accepted phrase 'a canon within the canon' challenges those who claim that each sentence of the Bible carries the same weight and authority as any other, resting as it does upon its divinely inspired verbal inerrancy. So for Muhammad and his later interpreters to suggest that some earlier passages may have been 'superseded' by later ones is a continuation of already familiar hermeneutical discussions. Uncomfortable questions cannot, however, be entirely avoided: if revelation can be in some sense 'altered', does this imply that God himself is changeable – or does it suggest that the reception of his Word is subject to the fallibility of human understanding? Is the authority of scripture, in particular that of the Qur'an itself, thereby undermined? Is Muhammad's claim that he simply memorised the dictated *suras* a sufficient rejoinder?

An added complication is the observation that the earlier (supposedly Meccan) revelations tend to be couched in more general terms, whereas later (supposedly Medinan) teachings were often so contextualised as to be less universally binding. Arising from this, some therefore propose that abrogation applies only to practical and legal matters, not to fundamental issues of belief. It may be, therefore, that in so far as the Qur'an usually regards the truth of the Torah and of the Gospel as confirmed rather than abrogated, this refers principally to their belief in God and their rejection of false religion. The Qur'an's affirmation of earlier scriptures does, however, apparently depend upon the extent of Muhammad's knowledge (and interpretation) of them: as noted already, this was often significantly different from the versions received among Jews and Christians.

On the face of it, evolution of religious understanding over a period of several hundred years is easier to appreciate than significant changes of direction within the lifetime of a single prophet who sees his role simply as a mouthpiece of God. The most problematic issue is to determine with any assurance which qur'anic texts may be taken as abrogated. In Rabbinic Judaism it was possible to rely upon 'the judge who is in office *in those days*', who should be consulted along with 'the Levitical priests' for resolution of disputed issues (which might include the interpretation of biblical texts):

They shall declare to you the decision. [Deut 17.9]

But in Islam there is no court of appeal to determine such matters, which must be widely agreed by all the most qualified and learned jurists. In particular, this requires agreement upon the meaning of the texts and upon their chronological placement.

Not even one of the 137 verses commonly listed as abrogated has been abrogated. The jurists do concede that a number of *laws* in the early days of the community were abrogated. But there is continuing disagreement about whether any *qur'anic ordinances* were abrogated by other qur'anic verses ... The principal problem that modern Muslim scholars face is deciding whether or not to accept the judgement of past scholars that qur'anic verses *which deal with interfaith relations* have been abrogated.[38]

In formal religious discourse, Muslim theologians occasionally cited the Gospels in support of their ideas. For instance, the early Yemeni theologian Qasim ibn Ibrahim (died 860 CE) quotes Matthew 5.17-22 – Jesus' statement

---

[38] *CCTQ* 299-300

that no verse of the Torah will be eliminated – as decisive evidence that the abrogation of one qur'anic verse by another cannot mean the actual elimination of any revelations, but instead, strictly speaking, only their modification (*tasrif*) through explanation.[39]

A further issue already touched upon is whether within the Qur'an there is any hierarchy of sacred or spiritual principles. Within Christianity many would accept that there are key doctrines which lie at the heart of the faith, but other teachings known as *adiaphora* which may be of devotional or practical value within some traditions, without being of universal application. In the Gospels the question was put, 'Which commandment is the first of all?' [Mk 12.28] i.e. the most important, while in the sub-apostolic Church 'the rule of faith' drew out the main tenets of belief in summarising creeds. Comparable debates have also been held within Islamic history, the principal division being between *traditionalists* who understand the Qur'an as the literal, uncreated Word of God – in which therefore each verse is equally sacred – and *rationalists* who argue that the Word was manifested at different times in response to changing circumstances, allowing a distinction to be drawn between fundamental teachings and those of particular applicability. The latter also maintain that any suggestion of an 'eternal' Qur'an might seem to threaten God's own unicity.

The appeal to reason

In fact, the Qur'an itself appeals frequently to the use of reason. Often it is in directing attention to the 'signs' that may be observed in the order and fruitfulness of creation, which testify to their origin in a single beneficent God. Thus,

> In the creation of the heavens and the earth ... there are signs in all these for those who use their minds. [Q 2.164]
> Watch their fruits as they grow and ripen! In all this there are signs for those who would believe. [Q 6.99]

---

[39] Tobias Mayer: *A Muslim speaks to Christians* (Priests & People January 2003, 10)

All [neighbouring plots] watered with the same water, yet We make the yield of some better than others: there truly are signs in this for people who reason. [Q 13.4]

There is also reflection on animate beings (although advances taken place since Muhammad's time in understanding aerodynamics!):

Do they not see the birds made to fly through the air in the sky? Nothing holds them up except God. There truly are signs in those for those who believe. [Q 16.79]

Otherwise it is the very existence of 'life' that speaks powerfully of God:[40]

It is God who splits open the seed and the fruit stone: He brings out the living from the dead and the dead from the living – that is God – so how can you turn away from the truth? [Q 6.95]

Do not take life, which God has made sacred, except by right. This is what He commands you to do: so that you may use your reason. [Q 6.151]

Say, 'Who provides for you from the sky and the earth? Who controls hearing and sight? Who brings forth the living from the dead and the dead from the living, and who governs everything? They are sure to say, 'God.' Then say, 'So why do you not take heed of Him?' [Q 10.31]

---

[40] The Qur'an's reasoning here echoes much earlier Christian reflection, as in Paul's letter to the Romans: those who 'share the faith of Abraham' believe that God 'gives life to the dead and calls into existence the things that do not exist' [Rom 4.16-17]. Similar expressions occur in the 2nd century apologists e.g. Athenagoras: *De Resurrectione* and Tatian: *Oratio ad Graecos* cf. in the 4th century, Gregory of Nyssa: *On the Making of Mankind* – with related teaching in his dialogue *On the Soul and the Resurrection*. That 'reconstitution' of life was less challenging to God than its initial creation became widespread in Christian preaching. A particularly vivid expression occurs in Augustine: *In Johannis Evangelium Tractatus* VIII.1, probably a homily delivered in the winter of 406-7; 'It is a matter of greater wonder for one to be who was not before, than for one who was to come to life again.' Muhammad's words may perhaps be foreshadowed too in the early 6th century poetry of Romanos the Melodist, who initially hailed from Syria: 'A hymn to the Merciful, praise to the Lover of man, Since He has deemed us worthy of His future grace. Come, all creation, let us entreat the One Who governs creation.'

People, if you doubt the Resurrection, [remember] that we created you from dust, then a drop of fluid, then a clinging form, then a lump of flesh, both shaped and unshaped. [Q 22.5]

Those who 'disbelieve' are castigated for their obstinacy:

The disbelievers invent lies about God. Most of them do not use reason. [Q 5.103]

This includes any among the People of the Book who fall into error, despite receiving 'clear proof in matters' [Q 45.17]:

You think they are united but their hearts are divided because they are people devoid of reason. [Q 59.14]

The use of reason is here particularly commended in matters of 'fundamental theology', but sometimes includes a wider reference to moral issues. The implication is that the revelations received by Muhammad are indeed of a rational character, in line with what prophets before him have taught since the days of Abraham:

Who but a fool would forsake the religion of Abraham? [Q 1.130]

There were obviously a good number of his contemporaries, especially early on in Mecca, who challenged Muhammad's credentials. Since he had no 'signs' to offer such as healing miracles or other forms of wonder-working, the veracity of his message was confirmed by the signs already evident in nature, by human reason, and by what was 'foretold in the scriptures of earlier religions' [Q 26.196] – making the Qur'an 'the truth confirming what they already have' [Q 2.91 cf 3.3]. Its divine origin was evident in its unique (but poetic) style: however –

We have not taught the Prophet poetry, nor could he ever have been a poet. This is a revelation. [Q 36.69-70]
This is ... not the word of a poet – how little you believe – nor the word of a soothsayer – how little you reflect! [Q 69.40-42]
If they say, 'He has invented it himself,' say, 'Then produce ten invented *suras* like it.' [Q 11.13]

Several of the above quotations suggest what has been termed the 'self-declarative' nature of the Qur'an. Whereas both the Hebrew and the Christian writings known to us as the Old and New Testaments emerged over a considerable period of time, and were used and tested at length before being accepted as authoritative scriptures, the Qur'an was already given that status by Muhammad before its final documentation was complete. And while the authors of biblical material would themselves claim to be testifying to God's truth, the Bible in both its Testaments is conscious of the need to make careful discernment of their teachings, given the abundance of prophets and teachers who speak falsely in their own name:

The prophet who presumes to speak a word in my name which I have not commanded him to speak, or who speaks in the name of other gods, that same prophet shall die. [Deut 18.20]
Take heed that no one leads you astray. [Mk 13.5]
Many false prophets have gone out into the world. [1 Jn 4.1]

To subject the Qur'an to critical inquiry is not necessarily to bow to modern scepticism: rather it is to apply an important biblical principle and to heed the Qur'an's own plea for using one's reason in matters of faith. Additionally, it is worth noting that the Qur'an does not portray Muhammad as invariably beyond reproach – he is challenged to practise what he preaches (a test he himself applied to the People of the Book):

He [Muhammad] frowned and turned away when the blind man came to him – for all you know, he might have grown in spirit, or taken note of something useful to him. For the self-satisfied one you go out of your way – though it is not your responsibility if he does not attain purity – but from the one who has come to you full of eagerness and awe you are distracted. [Q 80.1-10]

146

12. The People of the Book

The historical presence of biblical faiths in Arabia

It is easy to imagine that until Muhammad transformed the scene Arabia knew little of monotheism, being relatively isolated from religious movements and developments elsewhere. Certainly there is evidence of traditional polytheism, which flourished in different guises among the various tribes who maintained their own shrines called *harams*, places where feuding and bloodshed was outlawed. Yet Arabia lies within reach of Jerusalem and Syria, with Ethiopia not far across the Red Sea; further afield, important trade routes connected it north-westwards to Egypt and thence Europe, or eastwards to India and beyond. And while Jews had migrated over the centuries into many parts of the ancient world (including Egypt and 'Babylonia') to form what was called their *diaspora*, Christianity, as a missionary faith, had also expanded widely by the 4th century to embrace most of Arabia's trading partners. As commercial enterprises flourished, no doubt so too did the influence of 'foreign' religious teachings and practices – not forgetting that the Qur'an claims several indigenous prophets (Hud, Salih, Shu'ayb) who already taught some Arabs the oneness of God.

Fred Donner summarises the situation in Arabia by the 6th century:

> Judaism had come to Arabia very early—probably immediately after the Roman destruction of the Second Temple in Jerusalem in 70 c.a. Communities of Arabic-speaking Jews were found in most parts of Arabia, particularly in the Yemen and in the oasis towns of northwestern Arabia— Tabuk, Tayma', Khaybar, Yathrib (Medina), and so on. These may have been descendants of Jewish migrants or refugees from Palestine or Babylonia, local converts, or an amalgam of both. Christianity was also found in Arabia, especially in Yemen (where it had become established in the fourth century through Byzantine proselytizing), in eastern Arabia, and on Arabia's northern fringes bordering on Syria and Iraq, where it seems to have gained a following even among some pastoral nomadic groups. There is less agreement among scholars on the prevalence of Christians in the Hijaz (the

147

mountainous western side of Arabia), although some stray references show that Christians were not unknown there.[41]

Among the factors leading to the further conversion of Arabs it is clear that Christian monks and ascetics played an important role, either because of merchants and princes encountering them on their travels or through active missionary work in Arabia itself. Simeon Stylites, the most famous of the pillar saints in Syria, was responsible for many such conversions, according to his biographer:

> It was impossible to count the Arabs, their kings and nobles, who came and acknowledged Jesus.

Alternatively, there are stories of how healing miracles were instrumental in persuading various other chiefs to adhere, along with their tribesmen, to the Christian faith. Several bishops were consecrated by Syrian bishops for service in Arabia, where religious leanings tended to change with competing political interventions:

> On the urging of the Byzantine emperor Justin, the Axumite king Ella Asbeha invaded Yemen around 523 CE and established a Christian ruler there. This invasion may have been in part a reaction to the activities of a Jewish king of the Himyarites, Dhu Nuwas, who had just beforehand engaged in a series of bloody clashes with Yemenite Christians, or it may have been mainly in order to facilitate Byzantine commerce with India. This Ethiopian regime in Yemen, which soon became independent of Axum, dominated the country for a half-century; its most important leader was the king Abraha, who attempted to extend his rule into north-central Arabia and is reported by tradition to have mounted an unsuccessful siege on Mecca around the time of Muhammad's birth. The Sasanians (Persians) were not about to allow this indirect Byzantine presence in South Arabia to stand unchallenged, however. In the 570s, Great King Khosro II sent an expeditionary force that occupied Yemen and made it a province of the empire, administered directly by a Sasanian governor with a strong garrison. By the end of the sixth century, then, the Sasanians had enclosed Arabia almost completely on its eastern and southern sides; only the Red Sea littoral and its extension into

---

[41] Fred Donner: *Muhammad and the Believers* (Harvard 2012, 30)

southern Syria was free of their control. The Byzantine Empire, on the other hand, was especially influential in northwestern Arabia.[42]

The repulsed siege of Mecca apparently involved the use of war elephants. One objective may have been the destruction of its Ka'ba sanctuary (diverting pilgrims to the new cathedral in San'a?). It may explain *sura* 105:

> Do you not see how your Lord dealt with the army of the elephant? [Q 105.1]

The vast interior of the Arabian peninsula was of course mainly arid desert occupied by nomadic Bedouin tribes, but the coastal areas were populated with towns and villages sometimes boasting palaces and temples (such as the Ka'ba) built with stone cut from nearby mountain quarries. The city of Marib also boasted an impressively engineered dam which supplied water to a number of oases – surely a wonder of the ancient world. Yet as the 6th century progressed, this prosperous south-west corner of Arabia fell into economic decline, and around the year of Muhammad's birth the famous dam collapsed: where overland trade routes had once brought wealth to the area, now shipping largely bypassed it, taking advantage of monsoon winds to reach the northern ports of the Red Sea (such as Eilat or Myos Hormos) instead. So wealth relied on Arab merchants trading in Syria and elsewhere (notably Gaza), if not more readily on Arab tribesmen raiding their neighbours and any passing camel trains. The Qur'an, however, interprets the collapse of the Marib dam not in socio-political terms but as divine judgement on the people's continuing idolatry:

> There was a sign for the people of Sheba, too, in their dwelling place: two gardens, one on the right, one on the left ... But they paid no heed, so We let loose on them a flood from the dam and replaced their two gardens with others that yielded bitter fruit, tamarisk bushes, and a few lote trees. [Q 34.15-16]

What then did Muhammad himself know of Judaism or Christianity? He was born at Mecca into the dominant Quraysh tribe, but was orphaned at

---

[42] Donner 34

an early age and raised by his uncle Abu Talib, chief of the Hashim clan. Mecca was not in an oasis, although its well provided sufficient water for modest needs. Much of its food needed to be bought elsewhere, but here its status as a *haram* (a place where bloodshed was banned) enabled it to become an important commercial and religious centre, where animal hides and foodstuffs were available (there may have been some trade in locally mined gold as well). Muhammad was fortunate as a young man to marry Khadija, and to take on the management of her caravan trading ventures. This took him further afield, and exposed him to a variety of religious beliefs and practices, as well as introducing him to a wide network of contacts. One thing that stands out in the Qur'an is its awareness of divisions among Jews and Christians alike:

> As for those who have divided their religion and broken up into factions, have nothing to do with them. [Q 6.159]
>
> We gave Moses the Scripture before you, but differences arose about it. [Q 11.110]
>
> But factions have differed among themselves (Christians). [Q 19.37]
>
> But they (Christians) have split their community into sects, each rejoicing in their own. [Q 23.53]
>
> We enjoined on Abraham and Moses and Jesus: 'Uphold the faith and do not divide into factions within it.' [Q 42.13]
>
> When Jesus came with clear signs he said, 'I have brought you wisdom; I have come to clear up some of your differences for you' ... Yet still the different factions among them disagreed. [Q 43.63, 65]
>
> We gave scripture, wisdom, and prophethood to the Children of Israel ... They differed among themselves out of mutual rivalry, only after knowledge came to them. [Q 45.16-17]
>
> There is much hostility between them (the faithless among the People of the Book): you think they are united but their hearts are divided because they are people devoid of reason. [Q 59.14]

Thomas Carlyle, in the lecture quoted previously, is sympathetic here:

> Mahomet's Creed ... I should say a better kind than that of those miserable Syrian Sects, with their vain janglings about Homoiousion and Homoousion. [Carlyle 55]

Since Carlyle's time, the 'sects' – whether Christian or Jewish – have continued to multiply; but the same is true of Islam, whose adherents dispute, even with violence, about its proper interpretation. Muhammad, one imagines, would have been extremely disturbed by this development. In his day, one of the principal issues among Christians was (as Carlyle indicates) that of Christology, a matter on which the Qur'an took its own reductionist stance. The Council of Chalcedon in 451 CE was intended to heal this longstanding sore, and many parts of the Christian Church, including Rome and the Byzantines, signed up to its *dyophysite* definition: that Christ had two natures, human and divine, in one single person. This was confused by those who nevertheless considered Christ to have but a single will – a teaching known as *monotheletism*, which was condemned at the 3rd Council of Constantinople in 680-1 CE, but began to be debated sixty years earlier within the Byzantine sphere of influence, including Syria. The Coptic Church, and hence too the Ethiopian Church, along with the Syriac Orthodox Church (Jacobites), rejected the Chalcedonian definition, preferring a *miaphysite* position in which Christ's single nature has both a divine and a human character. With the Nestorians, prominent in East Syria, Persia and beyond, matters came to a head at the earlier Council of Ephesus in 431 CE. They rejected the agreed description of Mary as *theotokos* (bearer of God), arguing in favour of the title *christotokos* (bearer of Christ) since they suspected the former of denying Christ's full humanity.[43] There were also Christian sects with a more Jewish leaning whose roots went back to the 1st and 2nd centuries. Jerome wrote in his *Letter 89* (to Augustine):

> What shall I say of the Ebionites who pretend to be Christians? To-day there still exists among the Jews in all the synagogues of the East a heresy which is called that of the Minæans, and which is still condemned by the Pharisees; [its followers] are ordinarily called 'Nazarenes'; they believe that Christ, the son of God, was born of the Virgin Mary, and they hold him to be the one who suffered under Pontius Pilate and ascended to heaven.

---

[43] Jacobites are named after Jacob Baradeus, bishop of Edessa in the mid 6th century. Similarly, the term Nestorian derives from Nestorius, the early 5th century Patriarch of Constantinople. Maronites are a Lebanese ethno-religious group in communion with Rome, who trace their origins back to St Marun in the 4th century.

Some have suspected a certain 'Nazarene' influence upon Muhammad, but this seems unlikely, given the reference here to Christ's 'suffering' (which needs clarification) and his description as 'son of God' (which is strongly denied throughout the Qur'an).

Yet contact in some form or other with Christians of these varied persuasions, whether in Mecca or on Muhammad's journeying, is plausible; while a lively Jewish presence in some places is undeniable – in Yathrib (Medina) tradition mentions three prominent Jewish tribes, the Qaynuqa', the Nadir and the Qurayza. Again, particular individuals are recorded in the *hadith* as having been of assistance to Muhammad: one of the earliest (mentioned several times in *Sahih Al-Bukhari*) was Khadija's cousin Waraqa b. Nawfal who – according to Ibn Ishaq's 8th century account – 'had become a Christian and read the scriptures and learned from those who follow the Torah and the Gospel'. In Medina the story goes that Muhammad enlisted the help of a literate Jew named Zayd b. Thabit. There were certainly those who made malicious comments about such contacts, which the Qur'an addresses more than once:

> We know very well that they say, 'It is a man who teaches him.' [Q 16.103]
> The disbelievers say, 'These are nothing but old fables.' [Q 6.25]
> They say, 'It is just ancient fables, which he has had written down: they are dictated to him morning and evening.' [Q 25.5]

One verse of *sura* 26, however, while tacitly admitting some contact with local Jews, turns it to advantage:

> This Qur'an has been sent down by the Lord of the Worlds ... so that you could bring warning in a clear Arabic tongue. This was foretold in the scriptures of earlier religions. Is it not proof enough for them that the learned men of the Children of Israel have recognised it? [Q 26.192-7]

Questions certainly arise concerning the extent of his informants' knowledge about their faith and the character of the 'scriptures' with which they were conversant. In what version were they known? How extensive were they?

The fact that the Qur'an contains words which are not of Arabic origin provides an indication that Jewish and Christian scriptures, the latter probably in Syriac, were known in both Mecca and Medina. [CCTQ 43]

We must still come to terms with the possibility that numerous passages in the Qur'an should, in fact, be read as Aramaic phrases embedded in an otherwise Arabic matrix. [TQHC 39]

Oral lore was communicated to Muhammad in his mother tongue, but its original forms were in Syriac, Aramaic, Ethiopian and Hebrew materials, as evidenced by the vocabulary of foreign origin to be found in the Arabic Qur'an. [*ibid* 70]

The picture is, however, somewhat modified by research which indicates that the Qur'an was not alone in using some of these foreign words, which have been found in pre-Islamic Arabic texts as well. The conclusion seems to be that the language of the Qur'an 'is essentially a literary Arabic close to that of the pre- and early Islamic poetry'.[44] The fact that words were imported from elsewhere lends weight to the thesis that Arabia was not isolated from other ideas and influences. Indeed, Arabic writing is considered to be a derivation of Nabataean script.[45]

Several arguments have been proposed linking qur'anic knowledge of the gospels with the standard 'harmony' of texts that circulated in Syria viz. Tatian's *Diatessaron*, dating back to the 2nd century, e.g.

The only Old Testament personages named in the Qur'an are those whose names also appear in the Diatessaron. [TQHC 112]

This text (Q 48.29) combines two Gospel pericopes – Mark 4.26-7 and Matthew 12.23 – the same amalgam that the Diatessaron makes. [*op.cit.* 99]

However, the similarities may be explained otherwise, and in any case readers of the Qur'an cannot fail to notice that many of its biblical stories and references differ significantly from the accepted texts of the Bible itself, and indeed include narratives from the later apocryphal tradition. There is no need to suppose *written* versions of these extra-canonical texts were in circulation in the Hijaz (western Arabia), since by now a popular *oral* culture

[44] Harold Motzki: *Alternative Accounts of the Qur'an's Formation* (CCTQ 2006, 68)

[45] Robert Hoyland: *Epigraphy and the Linguistic Background to the Qur'an* (TQHC 2008, 53)

was spreading across the Christian world. Probably encouraged by bishops and holy men, people of all walks of life had begun to share miracle tales and Bible stories orally instead of relying upon written sources which were accessible only to the few. Scriptural 'boundaries' inevitably became more fluid (as is also evident in contemporary Christian art). Much the same can be seen in Jewish circles too, where biblical material had become much embroidered. Some examples as reflected in the Qur'an will be considered later. In its own words,

We tell you the best of stories in revealing this Qur'an to you. [Q 12.3]

Respect for Torah and Gospel

Nevertheless, it is the 'scriptures' of Jews and Christians – God's teachings 'sent down' and duly recorded in writing – that are accorded proper respect in the Qur'an:

Believe in the message I have sent down, confirming what you already possess. [Q 2.41]
Step by step, He has sent the Scripture down to you with the Truth, confirming what went before: He sent down the Torah and the Gospel earlier as a guide for the people. [Q 3.3]
We believe in God and in what has been sent down to us and to Abraham, Ishmael, Isaac, Jacob, and the Tribes. We believe in what has been given to Moses, Jesus, and the prophets from their Lord. We do not make a distinction between any of them. [Q 3.84]
We gave Moses the Scripture, so that they might be rightly guided. [Q 23.49]
We sent Jesus, son of Mary. We gave him the Gospel. [Q 57.27]
All this is in the earlier scriptures, the scriptures of Abraham and Moses. [Q 87.18-19]

The perhaps surprising reference to a scripture 'of Abraham' will be taken up later. Otherwise the Qur'an mentions by name over fifty characters who appear in the Bible. An entire *sura* is devoted to the story of Joseph, which has many parallels with the account in Genesis. Moses' example, by contrast, is appealed to throughout the Qur'an, and his confrontation with Pharaoh occurs no less than twenty-seven times. *Sura* 18 includes a lengthy story unknown to the Bible of a journey undertaken by Moses with several curious encounters that prove baffling to him at the time; the explanation is eventually given, but with a rebuke for his impatience. The moral seems to be that God alone knows what he is doing.

Variations on biblical names are very common too: for example, Abraham is *Ibrahim*, Noah is *Nuh*, Joseph is *Yusuf*, Moses is *Musa*, Jonah is *Yunus*, while Satan is *Iblis*. In the New Testament Mary (the only woman to be named in the Qur'an) is *Maryam* and – surprisingly to Christians – her father is called *Imran*. This name appears to be derived from that of Amram, described in Exodus 6.20 as the father of Moses and Aaron, extended in 1 Chronicles 6.3 to include their sister Miriam. (He was much earlier the subject of a fragmentary Aramaic document *The Testament of Amram* [4Q543-9] found at Qumran, and features too in Josephus' *Antiquities* 2.9.2-3.) So Mary, if not actually a close blood relation of Moses and Aaron, is seen spiritually as closely related to them, a connection often drawn out in Christian teaching from at least the time of Gregory of Nyssa in the late 4th century. In particular, Mary is addressed as 'sister of Aaron' soon after giving what is assumed to be an 'unchaste' birth; but the newborn Jesus speaks in her defence, revealing his vocation and thus upholding the honour and purity of her title [Q 19.27-32].

Jesus himself is known as *Isa*. He is described as *nabi* (prophet) and God's servant [Q 2.136; 19.30]. The term Messiah is also allowed:

The Messiah, Jesus, son of Mary, was nothing more than a messenger of God, His word directed to Mary, and a spirit from Him. [Q 4.171]

Yet while he is much revered in the Qur'an (with his eschatological role taken up in the *hadith*), he makes fewer appearances than Moses. Despite that, several key features of the biblical testimony are included – with some omissions:

We gave Jesus, son of Mary, clear signs and strengthened him with the holy spirit. [Q 2.87]
The angels said, 'Mary, God gives you news of a Word from Him, whose name will be Messiah, Jesus, son of Mary, who will be held in honour in this world and the next. [Q 3.45]
We made the son of Mary and his mother a sign. [Q 23.50]

[Jesus] said, 'Who will help me in God's cause?' The disciples said, 'We will be God's helpers.' [Q 3.52]

By My leave, you (Jesus) healed the blind person and the leper ... by My leave, you brought the dead back to life. [Q 5.110]

In God's eyes Jesus is just like Adam: He created him from dust, said to him, 'Be', and he was. [Q 3.59]

Peace was on me (*the infant Jesus speaks from Mary's arms*) the day I was born, and will be on me the day I die and the day I am raised to life again. [Q 19.33]

They did not kill him, nor did they crucify him, though it was made to appear like that to them ... No! God raised him up to himself. [Q 4.157-8]

This last assertion was of course not unknown among heretical Christian sects. Here it is not, as has sometimes been suggested, a form of docetism, as the previous citation ('created from dust') makes clear. But Muhammad may have learnt of similar deviant interpretations reaching back as far as the 2nd century Gnostic Basilides, who taught (according to Irenaeus) that

[Jesus] did not himself suffer death, but Simon, a certain man of Cyrene, being compelled, bore the cross in his stead. [*Adv Haer* 1.24.4]

It is strange, therefore, that elsewhere the martyrdom of prophets is accepted:

[The Israelites] persistently rejected [God's] messages and killed prophets contrary to all that is right. [Q 2.61]

Whenever a messenger brings you something you do not like, you become arrogant, calling some imposters and killing others. [Q 2.87]

The prospect of Muhammad himself being killed is even raised [Q 3.144]. So the denial of Jesus' crucifixion seems inconsistent, in any case flying in the face of overwhelming Christian testimony and that of contemporary historians:

Nero fastened the guilt [for Rome's fire in 64 CE] and inflicted the most exquisite tortures on a class hated for their abominations, called Christians by the populace. Christus, from whom the name had its origin, suffered the extreme penalty during the reign of Tiberius at the hands of one of our procurators, Pontius Pilatus. [Tacitus, *Annals* 15.44]

156

when Pilate, at the suggestion of the principal men amongst us, had condemned him to the cross, those that loved him at the first did not forsake him; for he appeared to them alive again the third day. [Josephus, *Ant* 18.3]

Of course, the authenticity of this latter *Testimonium Flavianum*, cited later by the church historian Eusebius, has been much discussed; but, although the passage may have been enhanced subsequently by Christian interpolations, the majority view believe the mention of Christ's crucifixion to be Josephus' own record. The same holds for the reference in Tacitus. It is surely significant too that Paul, initially a fierce critic and opponent of the Church, was later convinced of the truth of the Christian message and performed a *volte face*.[46]

The Qur'an nevertheless stresses that it 'confirms' – rather than corrects or contradicts – the Bible itself in both Old and New Testaments (so far as this was known to Muhammad). Yet this is often only possible because verses are given interpretations quite different from those familiar to Jews or to Christians. Where, for example, Christians find messianic prophecies in the Old Testament which for them point to the coming of Jesus, Muslim exegetes would see them as prefiguring Muhammad's mission instead. This is particularly true of several Isaianic passages; or again, references to the 'desert' are often applied to events in and around Mecca. In other words, just as Christians argued that Christ was the key to understanding the Old Testament, so Muslims saw the Qur'an as its true fulfilment. Sometimes the accusation was made that Jews or Christians had 'altered' the text to suit

---

[46] Something similar may have happened with Jesus' own family, who initially seem to have distanced themselves from his ministry – going to 'seize' him on one occasion [Mk 3.21] – yet later were among his closest supporters: Mary remained by him at the cross, and James his brother ('the Just', as Hegesippus described him in the 2nd century) became leader of the Jerusalem church. James' earlier disbelief [Jn 7.5] must certainly have been challenged by his encounter with the risen Jesus [1 Cor 15.6], if not sooner: according to John [20.24-29] a similar encounter persuaded 'doubting' Thomas. James' faith fortified him for later martyrdom [Josephus: *Antiquities* 20.9.1]. According to Matthew [28.17], there were others among the eleven disciples who also had initial doubts about the resurrection, which can only have been entertained if they were convinced of the reality of his death by crucifixion.

their own readings (usually to hide their applicability to the Prophet or – as with Moses' replacement of the tablets of the Decalogue – to omit qur'anic teachings):

> People of the Book, Our Messenger has come to make clear to you much of what you have kept hidden of the Scripture. [Q 5.15]

More commonly the dispute was about the refusal to acknowledge that, properly understood, the true subject of biblical revelation was actually Muhammad himself, who would also be its authoritative interpreter. In one important instance the two aspects came together, when Jesus' promise of the Paraclete is presented in a radically different qur'anic version:

> Jesus, son of Mary, said, 'Children of Israel, I am sent to you by God, confirming the Torah that came before me and bringing good news of a messenger to follow me whose name will be Ahmad.' [Q 61.6]

This variant reading is justified by the argument that the Johannine Greek term *parakletos* was an alteration of a similar sounding word *periklutos*, which (like the Arabic *Ahmad*) means 'praised one'.

However, the Qur'an's chief complaint is not about the biblically preferred text but against the conduct and attitude of some (but not all) Jews and Christians, together known as the People of the Book (a term used over fifty times, rather more than the forty references to the Children of Israel – whereas Nazarenes are so mentioned just fourteen times and 'the people of the Gospel' only once). Those who faithfully follow their own revealed teachings (as interpreted by Muhammad) are repeatedly commended:

> The believers, the Jews, the Christians and the Sabians (evidently a monotheistic sect, mentioned twice more) – all those who believe in God and the Last Day and do good – will have their rewards with their Lord. [Q 2.62]
> Some of the People of the Book believe in God ... These people will have their rewards with their Lord. [Q 3.199]
> There is a group among the people of Moses who guide with truth and who act justly according to it. [Q 7.159]

You are sure to find that the closest in affection towards the believers are those who say, 'We are Christians,' for there are among them people devoted to learning and ascetics. These people are not given to arrogance. [Q 5.82]

The last of these tributes stands in contrast to the harsh condemnation that immediately precedes it:

The most hostile to the believers are the Jews and those who associate other deities with God. [Q 5.82]

So this verse of *sura* 5 mirrors something of Muhammad's own experience. At Mecca he and his followers met initially with violent opposition, and the tradition recounts how both in 613 and in 615 CE parties of believers fled by boat, and were well received in Christian Axum across the Red Sea; whereas when Muhammad himself made the *hjira* in 622 CE to Medina, it was certain Jews there who frustrated his plans:

It is not clear exactly how or why his relationship with the Jews went awry; the *sira* literature offers numerous tales of the Jews' opposition ... but also hints that desire to seize lands held by the Jews, perhaps to relieve the distress of the *muhijirun,* may have been one of Muhammad's motivations. [CCTQ 27]

From a Christian perspective, Muhammad's difficulties with some of the Jewish tribes are reminiscent of Jewish opposition both to Jesus and subsequently to his followers. Condemnatory language is also found in the New Testament e.g.

You are of your father the devil, and your will is to do your father's desires. [Jn 8.44]
I know ... the slander of those who say they are Jews and are not, but are a synagogue of Satan. [Apoc 2.9 cf. 3.9]

The negative appraisal here of those opposed to the Christian community does, however, indicate that the term 'Jew', apart from the minority bearing this name, was in itself regarded with respect. Paul, despite the violence he sometimes experienced at their hands, certainly regarded Jews as his 'brethren', inheritors of God's promises [Rom 9.3-4]. Yet he adds this qualification, similar to that of the Qur'an:

Not all are children of Abraham because they are his descendants. [Rom 9.7]

A comment from the Pontifical Biblical Commission, however, puts this within a broader perspective:

In the New Testament, the reproaches addressed to Jews are not as frequent or as virulent as the accusations against Jews in the Law and the Prophets.[47]

Again, the Qumran writings often fulminate against the Sadduccean hierarchy in Jerusalem, not least because, just over a century before the time of Christ, their own Teacher of Righteousness had narrowly escaped death at the hands of the High Priest. For his part, Josephus offers a more favourable opinion of these Essenes than he does of other Jewish parties:

There are three philosophical sects among the Jews. The followers of the first of which are the Pharisees; of the second, the Sadducees; and the third sect, which pretends to a severer discipline, are called Essenes. These last are Jews by birth, and seem to have a greater affection for one another than the other sects have. [*The Jewish War* 2.8.2]

The Qur'an criticises the 'unbelievers' among the People of the Book on several counts:

Some of them are uneducated, and know the Scripture only through wishful thinking. They rely on guesswork. So woe to those who write something down with their own hands and the claim, 'This is from God,' in order to make some small gain. [Q2.78-79] They do not believe in what came afterwards, though it is the truth confirming what they already have. [Q 2.91]

They say, 'Become Jews or Christians, and you will be rightly guided.' Say, 'No, the religion of Abraham, the upright, who did not worship any god besides God.' [Q 2.135]

Believe in God and His messengers and do not speak of a 'Trinity'. [Q 4.171]

---

[47] *The Jewish People and their Sacred Scriptures in the Christian Bible* (Vatican 2002, 87)

You will always find treachery in all but a few of them. Overlook this and pardon them: God loves those who do good. [Q 5.13]

When God says, 'Jesus, son of Mary, did you say to people, "Take me and my mother as two gods alongside God"? he will say, 'May you be exalted! I would never say what I had no right to say ... You know all that is within me, though I do not know what is within You.' [Q 5.116]

They did not kill him (Jesus), nor did they crucify him, though it was made to appear like that to them. [Q 4.157]

They take their rabbis and their monks as lords beside God, as well as Christ, the son of Mary. [Q 9.31]

Many rabbis and monks wrongfully consume people's possessions and turn people away from God's path. [Q 9.34]

Monasticism was something they invented ... they did not observe it properly. [Q 57.27]

While some of these faults may be 'overlooked' – and above all else the Qur'an stresses God's mercy, as in its opening *sura* recited several times each day – the prime error of Christians is seen as their Trinitarian belief, which misrepresents what Jesus taught. Clearly Muhammad never received a nuanced theological account; and if the popular version of his own day counted Mary as divine, it was surely a form of tritheism which rightly called for criticism. Less defensible is the Qur'an's denial of the crucifixion (reminiscent of the 2nd century Gnostic *Gospel of Basilides*), likewise its claim that Muhammad's role as God's messenger was predicted by Jesus (above, pp 155-6):

Jesus, son of Mary, said, 'Children of Israel, I am sent to you by God, confirming the Torah that came before me and bringing good news of a messenger to follow me whose name will be Ahmad.' [Q 61.6]

Yet Muhammad was sometimes prepared to acknowledge and discuss teachings other than his own:

Each community has its own direction (for prayer) to which it turns: race to do good deeds and wherever you are, God will bring you together ... There is no compulsion in religion. [Q 2.148, 256]

Say, 'People of the Book, let us arrive at a statement that is common to us all: we worship God alone ... [Q 3.71]

Argue only in the best way with the People of the Book, except with those who act unjustly. Say, 'we believe in what was revealed to us and in what was revealed to you; our God and your God is one.' [Q 29.46]

While the focus here is on what others believe and on how they live out their beliefs, the practice of worship does also gain a passing – and positive – mention in the Qur'an. *Sura* 5, although it deals with much else, actually gains its title *Al-Ma'ida* (The Table) from its reference to the Christian Eucharist:

> When the disciples said, 'Jesus, son of Mary, can your Lord send down a feast (*ma'idatan*) to us from heaven?' he said, 'Beware of (i.e. Fear) God if you are true believers.' They said, 'We wish to eat from it; to have our hearts reassured; to know that you have told us the truth; and to be witnesses of it.' Jesus, son of Mary, said, 'Lord, send down to us a feast from heaven so that we can have a festival – the first and last of us – and a sign from You. Provide for us: You are the best provider.' God said, 'I will send it down to you, but anyone who disbelieves after this will be punished with a punishment that I will not inflict on anyone else in the world.' [Q 5.112-115 cf. 1 Cor 11.29, where Paul insists that lack of 'discernment' will bring 'judgement' upon the unworthy participant]

Scholars have noted in the language here at least two different streams of Christian influence: *'id* (feast) is a Syriac borrowing, as is *aya* (sign), whereas *ma'ida* (table) is of Ethiopic origin. The term 'first and last of us' is equivalent to the liturgical formula 'for you and for many (or, for all)' based on a merger of the different New Testament texts. Perhaps of greatest significance is the use of the familiar qur'anic expression 'send down', otherwise applied to God's sending of his Word to the prophets. It surely indicates recognition of the divine origin of the Eucharist, which is counted among the 'signs' engendering faith and requiring Christian 'witness'.

13. The Seal of the Prophets

God's teaching confirmed

Muhammad was a prayerful man, who according to the *hadith* retreated regularly in his Meccan days to the Cave of Hira for periods of meditation – often 'two-thirds of the night' [Q 73.20].[48] It was here that he began to experience 'revelations' in words and visions so powerful that he was convulsed and unable to stay upright. Initially he was perplexed by the challenge to share the messages he had received, but his wife Khadija was convinced that this was a real prophetic calling and encouraged him to tell others what he had heard. Some were convinced by his testimony, but many were initially sceptical, if not insulted by the repudiation of their 'idolatry' and the accompanying threat of damnation (which embraced their ancestors as well). Although the many 'prophecies' returned again and again to this basic theme, their scope became far more extensive as they continued until his death in Medina in 632 CE. The Qur'an recalls that more than once Muhammad was rebuked by the angel Gabriel for being too hasty to repeat what he had heard:

> Do not rush your tongue in an attempt to hasten the recitation. It is for Us to make sure of its safe collection and recitation. When We have recited it, repeat the recitation and it is up to Us to make it clear. [Q 75.16-19 cf. 20.114]

It was not only Muhammad but growing numbers of his followers who committed the revelations to memory. Little by little they also began to be recorded in writing, on whatever materials came to hand – including palm leaves and even animal bones. Part of the impetus behind this may have been the need to compile material for a form of 'liturgy' to emancipate the worship of God from pre-Islamic cultic ceremonies. In this connection, it has been suggested that *sura* 15 played a crucial role,[49] with its reference to 'the seven oft-recited verses' [Q 15.87]. The names of Arabic letters placed

---

[48] In the biblical tradition both Moses and Elijah encountered God in caves [Exod 33.22; 1 Kgs 19.9].

[49] Harold Motzi: *Alterative Accounts of the Qur'an's Formation* (CCTQ 2006, 65)

as an introduction to some twenty-nine of the *suras* also serve 'to hint at a newly achieved cultic function for the recited text'.[50] (Various other interpretations of these letters, which vary from one up to five, have been offered; no single explanation, however, has commanded universal assent.)

How far Muhammad himself was literate is much debated: as one who had transacted business affairs and travelled as a merchant in his younger days, a basic level of literacy and numeracy seems likely. Yet Muslim tradition often prefers to regard him as 'illiterate', since this is felt to reinforce the revelatory nature of the words and visions he received. Much depends upon what particular words mean, but the initial revelation is agreed to be found in *sura* 96:

> Read! In the name of your Lord who created: He created man from a clinging form. Read! Your Lord is the Most Bountiful One who taught by the pen, who taught man what he did not know. [Q 96.1-5]

Sura 7.157 describes the Messenger as an 'unlettered prophet' while *sura* 29 mentions that he had never yet written any revelation down with his hand [Q 29.48]. Perhaps one may only conclude that Muhammad never had training like that of a Jewish rabbi, and when he needed documentation of any sort he employed others to do this work.

Muslim tradition holds that one of his later wives, 'A'isha, had a transcript of some of the revelations at the time of his death, and that attempts then followed to complete the collection during the rule of the caliphs Abu Bakr and 'Umar who succeeded Muhammad. It appears, however, that systematic action using an editorial team was only undertaken under the next caliph 'Uthman (644-655 CE), resulting in the first official version. The story by no means ends there: as with the sayings of Jesus, variations on those of Muhammad were also in circulation, so that the 'recitation' (which is the meaning of Qur'an) was never entirely uniform. The order of *suras* may have varied slightly, and the longer ones certainly give the impression of being a merger of separate revelations received at different times. Other 'canonical' versions are therefore also found in use backed by different authorities e.g. by the 10th century these were to be found in the principal cities of Medina, Mecca, Damascus, Basra, and Kufa (where three different

---

[50] Angelika Neuwirth: *Structural, Linguistic and Literary Features* (CCTQ 2006, 109)

transmissions were recognised, thus making seven in all, according to the scholar Ibn Mujahid who died in 936 CE).

Many passages in the Qur'an make reference to biblical stories and characters, and it is clear that Muhammad was sufficiently influenced by his contacts with informed Jews and Christians to see himself as a further 'messenger' in the long line of biblical prophets. There are verses which suggest that his mission was principally to extend God's message to the Arab tribes i.e. to deliver it in Arabic:

> We have sent down the Qur'an to give judgement in the Arabic language. [Q 13.37]
> We have never sent a messenger who did not use his own people's language to make things clear for them. [Q 14.4]
> The scripture of Moses was revealed before it as a guide and a mercy, and this is a scripture confirming it in the Arabic language to warn those who do evil and bring good news for those who do good. [Q 46.12]
> The trustworthy Spirit brought it down to your heart, so that you could bring warning in a clear Arabic tongue. [Q 26.193-4 cf. 43.3]

So Muhammad evidently perceived Christianity (which 'confirms the Torah') as a later variant of Judaism and seems to have understood his core message as a distillation of what both these faiths taught:

> Say, 'I am nothing new among God's messengers. I do not know what will be done with me or you; I only follow what is revealed to me; I only warn plainly.' [Q 46.9]

Yet with the Hour of God's judgement much nearer now in time he could also believe himself to be God's final and definitive messenger – the 'seal of the prophets' [Q 33.40]. If so, two implications perhaps follow:

- Previous 'scriptures' may be subject to amendment:

  > There was a Scripture for every age: God erases or confirms wherever He will, and the source of Scripture is with Him. [Q 13.39]

- Muhammad's message was not limited to those of Arab tongue:

  > This is a message to all people, so that they may be warned by it. [Q 14.52]

165

> Say, 'People, I am the Messenger of God to you all, from Him who
> has control over the heavens and the earth.' [Q 7.158]

There are many indications that he conceived the Last Day (or the Hour, a term used some forty-eight times) to be approaching rapidly:

> That is a Day in which all people will be gathered together, a Day for all to see. We are delaying it only for a specified period. [Q 11.103-4]
> When the peoples of Gog and Magog are let loose and swarm swiftly from every highland, when the True Promise draws near, the disbelievers' eyes will stare in terror, and they will say, 'Woe to us! We were not aware of this at all. We were wrong.' [Q 21.96-97]
> The disbelievers will remain in doubt about it until the Hour suddenly overpowers them. [Q 22.55]
> People ask you about the Hour. Say, 'God alone has knowledge of it.' How could you know? The Hour may well be near. God has rejected the disbelievers and prepared a blazing fire for them. [Q 33.63-64]
> The imminent Hour draws near and only God can disclose it. [Q 53.57-58]
> The disbelievers think it (the Day) is distant, but we know it to be close [Q 70.6-7]

In addition, there is a verse [Q 43.61] with an ambiguous pronoun '*hu*', interpreted by some to mean the Qur'an itself, but by others to continue the previous reference to Jesus. The possible meanings are thus twofold:

> *This* (i.e. the Qur'an *or* Jesus) is knowledge for the Hour: do not doubt it.

Even if the former reading is intended, the 'imminence' and 'unexpectedness' certainly cohere with Jesus' teaching in the Gospels, as does the assertion that 'God alone knows'. Where the latter reading is preferred, commentators usually take it as a reference to Jesus' Second Coming.

It may further be noted that, according to the Qur'an, it is not only individuals who are answerable for their deeds, but the (religious) communities to which they belong:

> The day will come when We raise up in each community a witness against them, and We shall bring you as a witness against these people, for We have

sent the Scripture to you explaining everything, and as guidance and mercy and good news to those who devote themselves to God. [Q 16.89]

So Muhammad is passionate in his conviction and in his desire to warn 'disbelievers' of the peril they are in. This particular group of people obviously includes the idolaters, who worship other gods, but also those who distort beliefs about the one true God or who fail to take their faith seriously.

But the Qur'an offers a way out. It carries much practical advice and wise counsel on godly living (e.g. prayer, pilgrimage, family matters, inheritance, fasting, food and drink): it not only challenges the disbelievers but also encourages the believers. Thomas Carlyle once again glimpses a little of its wisdom:

> The sublime forgiveness of Christianity, turning of the other cheek when the one has been smitten, is not here: you are to revenge yourself, but it is to be in measure, not overmuch, or beyond justice. On the other hand, Islam, like any great Faith, and insight into the essence of man, is a perfect equalizer of men: the soul of one believer outweighs all earthly kingships; all men, according to Islam too, are equal. Mahomet insists not on the propriety of giving alms, but on the necessity of it: he marks down by law how much you are to give, and it is at your peril if you neglect. The tenth part of a man's annual income, whatever that may be, is the property of the poor, of those that are afflicted and need help. [Carlyle 64]

His evident appreciation, which helps to explain how Muhammad came to be acclaimed not just as a prophet but as a trusted political leader, does however leave an unanswered question: why does the Qur'an not refer more readily to biblical teachings about justice and compassion, or engage more fully with the scriptures it endorses? It hails Mary's piety in the Bible, and the righteousness of others, but its main emphasis seems to be on the militancy of the prophets. Does this reflect the Judaism and Christianity that Muhammad encountered, or was it a deliberately partial reading of their scriptures? Put differently, we may ask: if Muhammad had been treated well by devout practising Jews or had known a faithful Christian community (instead of observing factious divisions and bellicose rulers), might he not have become a Jew or a Christian, and have learnt much more about their beliefs and practices? According to Sozomen, the 5th century historian, some Arabs, identifying with Abraham's son Ishmael, had by then already 'returned' to his religious practices, which they took to be the Jewish faith:

> This is the tribe which took its origin and had its name from Ishmael, the son of Abraham; and the ancients called them Ishmaelites after their progenitor ... Such being their origin, they practice circumcision like the Jews, refrain from the use of pork, and observe many other Jewish rites and customs. If, indeed, they deviate in any respect from the observances of that nation, it must be ascribed to the lapse of time, and to their intercourse with the neighbouring nations ... Some of their tribe afterwards happening to come in contact with the Jews, gathered from them the facts of their true origin, returned to their kinsmen, and inclined to the Hebrew customs and laws. From that time on, until now, many of them regulate their lives according to the Jewish precepts. [*Hist Eccl* 6.38]

Abrahamic faith

However, although the Qur'an commends both Jewish and Christian scriptures it distances itself from them by revering Abraham as its own proper mentor; he features in no less than twenty five *suras*:

> People of the Book, why do you argue about Abraham when the Torah and the Gospels were not revealed until after his time? ... Abraham was neither a Jew nor a Christian. He was upright and devoted to God, never an idolater, and the people who are closest to him are those who truly follow his ways, this Prophet (Muhammad), and believers. [Q 3.65, 67-8]

This touches a debate that was live in New Testament times. Jews maintained that they were the heirs of Abraham, to whom God's promises were made [Gen 12.1-3], while Paul takes issue with them in his Letter to the Galatians and again in his Letter to the Romans:

> Those who are men of faith are blessed with Abraham who had faith. [Gal 3.9]
> If you are Christ's, then you are Abraham's offspring, heirs according to promise. [Gal 3.29]

The promise to Abraham and his descendants, that they should inherit the world, did not come through the law but through the righteousness of faith. [Rom 4.13]

He employs a 'rabbinical' approach (that hangs on a single grammatical detail) to demonstrate how Christ is Abraham's one true 'offspring'. Matthew endorses this by his careful construction of Jesus' genealogy, claiming him as 'son of David, son of Abraham' [Mt 1.1]; whereas in John's Gospel Jesus himself concludes an argument with the Jews by declaring 'before Abraham was, I am' [Jn 8.58]. There are in all about a dozen occasions in the Gospels when Jesus mentions Abraham – often as 'father' Abraham, each time with evident respect.

For its part, the Qur'an claims Abraham for the Arabs, seeing him as the prophet who first established monotheism (cf. Josh 24.2-3), henceforth to be their 'traditional' religion:

When Abraham's Lord tested him with certain commandments, which he fulfilled, He said, 'I will make you a leader of people.' Abraham asked, 'And will You make leaders from my descendants too?' God answered, 'My pledge does not hold for those who do evil.' We made the House a resort and a sanctuary for people, saying, 'Take the spot where Abraham stood as your place of prayer' ... As Abraham and Ishmael built up the foundations of the House ... 'Our Lord, make a messenger of their own rise   up   from among them, to recite Your revelations to them.' [Q 2.124-   5,127, 129]

The Sacred House, whose site was 'shown' to Abraham [Q 22.26], is identified in sura 5 as 'the Ka'ba', which means the cube, and is also called 'the Sacred Mosque' [Q 8.34]. Because 'those mindful of God' were debarred from it for a period of Muhammad's life by disbelievers, the location of the House can with some confidence be identified as Mecca, rather than some other Ka'ba in the region, although the Qur'an terms this place Bakka:

The first House to be established for people was the one at Bakka. It is a blessed place; a source of guidance for all people; there are clear signs in it; it is the place where Abraham stood to pray; whoever enters it is safe. [Q 3.96-97]

It is certain that the Ka'ba pre-dated Muhammad as a focal point for tribes to come and worship,[51] although what disbelievers practised there with their idols might well be 'disgraceful' [Q 7.28]:

> Their prayers before the House are nothing but whistling and clapping. [Q 8.35]

Whether its construction was anything like as ancient as the time of Abraham is much disputed. Nevertheless it is not the only possible connection of his with Arabia. His firstborn was Ishmael, 'a wild ass of a man' [Gen 16.12], whose descendants are depicted as Arab traders, perhaps from western Arabia where gold was to be mined:

> They saw a caravan of Ish'maelites coming from Gilead. [Gen 37.25]
> They had golden earrings, because they were Ish'maelites. [Judg 8.24]

Another of Abraham's children is listed in the Bible as an Arab viz. Mid'ian [Gen 25.2] – the name also of a tribal territory, probably somewhere east of Aqaba in the Hijaz. It was in Mid'ian that Moses is recorded as taking refuge from Pharaoh, later to experience 'the God of your father, the God of Abraham ...' [Exod 3.6] in the burning bush episode, within sight of mount Horeb. Biblical place names associated with Abraham himself are mainly in the Judaean region (e.g. his encounter with the enigmatic figure of Melchizedek, 'priest of God Most High'), and we read that after his death

> Isaac and Ish'mael his sons buried him in the cave of Mach-pe'lah, in the field of Ephron the son of Zohar the Hittite, east of Mamre. [Gen 25.9 cf. 14.13 which describes Abraham as then 'living by the oaks of Mamre']

Mamre is just north of Hebron (30 miles due south from Jerusalem), and according to Sozomen was the location of an important *caravanserai*:

> The place is presently called the Terebinth, and is situated at the distance of fifteen stadia from Hebron ... There every year a very famous festival is held in the summer time, by people of the neighbourhood as well as by the

---

[51] A biblical parallel appears in the story of Jacob, who set up a stone pillar at Bethel to be 'God's house'. [Gen 28.18-22]

inhabitants of more distant parts of Palestine and by Phoenicians and Arabians. Very many come there for the sake of business, some to sell and some to buy. The feast is celebrated by a very big congregation of Jews, since they boast of Abraham as their forefather, of heathens since angels came there, of Christians since he who should be born from the Virgin for the salvation of humankind appeared there to that pious man. Everyone venerates this place according to his religion.[52] [*Hist Eccl* 2.4]

Not long before Muhammad was born (570 CE) the 'Terebinth' was sufficiently notable to be marked on the famous Madaba Mosaic map, still preserved in Jordan. Abraham was venerated at Mamre as the father of Jews and Christians alike, allowing his fame to be known much further afield, including in the Arab world. As for his dates, little is certain – the biblical stories about him may have been fully incorporated into Israel's ideology as late as the time of the Babylonian exile, given the paucity of references to him in pre-exilic writings. Whether he was also connected with the Ka'ba seems unlikely, since Mecca lies a long way south from other places associated with him. In his classic study of these issues Thomas Thompson finds that 'Abraham' is a relatively common West Semitic name, both in the first and second millennia BCE, but warns:

Any attempt to find movements analogous to Abraham's in the history of the Near East are essentially misdirected for the purposes of biblical (hence also qur'anic) interpretation.[53]

According to the Qur'an, a tradition of monotheism existed in Arabia long before Muhammad's time. Among the religious groups both Sabians and Magians are listed along with Jews and Christians [Q 22.17 cf. 2.62, 5.69] as those 'who believe in God and the Last Day and do good': little is known about the Sabians, who may have been astrologically-minded spiritualists, but the Magians are generally thought to have been

---

[52] The 'Terebinth' – more plausibly translated in the RSV as 'the oaks' of Mamre [Gen 18.1] – was the location where 'three men' were offered hospitality by Abraham: they were understood by some to have been angels, but in later Christian tradition as the holy Trinity.

[53] Thomas Thompson: *The Historicity of the Patriarchal Narratives – the Quest for the Historical Abraham* (Harrisburg PA 2002, 315)

Zoroastrians, otherwise prominent in neighbouring Persia. Again, in the qur'anic listings of Muhammad's prophetic predecessors, many of the names – which go back to Abraham – are familiar from the Bible, even if some of the stories recounted are different. There are three, however, unknown outside the Qur'an:

> To the people of 'Ad We sent their brother, Hud ... To the people of Thamud We sent their brother, Salih ... To the people of Midian We sent their brother, Shu'ayb. [Q 7.65, 73, 85]

Of 'Ad and Thamud – renowned for its rock carvings [Q 89.6-9], which have been compared with those of Petra – little is known; but Midian features here once again, this time as a place where monotheistic ideas had flourished. It is indeed credible that Yahwism itself originated in this area, whence it passed (as previously noted) to Moses. The existence here of prophets upholding this tradition is certainly not contrary to the biblical picture, which allowed that genuine prophets might be found beyond Israel's frontiers (for of course God himself, as it came eventually to be appreciated, was not confined to one territory alone):

> Balak the son of Zippor, who was king of Moab at that time, sent messengers (with elders from Mid'ian) to Balaam the son of Be'or at Pethor, which is near the River, in the land of Amaw. [Num 22.4-5]

Many centuries later, whereas prophecy had largely died out elsewhere in the Near East, there were still Montanists active in this way in Asia Minor, with various offshoots of Manichaeism continuing to thrive on its native Persian soil:

> At the time of Muhammad's preaching in the early 7th century, moreover, there were a number of other figures in Arabia who, like him, presented themselves as prophets bearing a divine message. All of this points to the vitality of the tradition of active prophecy, particularly in Arabia, and helps us understand the way in which people in Arabia may have received Muhammad's claims to be a prophet.[54]

---

[54] Donner 31

172

Thus, it is not without foundation that the Qur'an can portray Muhammad as the spiritual heir of Abraham, the first to prophesy in the name of the one true God. Yet those to whom the word 'prophet' suggests someone in the biblical mould of Amos, Micah or Isaiah may be a little surprised to find this label attached to Abraham, usually regarded in the different category of 'patriarch'; but in fact the Hebrew Bible itself offers this description in one place – an example of its growing tendency so to term any who understood God's ways and were approved by him:

> He (Abraham) is a prophet, and he will pray for you, and you shall live. [Gen 20.7]

However, even apart from linking him with the Ka'ba, the Qur'an recounts several other incidents in his life that are quite unknown to the Bible (as does the late Jewish composition, the book of Jubilees) e.g.

- (Abraham) said ... 'By God I shall certainly outwit your idols as soon as you have turned your backs!' He broke them all into pieces, but left the biggest one for them to return to. [Q 21.57-58]

  The story, similar to the Jewish midrash *Genesis Rabbah* 38.13, continues with Abraham pretending that the biggest idol had caused the damage, and inviting the people then to extract a confession from that idol – at which point they are forced to admit that all their idols are dumb.

- And when Abraham said, 'My Lord, show me how You give life to the dead,' He said, 'Do you not believe, then?' 'Yes,' said Abraham, 'but just to put my heart at rest.' So God said, 'Take four birds and train them to come back to you. Then place them on separate hilltops, call them back, and they will come flying to you.' [Q 2.260]

- We showed Abraham (God's) mighty dominion over the heavens and the earth, so that he might be a firm believer. When the night grew dark over him he saw a star and said, 'This is my Lord,' but when it set, he said, 'I do not like things that set.' And when he saw the moon rising he said, 'This is my Lord,' but when it too set, he said, 'If my Lord does not guide me, I shall be one of those who go astray.' Then he saw the sun rising and cried, 'This is my Lord! This is greater.' But

173

when the sun set, he said, 'My people, I disown all that you worship beside God. I have turned my face as a true believer towards Him who created the heavens and the earth. I am not one of the polytheists.' [Q 6.75-79]

Again, in the story [Q 37.99-111] of Abraham's call to sacrifice his son, there are many variations on the familiar biblical version, and since Isaac is introduced afterwards at verse 112 it appears that it is Ishmael who is ransomed 'with a momentous sacrifice' [v107]. It is arguable that the qur'anic account in this respect makes better sense than the biblical text, which refers to the offering of Abraham's 'only son' [Gen 22.2]. The point of all these narratives, however, is not their 'factual' accuracy, but their value as 'midrash' – or it might be suggested, in more familiar English, as sermon illustrations to emphasise the strength of Abraham's faith.

Qur'anic sources

Much of the biblical material (including the many references to Moses and to Mary) is similarly embellished, sometimes using apocryphal writings. The Qur'an thereby illustrates its message by using stories that were probably familiar to some at least of its audience, an oral repertoire whose likely or possible sources are quite diverse. Among these extra-biblical reminiscences may be named *the Jewish Mishnah, the Babylonian Talmud, the Life of Adam and Eve, the Apocalypse of Abraham, the Apocryphon of Jannes and Jambres the Magicians, the Book of Jubilees, the Diatessaron, the Proto-Evangelium of James, the Gospel of Pseudo-Matthew, the Infancy Gospel of Thomas.* While these Jewish / Christian writings mostly originated in the 2nd century CE or soon after, they were often altered or embellished subsequently, sometimes in translation. Even so, the versions in oral circulation did not necessarily conform altogether with any known extant text. There is a possibility that some later written versions may in turn reflect details found in the Qur'an.

Further examples of their influence upon qur'anic material appear in the two main *suras* that feature Mary: thus, *sura* 3 (Al-'Imran) includes the birth of Mary prior to the annunciations to Zechariah and to Mary herself, which is the same sequence as in the *Proto-Evangelium of James*; *sura* 19

(Maryam), however, omits her birth, and adheres more closely to Luke's Gospel (and correspondingly to the *Diatessaron*). Yet the latter *sura* also recounts the story of Mary seeking refuge under a palm-tree – here to give birth to Jesus; this is similar to the post-natal story found in the *Gospel of Pseudo-Matthew.*

There is also a famous non-biblical legend in *sura* 18, which tells of the young men who took refuge in a cave to escape persecution on account of their (originally Christian) faith; here they fell asleep – and woke three hundred years later [v25]. The story goes back to the time of the emperor Decius around 250 CE, and is known as the 'Seven Sleepers of Ephesus'; it is thought to have been first written down by bishop Stephen of Ephesus in the middle of the 5th century, with Syriac texts extant from the 6th century. These probably circulated in Jacobite circles, whose beliefs were shared by some Christians in southern Arabia, namely, at Najran. The story's popularity evidently spread, because the *sura* notes some of its disputed points:

> (Some) say, 'The sleepers were three, and their dog made four,' others say, 'They were five, and the dog made six' – guessing in the dark – and some say, 'They were seven, and their dog made eight.' Say, My Lord knows best how many they were.' [Q 18.22]

Mention of the 'dog' appears to be limited to the qur'anic version. Here at any rate is one particular example of the Christian lore that was current in Muhammad's milieu, providing him with well-known tales whose true meaning could then be revealed to his hearers; in this instance, the assurance offered was that 'they (believers) have no one to protect them other than Him' [v26].

If many of the *suras* seem therefore to have the character of 'sermons' conveying an urgent message for Muhammad's contemporaries, the point is often driven home with vivid illustrations that tell of the rewards of faith or, contrariwise, the consequences of disobedience.

14. Some Qur'anic Themes

Prayer

The Qur'an begins and ends with prayer: it opens with the *Fatiya*, which may have been added to the other *suras* in order to make a suitable preface to the whole collection. Every Muslim knows this by heart and recites it several times each day as well as on most religious occasions:

> In the Name of Allah, the Lord of Mercy, the Giver of Mercy. Praise belongs to God, Lord of the worlds, the Lord of Mercy, the Giver of Mercy, Master of the Day of Judgement. It is You we worship; it is You we ask for help. Guide us to the straight path: the path of those You have blessed, those who incur no anger and who have not gone astray.

Because those who pray are in the presence of the Lord, instructions are given about their necessary preparation for this sacred encounter:

> You who believe, when you are about to pray, wash your faces and your hands and arms up to the elbows, wipe your heads, wash your feet up to the ankles, and, if required, wash your whole body. [Q 5.6]

Prayer is advocated at regular intervals throughout day and night, to keep the heart and mind focused on what matters most:

> Celebrate the praise of your Lord, before the rising and setting of the sun, celebrate His praise during the night, and at the beginning and end of the day, so that you may find contentment and do not gaze longingly at what We have given some of them to enjoy, the finery of this present life. [Q 20.131-2]

There was evidently some controversy about the direction of prayer, which Muhammad regarded as a relatively minor matter:

> The East and the West belong to God: wherever you turn, there is His Face. [Q 2.115]

Since 'each community has its own direction' [Q 2.148] – probably meaning Jerusalem for the Jews and east for the Christians – the 'believers' were eventually instructed to distinguish themselves [Q 2.143] by facing towards the Ka'ba. When the change occurred, there were some rumblings – even the concern that prayers had previously been 'wasted'.

Foolish people will say, 'What has turned them away from the prayer direction they used to face?' [Q 2.142]

Yet in the Qur'an it is never the ritual that counts, so much as the inner disposition:

We have made camels part of God's sacred rites for you. It is neither their meat nor their blood that reaches God but your piety. [Q 22.36-37]

Since the apparent need for 'camels' here is clearly incapable of being put into universal practice, the use of reason commended elsewhere in the Qur'an at once indicates that its text need not be taken literally. It is the piety, rather than the camel, that actually matters. So, true prayer is not possible in a drunken state:

You who believe, do not come anywhere near the prayer if you are in drunken state. [Q 4.42]
With intoxicants and gambling, Satan seeks only to cite enmity and hatred among you, and to stop remembering God and prayer. Will you not give them up? [Q 5.91]
They ask you about intoxicants and gambling: say, 'There is great sin in both, and some benefit for people: the sin is greater than the benefit.' [Q 2.219]

There may be times when prayer should be accommodated to the situation at hand:

When you are travelling in the land, you will not be blamed for shortening your prayers, if you fear disbelievers may harm you. [Q 4.101]

In fact, although the Qur'an sets out exemplary patterns of prayer and of behaviour generally, it is not legalistic; circumstances can vary:

He has only forbidden you carrion, blood, pig's meat, and animals over which any name other than God's has been invoked. But if anyone is forced to eat such things by hunger, rather than desire or excess, he commits no sin: God is most merciful and forgiving ... For those who can fast only with

177

extreme difficulty, there is a way to compensate – feed a needy person. [Q 2.173, 184]

It is advisable to pray not just at the specified times, but as the occasion demands, for example, when difficulties or dangers arise:

If you are in danger, pray when you are out on foot or riding; when you are safe again, remember God, for He has taught you what you did not know. [Q 2.239]

Two prayers seeking God's protection bring the Qur'an to a suitable close:

In the name of God, the Lord of mercy, the Giver of Mercy –
Say, 'I seek refuge with the Lord of daybreak against the harm of what He has created, the harm of the night when darkness gathers, the harm of witches when they blow on knots, the harm of the envier when he envies.' [Q 113]
Say, 'I seek refuge with the Lord of people, the Controller of people, the God of people, against the harm of the slinking whisperer – who whispers into the hearts of people – whether they be jinn or people. [Q 114]

Yet the focus of prayer should never be simply the here and now. Mindfulness of God and awareness of one's ultimate destiny in his hands are fundamental:

There are some who pray, 'Our Lord, give us good in this world,' and they will have no share in the Hereafter; others pray, 'Our Lord, give us good in this world and in the Hereafter, and protect us from the torment of the Fire.' They will have the share they have worked for. [Q 2.200-2]

So there is a very brief prayer which, according to tradition, Muhammad reckoned to equal one-third of the entire Qur'an; it expresses total devotion to God:

He is God the One, God the eternal. He begot no one nor was He begotten. No one is comparable to Him. [Q 112]

Faith

Today I have perfected your religion for you, completed My blessing for you, and chosen as your religion total devotion to God. [Q5.3]

The deeds of anyone who rejects faith will come to nothing, and in the Hereafter he will come to nothing. [Q5.5]

So the Qur'an emphasises faith even more than good works. While the term *muslim* – one who submits – appears about seventy times in the text, it is far outnumbered by the one thousand references to the *mu'minum* – the Believers – and the difference in meaning is made explicit:

The desert Arabs say, 'We have faith.' Tell them, 'You do not have faith. What you should have said instead is, "We have submitted," for faith has not yet entered your hearts' … The true Believers are the ones who have faith in God and His Messenger and leave all doubt behind, the ones who have struggled with their possessions and their persons in God's way: they are the ones who are true. [Q 49.14-15]

Of course, faith has an intellectual dimension – chiefly the acceptance that God is one, and has no partners nor any rivals. But although it also entails submission to his will, this is more than an attitude of obedience: it implies a prayerful trust.

Do not say of anything, 'I will do that tomorrow,' without adding, 'God willing,' and, whenever you forget, remember your Lord and say, 'May my Lord guide me closer to what is right.' [Q 18.23-24]

One exemplar in the Qur'an of trusting submission is Mary, 'chosen above all women' [Q 3.42], 'a virtuous woman' [Q 5.75] who 'guarded her chastity' [Q 21.91 cf. 66.12]. She is esteemed more highly here than is immediately apparent within the New Testament, paradoxically perhaps as a way of lessening the difference between her standing and that of Jesus, who in qur'anic teaching is – like herself – a human being called into God's service.

Mary, be devout to your Lord, prostrate yourself in worship, bow down with those who pray. [Q 3.43]
We breathed into her from Our Spirit and made her and her son a sign for all people. [Q 21.91 cf. 23.50]
She accepted the truth of her Lord's words and Scriptures: *she was truly devout*. [Q 66.12]

Mary's inclusion 'with those who pray' is a reminder that the Qur'an is addressed to men and women alike. In this it is quite different from the disparagement of women found in some Gnostic writings such as the *Gospel of Thomas*, which concludes with notoriously chauvinistic words:

> Simon Peter said to them, 'Let Mary leave us, because women are not worthy of life.' Jesus said, 'Look, I shall lead her so that I will make her male ... For every woman who makes herself male will enter the kingdom of heaven.' [Coptic version of *Gospel of Thomas* 114]

By contrast, one verse above all in the Qur'an is quite emphatic in its inclusiveness:

> For men and women who are devoted to God – believing men and women, obedient men and women, truthful men and women, steadfast men and women, humble men and women, charitable men and women, fasting men and women, chaste men and women, men and women who remember God often – God has prepared forgiveness and rich reward. [Q 33.35]

(While it is true that Muhammad's wives were expected to be extra-zealous in their behaviour and to stay at home [Q 33.33], it is specifically stated that they were 'not like any other woman' [Q 33.32]. Nevertheless, the restrictions placed upon them were extended, as Muslim tradition developed, to other women as well. One particular verse [Q 4.34] which mentions 'high-handedness' in wives and their need for 'obedience' has been subject to much commentary; but 'high-handedness' is also seen as a potential fault in husbands [Q 4.128], while the usual focus of 'obedience' in the Qur'an is God himself. The verse does perhaps allow that 'high-handedness' in a wife may merit a slap, although the verb *daraba* used here can also mean 'to set an example'. At the very least, it differs from a similar verb *darraba*, 'to strike repeatedly', and thus disallows any unchecked violence against women.)

Charity

One of the shorter *suras* is entitled 'Common Kindnesses'. It is critical of piety that is mere outward display:

Woe to those who pray but are heedless of their prayer; those who are all show and forbid common kindnesses. [Q 107.4-6 cf. Matt 6.1]
Do not strut arrogantly about the earth. [Q 17.37]

Similar points are made at greater length elsewhere:

Goodness does not consist in turning your face towards East or West. The truly good are those who believe in God and the Last Day, in the angels, the Scripture, and the prophets; who give away some of their wealth, however much they cherish it, to their relatives, to orphans, the needy, travellers and beggars, and to liberate those in bondage; those who keep up the prayer and pay the prescribed alms; who keep pledges whenever they make them; who are steadfast in misfortune, adversity, and times of danger. These are the ones who are true, and it is they who are aware of God. [Q 2.177]

Kindness — a charitable disposition — has many different avenues by which to express itself:

When you are offered a greeting, respond with a better one, or at least eturn it. [Q 4.86]
A kind word and forgiveness is better than a charitable deed followed by hurtful. [Q 2.261]
Your Lord has commanded that you should worship none but Him, and that you be kind to your parents. If either or both of them reach old age with you, say no word that shows impatience with them, and do not be harsh with them, but speak to them respectfully and lower your wing in humility towards them in kindness and say, 'Lord, have mercy on them, just as they cared for me when I was little' ...Give relatives their due, and the needy, and travellers – do not squander your wealth wastefully ... Do not be tight-fisted, nor so open-handed that you end up blamed and overwhelmed with regret. [Q 17.23-29]

There are occasionally verses that mirror Jesus' teaching:

If you give charity openly, it is good, but if you keep it secret and give to the needy in private, that is better for you. [Q 2.271 cf. Mt 6.3-4]

The Qur'an has a particular concern for the vulnerable, insisting that they should not be harmed or exploited:

God has allowed trade and forbidden usury. [Q 2.276 cf. Exod 22.25, Deut 23.19-20, Lev 25. 35-38, Ps 15.5]

Give full measure when you measure, and weigh with accurate scales. [Q 17.35]

What will explain to you what the steep path is? It is to free a slave, to feed at a time of hunger an orphaned relative or a poor person in distress, and to be one of those who believe and urge one another to steadfastness and compassion. [Q 90.12-17]

Do not kill your children for fear of poverty – We shall provide for them and for you – killing them is a great sin. [Q 17.31]

When the baby girl buried alive is asked for what sin she was killed ... then every soul will know what it has brought about. [Q 81.8,14]

Muhammad confesses how his own heart is distraught when he sees others afflicted around him:

A Messenger has come to you from among yourselves. Your suffering distresses him: he is deeply concerned for you and full of kindness and mercy towards the believers. [Q 9.128]

How far should one's responsibilities stretch? The Qur'an insists that all human beings should be respected, including slaves: thus, 'freeing a slave' is recommended in *sura* 90 (as above) – and there is criticism of those who do not treat their slaves well:

It is God who has given some of you more provision than others. Those who have been given more are unwilling to pass their provision on to the slaves they possess so that they become their equals. How can they refuse to acknowledge God's blessings? [Q 16.71]

Any slaves who want to gain their freedom should be financially assisted too:

If any of your slaves wish to pay for their freedom, make a contract with them accordingly, if you know they have good in them, and give them some of the wealth God has given you. [Q 24.33]

One may wonder indeed whether the Qur'an might not have challenged the sexual rights slave-owners traditionally claimed over their slaves – had not Abraham already confirmed these earlier by his own conduct:

(The faithful) guard their chastity except with their spouses or their slaves. [Q 23.5]

Yet intercourse with slaves was evidently not seen as infidelity, which is roundly condemned – and subject to penalties:

Do not go anywhere near adultery: it is an outrage, and an evil path. [Q 17.32]
Strike the adulteress and the adulterer one hundred times. [Q 24.2]

Temptation is best avoided here by chaste behaviour and modest dress:

Tell believing men to lower their eyes and guard their private parts: that is purer for them. God is well aware of everything they do. And tell believing women that they should lower their eyes, guard their private parts, and not display their charms beyond what (it is acceptable) to reveal; they should draw their coverings over their necklines and not reveal their charms except to their husbands, their fathers (and other close family members). [Q 24.30-31]

The sanctity of life

On the fundamental right to life, the Qur'an is firm:

Do not take life, which God has made sacred, except by right. [Q 17.33]

The 'exceptional' clause is not easy to pin down, even though it is illustrated in several other qur'anic passages. In most instances, it is the right to self-defence that is being upheld, but even this has qualifications:

Fight in God's cause against those who fight you, but do not overstep the limits. [Q 2.190]
How could you not fight a people who have broken their oaths, who tried to drive the Messenger out, who attacked you first? [Q 9.13]
You may fight the idolaters at any time, *if they first fight you*. [Q 9.36]
There is no cause to act against anyone who defends himself after being wronged, but there is cause to act against those who oppress people and transgress in the land against all justice – they will have an agonizing torment – though if a person is patient and forgives, this is one of the greatest things. [Q 42.41-43]

The reminder inserted in this last quotation, that retribution for wrongdoing ultimately lies with God, is a warning against vengefulness. Elsewhere similar restraint is advocated (indeed, Muhammad understood that human divisions were not part of God's original plan – 'all people were originally one single community' Q 10.19):

> You who believe, be careful when you go to fight in God's way, and do not say to someone who offers you a greeting of peace, 'You are not a believer.' [Q 4.94]
> We decreed to the Children of Israel that if anyone kills a person – unless in retribution for murder or spreading corruption in the land – it is as if he kills all mankind, while if any saves a life it is as if he saves the lives of all mankind. [Q 5.32]

The Jewish writer Isaac Bashevis Singer is far from convinced that modern Israel heeds this message. It uses Hebrew 'but it's no longer the Sacred Tongue':

> A language used to build ships and airplanes and to manufacture guns and bombs cannot be a Sacred Tongue.[55]

So too in his own day Muhammad sometimes faced criticism over his call to arms. Initially there were apparently those who had been told:

> Restrain yourselves from fighting, perform the prayer, and pay the prescribed alms. [Q 4.77]

When circumstances changed and 'fighting was ordained for them', those who demurred were then castigated as frightened:

> Some of them feared men as much as, or even more than, they feared God. [Q 4.77]

There may indeed be some truth in this, and Muhammad was well aware that whereas they attributed all good fortune to God, any reversals were blamed on himself! They were reminded therefore that death comes

---

[55] Isaac Bashevis Singer: *The Penitent* (Harmondsworth 1986, 69)

eventually to all, and that a key component of faith is the belief in God's future rewards:

> The Hereafter is far better for those who are mindful of God. [Q 4.77-78]
>
> Do not say that those who are killed in God's cause are dead; they are alive, though you do not realise it. [Q 2.154 cf. 3.156,169]

Elsewhere he offers what may be considered an *ad hominem* argument:

> If God did not repel some people by means of others, many monasteries, churches, synagogues, and mosques, where God's name is much invoked, would have been destroyed. [Q 22.40]

This verse speaks up in defence, not only of the believers, who worship in mosques, but of other monotheists viz. Jews in their synagogues and Christians in their monasteries and churches, where the Qur'an notes approvingly there are 'people devoted to learning and ascetics' [Q 5.82]. How any believing Muslim could therefore read the Qur'an today and then proceed to attack Christian places of worship in (e.g.) Nigeria or Egypt is inconceivable. The only justification might be found in a verse that in effect denounces some People of the Book as insincere:

> Fight those of the People of the Book who do not believe in God and the Last Day, who do not forbid what God and His Messenger have forbidden, who do not obey the rule of justice, until they pay the tax promptly and agree to submit. [Q 9.29]

The principle here is expressed in a later verse of the same *sura*:

> God will not forgive them even if you ask seventy times, because they reject God and His Messenger. God does not guide those who rebel against Him. [Q 9.80 cf. Matt 18.21-22]

So hostile action is seen as imperative, not necessarily just in self-defence, but because of the affront to God:

> If God did not drive some back by means of others the earth would be completely corrupt. [Q 2.251]

It is as if the believers have been recruited as 'mercenaries' into God's army:

God has purchased the persons and possessions of the believers in return for the Garden – they fight in God's way: they kill and are killed – this is a true promise given by Him in the Torah, the Gospel, and the Qur'an. [Q9.111]

The believers fight for God's cause, while those who reject faith fight for an unjust cause. [Q 4.76]

The Arabic word translated here as 'unjust cause' is *taghut*, which may mean 'idols', 'tyrants' or 'opponents'. Yet, if there is an offer of peace, it should be accepted in line with God's own readiness to forgive (a theme repeated no less than 500 times in the Qur'an cf. the 'covenant of the thirteen attributes' in Exodus 34.6-7, of which most refer to God's mercy):

If they withdraw and do not fight you, and offer you peace, then God gives you no way against them. [Q 4.90]

If they incline towards peace, you must also incline towards it, and put your trust in God. [Q 8.61]

God may still bring about affection between you and your [enemies] – God is all powerful, God is most forgiving and merciful – and He does not forbid you to deal kindly and justly with anyone who has not fought you for your faith or driven you out of your homes. [Q 60.7-8]

It should not be forgotten that Muhammad, living as he did some three centuries after the conversion of Constantine, which marked a turning point in the fortunes of the Church and a weakening of its hitherto universal pacifism, was familiar with the forced imposition of Christian faith under the rule of Byzantines and others. Patricia Crone, in a 2007 article *Jihad: idea and history*[56], makes the important observation that the bellicosity urged upon Israelites in the Old Testament and seen too in neighbouring Assyrian and Moabite regimes was invariably for themselves rather than for 'the good of the victims'; in other words, a manifestation of tribalism:

They fought for the greater glory of their own god and their own community, not to save anyone else ... But in classical Islam, the divine command to go and fight is no longer addressed to an ethnic group, only to believers, whoever they may be.

---

[56] www.opendemocracy.net/faith-europe_islam/jihad

She goes on to argue that *jihad* 'is linked to a religious *mission civilisatrice*' in which 'the believers conquer in order to save souls'. This is surely overstated, given the oft-cited verse of *sura* 2 that 'there is no compulsion in religion'. The emphasis of the Qur'an lies rather on the nullifying of 'disbelief'; indeed, in *sura* 80 Muhammad is rebuked for giving more attention to (disbelieving) nobles than to a blind man who was seeking further instruction:

> For the self-satisfied one you go out of your way – though *it is not your responsibility* if he does not attain purity – but from the one who comes to you full of eagerness and awe you are distracted. [Q 80.5-8]

The last judgement – and beyond

What remains unclear, because Muhammad's view of the People of the Book does seem to have become generally less favourable as time went on, is how flexibly the category of 'believers' can be interpreted. The key doctrinal test of monotheism seems to have been extended over the years to include related teachings, in a manner somewhat analogous to the Christian extension of the simple confession 'Jesus is Lord' to increasingly complex credal statements. There is, however, the recognition that the final judgement rests with God:

> Say, 'God is our Lord and your Lord – to us our deeds and to you yours, so let there be no argument between us and you – God will gather us together, and to Him we shall return.' [Q 42.15]
> On the Day of Resurrection, your Lord will judge between them regarding their differences. [Q 45.17]

What then is the qur'anic vision of the afterlife?

> Bear in mind that the present life is just a game, a diversion, an attraction, a cause of boasting among you, of rivalry in wealth and children ... So race for your Lord's forgiveness and a Garden as wide as the heavens and earth, prepared for those who believe in God and His messengers. [Q 57.20-21]

There are abundant references to the Last Day, regarded as a key doctrine governing the full accountability of human life, alongside verses explicitly directed to those who are sceptical about the idea of resurrection. The

187

latter are reminded of the many natural phenomena which in one way or another display God's creative powers and his ability to bring or restore life where there was none before. As for Paradise, it is frequently depicted as a garden:

> God has promised the believers, both men and women, Gardens graced with flowing streams where they will remain; good, peaceful homes in Gardens of lasting bliss; and – greatest of all – God's good pleasure. [Q 9.72] They will enter perpetual Gardens, along with their righteous ancestors, spouses, and descendants. [Q 13.23]

Another *sura* spells out the meaning of 'righteous', which may entail hardships:

> Any who direct themselves wholly to God and do good will have their reward with their Lord ... Do you suppose that you will enter the Garden without first having suffered like those who passed away before you? [Q 2.112, 214]

Repentance is expected of any 'who neglected prayer and were driven by their own desires' [Q 19.60] – or who sought 'superiority on earth or spread corruption' [Q 28.83]. The accoutrements of Paradise are then elaborated imaginatively:

> They will have Gardens of lasting bliss graced with flowing streams. There they will be adorned with bracelets of gold. There they will wear green garments of fine silk and brocade. There they will be comfortably seated on soft chairs. [Q 18.31]
> The people of Paradise today are happily occupied – they and their spouses – seated on couches in the shade.   [Q 36.55-56]
> But those mindful of God will be in a safe place amid Gardens and springs, clothed in silk and fine brocade, facing one another: so it will be. We shall pair them with maidens with beautiful eyes. [Q 44.51-54]

The text here has obviously become a little less chaste, with its switch from 'spouses' to 'beautiful-eyed maidens', repeated in further *suras*:

> They are comfortably seated on couches arranged in rows; We pair them with beautiful-eyed maidens. We unite the believers with their offspring who followed them in faith. [Q 52.20-21]

For those who are aware of God there is supreme fulfilment: gardens, vineyards, maidens of matching age. [Q 78.31-32]

And there is a further development in which Paradise is subdivided according to one's faith and works. It has an upper and a lower heaven, both of which are contrasted with hell, a scenario similar to those found in later Jewish and Christian apocryphal writings:

Then you will be sorted into three classes. Those on the Right—what people they are! Those on the Left—what people they are! And those in front— ahead indeed! For these will be the ones brought nearest to God in Gardens of Bliss: many from the past and a few from later generations. On couches of well-woven cloth they will sit facing each other; everlasting youths will go round among them with glasses, flagons, and cups of a pure drink that causes no headache or intoxication; any fruit they choose; the meat of any bird they like; and beautiful-eyed maidens like hidden pearls: a reward for what they use to do. [Q 56.8-24]
For those who fear (to) stand before their Lord there are two gardens ... [Q 55.46]
A wall with a door will be erected between them (the believers and the hypocrites): inside it lies mercy, outside lies torment. [Q 57.13]

Ultimately though, even if the pious anticipate their reward in the shape of delightful gardens and couches, with 'rivers of water forever pure', 'milk forever fresh', 'wine a delight for those who drink', 'honey clarified and pure', with 'fruit of every kind' [Q 47.15], such imagery is only a symbol for their acceptance with God:

The final return is to God. [Q 3.28]
They will find forgiveness from their Lord. [Q 47.15]

189

15. Early Christian Responses

Initial reactions

When Muhammad died in 632 CE, the Qur'an had only a rudimentary written form, but its *suras* had been memorised by many of his followers. How much of its message had been properly appreciated is another question, but it was the witness borne by the 'believers' that was initially responsible for spreading abroad the teachings of the Qur'an. From the limited evidence available it seems that the emphasis was upon God as 'compassionate' and 'merciful', the Lord of the world, whose earthly commander unites all true believers. There was in this early period relatively little reference to Muhammad himself, although the *muhajirun* certainly dated their calendar from 622 CE when the *hjira* took place. At least some of Muhammad's supporters were attracted less by any particular teachings than by the ensuing military and political successes ('God helped you at Badr when you were very weak' Q 3.123), which brought them both land and booty (even if 'one-fifth' belonged 'to God and the Messenger, to close relatives and orphans, to the needy and travellers' Q 8.41). Following the conquest of Mecca in 630 came the 'year of delegations' when tribes throughout Arabia made their peace with him; various raids were carried out elsewhere (see map on p193) and the seeds were sown for migration to continue in occupied territories. So Christians in Syria gained their first experience of what came to be known as Islam under a wave of Arab attacks – yet as the aggression escalated so too did the unfavourable impressions of this religious awakening. A Christian named Jacob, formerly a Jew, received a letter in July 634 from his brother Abraham written from Caesarea which commented on how the Saracens had killed a member of the imperial guard:

> And they were saying that the prophet had appeared ... proclaiming the advent of the anointed one ... So I, Abraham, inquired and heard from those who had met him that there was no truth to be found in the so-called prophet, only the shedding of men's blood. He says also that he has the keys of paradise, which is incredible. [*Doctrina Jacobi* 5.16.209]

Again, Sophronius, Patriarch of Jerusalem, noted continuing bloodshed two years later; like other contemporary Christians, he interpreted this as one of the 'End signs', in fact, as a warning to those who failed to live up to their professed faith:

> The vengeful and God-hating Saracens, the abomination of desolation clearly foretold to us by the prophets, overrun the places which are not allowed to them, plunder cities, devastate fields, burn down villages, set on fire the holy churches, overturn the sacred monasteries, oppose the Byzantine armies arrayed against them ... unrestrainedly imitating their leader, who is the devil ... Yet these vile things would not have been accomplished ... unless we had first insulted the gift (of baptism). [*On Holy Baptism* 166-7]

He added:

> Through repentance we shall blunt the Ishmaelite sword and break the Hagarene bow, and see Bethlehem again.

Corroboration of much turbulence and distress, affecting Christian, Jew and Samaritan alike, in Syria and even Persia is found in the contemporary *Chronicle* of Thomas the (Jacobite) Presbyter:

> The Arabs climbed the mountain of Mardin and killed many monks there in the monasteries of Qedar and Bnata. There died the blessed man Simon, doorkeeper of Qedar, brother of Thomas the priest.
> In January [636] the people of Homs took the word for their lives and many villages were ravaged by the killing of the Arabs of Muhmd and many people were slain and taken prisoner from Galilee as far as Beth.

Yet this grim picture seems by recent and extensive archaeological evidence to have been a considerable exaggeration of what actually happened. In many places, for example, churches were not destroyed and continued in use – sometimes, according to later Muslim tradition, shared with the new settlers (in particular, in Jerusalem, Damascus and Homs). Indeed, new churches were also built at this time, with (datable) mosaic floors. The inscription on the floor of St Menas Church, Rihab in Jordan mentions the year of its construction as 635 CE. It is possible that some of the above-mentioned devastation resulted from raids quite unconnected with the Believers' movement.

Later in the 7th century other Christian authors, while agreeing to see the invasion as divine punishment, explained it more variously. The Chalcedonian author of *The Life of Maximus* thought that dyothelitism was the root fault, exemplified in Maximus and his followers; whereas the dyothelite Anastasios of Sinai, who was especially concerned about the Arab incursions into Palestine, attributed it to the Byzantine emperor's pro-monothelite stance. John of Phenek, a Nestorian, recorded in his *Summary of World History* [Bk 15] that 'among them (the Arabs), there are many Christians, some of whom are from the heretics, others from us', and considered that while Christian heresies were partly to blame, yet widespread laxity of faith also needed chastising:

> God called the Arabs from the end of the earth, to destroy through them a sinful kingdom.

He reported that those who violated Muhammad's teachings (which he understood to be based upon the 'old Law' i.e. the Torah) were subject to the death penalty. Among the (perhaps much exaggerated) 'crimes' of Christians he notes the following :

- The bishops ... dictated orders and shouted loudly as archons, and sent the terror of their voices to their subjects, like animals without reason. They drew their strength and power not from Christ, but from the civil courts.
- But, what of those who come behind them, the phalanx of priests and deacons, who serve not Christ but their belly.
- Shrines are built, and there is no one to open the doors. Altars are erected, and they are covered with cobwebs.
- There was no difference between pagan and Christian, the believer was not distinct from the Jew, and did not differ from the deceiver.
- At Babel, the soothsayers and diviners were not so numerous as they are now, within the Christian people.
- You can still see desecrations greater than these: contempt for holy shrines, mockery of the divine sacraments, mocking profanation of the holy day of Sunday, neglect of the meetings which are the feast days of Our Lord, transgression of the law, and of the apostolic canons.

Not only had God punished these many failings through the Arab incursion, but had also sent a recent plague upon his people, with devastating consequences. Yet he prophesied that the Arabs would in time be subdued by God: 'They have against them a people from distant countries'.

Map of Arabia and her Neighbours
at the time of Muhammad's death in 632 CE

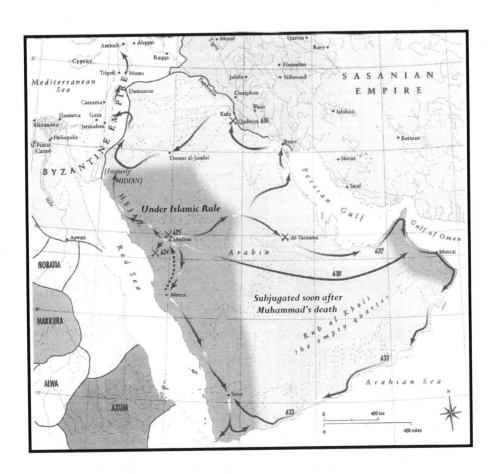

Mutual respect

When stability returned to the region, Christians who were prepared to deal with their new masters found it to their advantage. It seems that while Umar was still Caliph (from 634 to 644 CE) a treaty known as the Pact of Umar was concluded with the above-mentioned Sophronius. Because of its subsequent history, its authenticity remains uncertain; but it seems to have guaranteed the safety and religious freedom of both Jews and Christians (while forbidding them to be teachers of the Qur'an, although this may be a later addition). It was thus broadly in line with the famous agreement (known as the *umma* document) concluded a decade or more earlier between Muhammad himself and various Jewish tribes of Yathrib (i.e. Medina):

> The Jews of the tribe of 'Awf are a people with the Believers; the Jews have their *din* and the *muslimun* have their *din*.

The same tolerant spirit is later found in the letters of Isho'yahb, who became Patriarch of Adiabene within the Nestorian Church of Assyria:

> As for the Arabs, to whom God has at this time given rule over the world, you know how well they act towards us. Not only do they not oppose Christianity, but they praise our faith, honour the priests and saints of our Lord, and give aid to the churches and monasteries. [*Ep 14C*, 252]

Isho'yahb's letters include the earliest texts known so far to refer to Muslims as *mhaggre*, a term deriving from the Arabic *muhajir* – i.e. meaning those who have 'emigrated', as in the *hjira* to Medina. The *Letter of John of Sedreh* also refers to these *Mhaggraye*, and reports a discussion, held several years before his death in 648 CE, when he was summoned as the Syrian Orthodox Patriarch before the Arab ruler (or Amir) in Homs:

> The blessed one (the Patriarch) responded, 'Just as the Torah is one and the same and is accepted by us Christians and by you *Mhaggraye*, and by the Jews and the Samaritans, and each is distinct in belief; likewise concerning faith in the Gospel, each heretical group understands and interprets it differently, and not like us (Orthodox). [II]

194

The glorious Amir did not accept these proofs from the prophets, instead, he demanded proof from Moses (i.e. the Torah) that Christ is God. The blessed one, therefore, cited Moses in many things, (e.g.) that 'the Lord let fire and sulphur come down from the Lord on Sodom and Gomorrah.' The glorious Amir demanded that this be shown in the book. Immediately, our father showed it in the complete Greek and Syriac texts. [VII cf. Gen 19.24]

It is quite clear from his letter that the *Mhaggraye* accepted the authority of the Torah, above any other biblical writings, and made no appeal to the Qur'an itself: this implies that the Qur'an was not yet available as an agreed and authoritative book of scripture. The discussion indeed indicates that the Amir was not so well informed about his faith that he could challenge the Patriarch's version of it:

Again the glorious Amir asked him, 'What kind of belief and faith did Abraham and Moses hold?' Our blessed Father answered, 'It is the belief and faith of Christians that they held.' [V]

About twenty years later, Sebeos, a bishop in Armenia, wrote a chronicle of recent events, and included this account of Muhammad, whose picture is now somewhat amplified:

In that period a certain one of them, a man of the sons of Ishmael named Muhammad, a merchant, became prominent. A sermon about the Way of Truth, supposedly at God's command, was revealed to them, and taught them to recognize the God of Abraham, especially since he was informed and knowledgeable about Mosaic history. Because the command had come from on high, he ordered them all to assemble together and to unite in faith. Abandoning the reverence of vain things, they turned toward the living God, who had appeared to their father, Abraham. Muhammad legislated that they were not to eat carrion, not to drink wine, not to speak falsehoods, and not to commit adultery. He said, 'God promised that country to Abraham and to his son after him, for eternity. And what had been promised was fulfilled during that time when (God) loved Israel. Now, however, you are the sons of Abraham, and God shall fulfil the promise made to Abraham and his son on you. Only love the God of Abraham, and go and take the country which God gave to your father, Abraham. No one can successfully resist you in war, since God is with you.' [*Hist* 30]

It is also interesting to learn from Sebeos' chronicle that, when the Believers first arrived in Jerusalem, the first governor they appointed there was a Jew. Although there was inevitably some instability and turmoil in the early years of conquest, by Sebeos' time (so we learn from another Christian author Bar Penkaye, writing shortly after 680 CE) there was peaceful cooperation and religious tolerance.

By the end of the 7th century, the situation had become complicated by issues such as apostasy and inter-marriage. One of the most learned Christians during this period was the Syrian Orthodox bishop, Jacob of Edessa. He was renowned for his strictness in canon law, and among his writings was a collection of ecclesiastical canons, some of which had a bearing upon relations with Muslims:

> We should not rebaptise a Christian who becomes a Muslim or pagan but then returns; the prayer of penitents is to be said over him by the bishop and a period of penance enjoined upon him. [*Replies to John* A13]
>
> A woman who is married to a Muslim, and who says that she will convert to Islam unless she is given the host, should be granted it, but with a penalty that is appropriate for her to receive. [*Replies to Addai* 75]

Jacob had some knowledge of Islamic teaching – in a letter to John the Stylite he mentions that Muslims turn towards the Ka'ba for prayer and comments on their acceptance of Jesus as Messiah – but this was apparently derived from observation rather than from any written sources.

Qur'anic teaching on the increase

Certain qur'anic texts were however now gaining wider circulation, not only to reinforce the faith of believers but also as a witness to Jews and Christians. Several public inscriptions have been identified dating from the 7th century: Robert Hoyland[57] mentions those on dams at Ta'if (680 CE) and Medina (670s CE), along with a tax demand written about the same time on marble in Northern Syria, commencing with the words 'In the name of God the Merciful the Compassionate'. References to the Qur'an on these

---

[57] Robert Hoyland: *New Documentary Texts and the Early Islamic State* [SOAS 69.3, London 2006, 395-416]

inscriptions are usually 'a collage of phrases' (e.g. at Medina a combination of texts from Q 26.24 and 73.9) – reminiscent of the form in which Christians often cited their own scriptures. In 685 CE 'Abd al-Malik became the Umayyad Caliph and coins issued during his rule then started to be inscribed with words rather than with images. The objective was to propagate qur'anic teaching: on one side would be a statement about God's uniqueness, surrounded by testimony to Muhammad as God's messenger, while the reverse contained *sura* 112:

> He is God the One, God the eternal. He begot no one nor was He begotten. No one is comparable to Him.

This was evidently intended to counter Christian belief in the Trinity.

Similarly, it was under 'Abd al-Malik that the Dome of the Rock was erected in Jerusalem around 692 CE. The site is mentioned in the Qur'an in the opening verse of *sura* 17, which describes Muhammad's celebrated 'night journey' from Mecca to Jerusalem.

> Glory to Him who made His servant travel by night from the sacred place of worship to the furthest place of worship. [Q 17.1]

The design of the Dome – perhaps surprisingly – followed the style of a Byzantine martyrium; this may have been chosen as a symbolic reminder of judgement and what lay in store beyond death. It was, however, the epigraphic decoration on both the inner and outer faces of its octagon that presented the greatest challenge to both Jews and Christians. The inscription band (240 metres long) carries a variety of texts drawn from the Qur'an, an indication that a written version of it had by now become established. One section reads as follows:

> The Messiah Jesus son of Mary was only a messenger of God, and His word which He committed to Mary, and a spirit from Him. So believe in God and His messengers and do not say 'three'; it is better for you. God is only one God; He is too exalted to have a son ... O God, incline unto your messenger and your servant Jesus son of Mary. Peace on him the day he was born and the day he dies and the day he shall be raised alive. Such was Jesus son of Mary; a statement of truth concerning which they are in doubt. It is not for Him to take a son, glory be to Him.

197

Christian engagement and critique

The weightiest Christian response to Islamic ideas came in the following 8th century from the renowned hand of St John of Damascus. He was both well-born and well-educated: his grandfather had been a high official in Damascus under the Byzantines, as was his father under the Saracen regime[58] – some sources suggest that he took over this position on his father's death before entering the monastery of Mar Saba near Jerusalem. There he wrote a masterful refutation of heresies, *The Fount of Knowledge.* It was not in fact his critique of Islam that attracted attention at the time so much as his attack on iconoclasm. Yet there is a link between these two issues: many Christians in the East had come to relate the rapid expansion of the new Arab empire to its rejection of 'images', and therefore they considered that, to win back divine favour, the churches should follow suit.

Nevertheless, the arguments John employed (in writing and evidently also in person) against Muslims are more specific than any previously recorded, and reveal a detailed knowledge of the Qur'an. He dismisses Muhammad's views as but a variation of Arianism:

> There is also the superstition of the Ishmaelites which to this day prevails and keeps people in error, being a forerunner of the Antichrist ... Down to the time of Heraclius they were very great idolaters. From that time to the present a false prophet named Mohammed has appeared in their midst. This man, after having chanced upon the Old and New Testaments and likewise, it seems, having conversed with an Arian monk, devised his own heresy. Then, having insinuated himself into the good graces of the people by a show of seeming piety, he gave out that a certain book had been sent down to him from heaven. He had set down some ridiculous compositions in this book of his and he gave it to them as an object of veneration.
>
> He says that there is one God, creator of all things, who has neither been begotten nor has begotten. He says that the Christ is the Word of God and

---

[58] Yet well-educated Christians and Jews who took such administrative posts under the new regime came progressively to loosen ties with their own faith community. Their eventual conversion would then undermine the morale of less affluent fellow-believers, who might well struggle to pay the extra dues now demanded of them (cf. R. Stephen Humphreys: *Christian Communities in Early Islamic Syria* ... in Money, Power and Politics in Early Islamic Syria, London 2010, 55).

His Spirit, but a creature and a servant, and that He was begotten, without seed, of Mary the sister of Moses and Aaron ... And he says that the Jews wanted to crucify Him in violation of the law, and that they seized His shadow and crucified this. But the Christ Himself was not crucified, he says, nor did He die, for God out of His love for Him took Him to Himself into heaven ... There are many other extraordinary and quite ridiculous things in this book which he boasts was sent down to him from God. But when we ask: 'And who is there to testify that God gave him the book? And which of the prophets foretold that such a prophet would rise up?'—they are at a loss ... When we ask again: 'How is it that when he enjoined us in this book of yours not to do anything or receive anything without witnesses, you did not ask him: "First do you show us by witnesses that you are a prophet and that you have come from God, and show us just what Scriptures there are that testify about you"'—they are ashamed and remain silent ...

They furthermore accuse us of being idolaters, because we venerate the cross, which they abominate. And we answer them: 'How is it, then, that you rub yourselves against a stone in your Ka'ba and kiss and embrace it?' Then some of them say that Abraham had relations with Agar upon it, but others say that he tied the camel to it, when he was going to sacrifice Isaac. And we answer them: 'Since Scripture says that the mountain was wooded and had trees from which Abraham cut wood for the holocaust and laid it upon Isaac, and then he left the asses behind with the two young men, why talk nonsense? For in that place neither is it thick with trees nor is there passage for asses.' And they are embarrassed, but they still assert that the stone is Abraham's ... This stone that they talk about is a head of that Aphrodite whom they used to worship and whom they called Khabár. Even to the present day, traces of the carving are visible on it to careful observers. [De Haeresibus C/CI 60-64]

This extract not only offers the counter-accusation that idolatry had not wholly ceased among Muslims, but raises the important issue of the apparently 'self-declarative' nature of the Qur'an. So John seems to present his arguments, not simply to buttress the faith of his fellow Christians, but to invite their Muslim rivals to engage in further reasoned debate.

Reasoned debate

Such debate was by no means out of the question, but it is not until later in 8th century that there is any record of measured discussion worthy of its profound subject matter. It was probably not until this time that Muslims had (for their part) begun to gain sufficient knowledge of Christian teaching: for example, it is during this century that biblical references begin to be more common in Islamic sources (even if they appear in considerably amended form): thus, a combination of words spoken by Jesus [Mt 7.12; 5.39 = Lk 6.31, 29] appears to be cited by Ja'far al-Sadiq, the 6th Shi'i Iman who died in 760 CE. Two decades later a famous meeting took place in Baghdad between the Nestorian Patriarch Timothy I and the third Abbasid Caliph al-Mahdi. Their dialogue, spread over two days, was conducted in an atmosphere of mutual respect and was afterwards recorded by Timothy. On the first day the starting point was the status of Christ, which led on to an examination of Trinitarian concepts. Then the Caliph embarked on another theme:

> How is it that you accept Christ and the Gospel from the testimony of the Torah and of the prophets, and you do not accept Muhammad from the testimony of Christ and the Gospel?

Timothy's reply was that there is not a single testimony from either 'which would refer to his name or his works'. So the Caliph raised the subject of 'the Paraclete'. After Timothy had cited texts which promised the gift of the Spirit and explained his role, the Caliph answered, 'All these refer to Muhammad.' Timothy then proceeded to demonstrate the weakness of this assertion:

> Further, the Paraclete searches the deep things of God, but Muhammad owns that he does not know what might befall him and those who accept him. He who searches all things even the deep things of God is not identical with the one who does not know what might happen to him and to those who acknowledge him. Muhammad is therefore not the Paraclete. Again, the Paraclete, as Jesus told His disciples, was with them and among them while He was speaking to them, and since Muhammad was not with them and among them, he cannot, therefore, have been the Paraclete. Finally, the Paraclete descended on the disciples ten days after the ascension of Jesus to heaven, while Muhammad was born more than six hundred years later, and this impedes Muhammad from being the Paraclete. And Jesus taught the disciples that the Paraclete is one God in three persons, and since Muhammad does not believe in the doctrine of three persons in one

Godhead, he cannot be the Paraclete. And the Paraclete wrought all sorts of prodigies and miracles through the disciples, and since Muhammad did not work a single miracle through his followers and his disciples, he is not the Paraclete.

The Caliph might at this point have challenged at least one of these arguments viz. that Jesus taught explicit Trinitarian doctrine, but instead he riposted:

There were many testimonies but the Books have been corrupted, and you have removed them.

Later in the discussion, having named the four Gospels, he asked:

Why are they different from one another and contradict one another?

To each question Timothy has a ready answer, and challenges the Caliph:

Where is it known, O King, that the Books have been corrupted by us, and where is that uncorrupted Book from which you have learned that the Books which we use have been corrupted?

Had he been better acquainted with the Qur'an, he might at this juncture have pointed to some of its own inconsistencies and variant readings. The Caliph, however, did ask him for his assessment of the Qur'an:

Do you not believe that our Book was given by God?
And (Timothy) replied to him: 'It is not my business to decide whether it is from God or not. But I will say something of which your Majesty is well aware, and that is all the words of God found in the Torah and in the Prophets, and those of them found in the Gospel and in the writings of the Apostles, have been confirmed by signs and miracles; as to the words of your Book they have not been corroborated by a single sign or miracle.

This was not a blanket condemnation, for Timothy goes on to say, just before the session ended:

The Arabs are to-day held in great honour and esteem by God and men, because they forsook idolatry and polytheism, and worshipped and honoured one God; in this they deserve the love and the praise of all; if,

201

therefore, there was an allusion to their Prophet in the Books, not only would we not have introduced any changes in it, but we would have accepted him with great joy and pleasure, in the same way as we are expecting the one of whom we spoke, and who is going to appear at the end of the world. We are not the correctors but the observers of the commandments of God.

And our Sovereign said with a jocular smile: We shall hear you about these at some other time, when business affairs give us a better opportunity for such an intimate exchange of words.

Indeed, a second meeting was held the next day, with the Caliph in 'a sweet and benevolent' mood. The most noteworthy exchange occurred early in the discussion:

Our gracious and wise King said to me: 'What do you say about Muhammad?'

And I replied to his Majesty: 'Muhammad is worthy of all praise, by all reasonable people, O my Sovereign. He walked in the path of the prophets, and trod in the track of the lovers of God. All the prophets taught the doctrine of one God, and since Muhammad taught the doctrine of the unity of God, he walked, therefore, in the path of the prophets. Further, all the prophets drove men away from bad works, and brought them nearer to good works, and since Muhammad drove his people away from bad works and brought them nearer to the good ones, he walked, therefore, in the path of the prophets.

'He trod in the track of the lovers of God.' Muslims would, of course, assert more than this. Their faith is summarised in the confession known as the *Shahadah*: 'I testify that there is no god but God and Muhammad is the messenger of God'. With the first of these statements Christians and Jews are in complete agreement; but while Muhammad can certainly be recognised as one of God's prophets, it would be difficult to ascribe complete infallibility to his teaching and therefore to call him *the* messenger of God. *Sura* 5.48 begins as follows:

We sent to you the Scripture with the truth, confirming the Scriptures that came before it, and *with final authority over them*.

The italicised clause is clearly unacceptable to the People of the Book, and surely too to anyone with an understanding of the historical processes that have led faith communities to their appropriation of divine truth. Indeed, it is arguable that Muhammad understood himself to be 'the seal of the prophets' primarily because of the rapidly approaching Hour of God's judgement, in which belief he was (like the earliest Christians) mistaken. Hence, even in qur'anic terms, it is legitimate to see God's revelation, including the process of scriptural interpretation, as continuing to unfold:

> There was a Scripture for every age: God erases or confirms wherever He will, and the source of Scripture is with Him. [Q 13.39]

Christians find their clearest guidance here in Jesus' 'farewell discourse':

> I have yet many things to say to you, but you cannot bear them now. When the Spirit of truth comes, he will guide you into all the truth; for he will not speak on his own authority, but whatever he hears he will speak, and he will declare to you the things that are to come. He will glorify me, for he will take what is mine and declare it to you. [Jn 16.12-14]

Thus, the Spirit of truth does not declare another Scripture, but reveals the deeper mysteries of Christ. The Islamic claim that the word *Paraclete* was a falsification of Gospel texts, whose intended reference was to the coming of Muhammad himself, is unsupported by manuscript evidence and thus lacks any serious critical foundation. Patriarch Timothy I was right to resist the Caliph at this crucial point, and the reasoned and courteous manner in which he did so has much to commend it.

The Christian faith teaches, as the Johannine saying 'before Abraham was, I am' reminds us, that Jesus was in fact no mere prophet, but a uniquely authoritative divine figure, whose life and teaching hold an abiding significance. His passion and subsequent resurrection remain the focus of God's revelation, however its contemporary meaning is interpreted. Hence a further key issue, as John of Damascus noted, is the Qur'an's *denial* of the reality of Christ's death and his path of suffering. Despite Muhammad's strong emphasis upon God's mercy and forgiveness, he became seemingly too inclined to advocate *militancy* as the way to advance God's cause, no doubt seeing the Cross as a sign of failure rather than (in Johannine terms) as God's ultimate victory:

> The light shines in the darkness, and the darkness has not overcome it. [Jn 1.5]
>
> I, when I am lifted up from the earth, will draw all men to myself. [Jn 12.32]

Perhaps too, in imitating his mentor Abraham [Gen 14.14-16], he had not entirely transcended tribal instincts?

Further, it is only the well-attested Christian witness to Christ's death and resurrection that offers a secure foundation to belief in God's loving purposes and the hope of eternal life. The Qur'an's arguments about judgement and life beyond the grave remain otherwise plausible, but of no more than theoretical standing: certainly God *could* revive the departed – the question is, on what evidential basis (other than the belief that they are his own creation) does the conviction arise that he *cares enough* about human beings to do so. The Christian faith is grounded, not in dreams and visions, nor on well-constructed analogies, nor even (as with Jews) on hopes arising from a long-standing covenantal relationship with God, but in the actual encounter with a Lord who has suffered on the Cross and has been raised from the dead.

EPILOGUE

A view of Toledo in Spain,
where for nearly seven centuries
Muslims, Jews, and Christians
lived together in an atmosphere of tolerance

16. Dialogue Today

Respectful co-existence

Despite the recent centuries of mutual suspicion and hostility – and despite the continuing wave of Western invasions of Muslim countries met with escalating acts of terrorism – it is possible to look back to earlier encounters between the Abrahamic faiths where respectful co-existence was fostered and where God's truth was seen as present in some measure within the treasured scriptures of other traditions. As recorded above, such a situation seems to have existed throughout most of 7th century Syria.

Perhaps the most commendable expression of such tolerance was in medieval Spain. Maria Rosa Menocal recently wrote a timely appreciation, *Ornament of the World* (New York 2002), of how Jews and Christians flourished economically and culturally from the 8th century onwards in Muslim Andalusia under the Ummayad dynasty. It is worthy of note that in Toledo especially 'the Mozarabs had preserved their own way of celebrating the Eucharist, not in Latin, the liturgical language of Western Christendom, but in Arabic'.[59] The same rite is still to be found there today.

Such a readiness to engage with other traditions was, as we have seen, already present in the Church from its beginnings. The Christian faith never repudiated its Jewish origins, despite attempts by Marcion and others to discount the Old Testament, whose liturgical use continued along with a hermeneutic developed from scribal practices. It is sometimes forgotten that Jews were in turn influenced by Christian teachings and practices. A pioneering work by Rabbi Michael Hilton, *The Christian Effect on Jewish Life* (London 1994), has many examples, not least the interaction between the formation of the Christian canon and that of the Hebrew Bible. Much later, the Jewish commentator Rashi drew upon Christian sources (somewhat paradoxically, given his experience of massacres committed by the Crusaders in 1096 CE) for his interpretation of Isaiah 53:

[Israel] was chastised that the whole world might have peace.

---

[59] Menocal 178

The Qur'an too explicitly builds upon what preceded it in the revered writings of Jews and Christians, even though it often seems to elucidate them differently. Despite the fact that Christians will never be able to accord the Qur'an any 'canonical' status, it may yet be seen as a possible *preparatio evangelica* (even as such on a par with the Old Testament?). Certainly those who have taken the trouble to read it have found it a source of much spiritual value, and when its teachings are practised by faithful Muslims their way of life and their prayer speak eloquently of its divine origin.

Contemporary initiatives

One 20th century landmark was surely the promulgation at the 2nd Vatican Council of the document *Nostra Aetate*:

> Upon the Moslems, too, the Church looks with esteem. They adore one God, living and enduring, merciful and all-powerful, Maker of heaven and earth and Speaker to men. They strive to submit wholeheartedly even to His inscrutable decrees, just as did Abraham, with whom the Islamic faith is pleased to associate itself. Though they do not acknowledge Jesus as God, they revere Him as a prophet. They also honour Mary, His virgin mother; at times they call on her, too, with devotion. In addition, they await the day of judgement when God will give each man his due, after raising him up. Consequently, they prize the moral life, and give worship to God especially through prayer, almsgiving, and fasting.
>
> Although in the course of the centuries many quarrels and hostilities have arisen between Christians and Moslems, this most sacred Synod urges all to forget the past and to strive sincerely for mutual understanding. On behalf of all mankind, let them make common cause of safeguarding and fostering social justice, moral values, peace and freedom.

The document continues by remembering 'the spiritual ties which link the people of the New Covenant to the stock of Abraham' and the 'common spiritual heritage' between Christians and Jews:

> [Mutual understanding and appreciation] can be obtained especially, by way of biblical and theological enquiry and through friendly discussions.

Joint exploration of the scriptures is particularly important in a world where religious belief of any sort is often challenged.[60] Despite many significant differences, the various custodians and messengers of God's Word must surely today witness more harmoniously to God's purpose for humanity.

Pope Francis has drawn attention to this in his recent Apostolic Exhortation *Evangelii Gaudium*:

> God continues to work among the people of the Old Covenant and to bring forth treasures of wisdom which flow from their encounter with his word ... There exists as well a rich complementarity which allows us [the Church] to read the texts of the Hebrew Scriptures *together* and to help one another to mine the riches of God's word ...
>
> Our relationship with the followers of Islam has taken on great importance ... The sacred writings of Islam have retained some Christian teachings ... Many [Muslims] also have a deep conviction that their life, in its entirety, is from God and for God ... In order to sustain dialogue with Islam, suitable training is essential for all involved ... Our respect for true followers of Islam should lead us to avoid hateful generalisations, for authentic Islam and the proper reading of the Koran are opposed to every form of violence.[61]

Such overtures have also been reciprocated in recent years by Muslim leaders, notably in 2006 when a body of Muslim scholars wrote an Open Letter to Pope Benedict XVI and a year later when a similar document was published entitled *A Common Word between Us and You*. This title is drawn from the Qur'an itself:

> People of the Book, let us arrive at a statement that is common to us all. [Q 3.64]

The document's Preface reads as follows, in terms very similar to those of the Catholic teachings cited above;

---

[60] The publication of *The Jewish Annotated New Testament* (Oxford 2011) was a noteworthy recent development. It remarks at one point that 'for all their profound theological differences and mutual conflict, early Christianity and rabbinic Judaism spoke much the same language' [p569].

[61] *Evangelii Gaudium* (Vatican 2013, 249ff)

Muslims and Christians together make up well over half of the world's population. Without peace and justice between these two religious communities there can be no meaningful peace in the world. The future of the world depends on peace between Muslims and Christians.

The basis for this peace and understanding already exists. It is part of the very foundational principles of both faiths: love of the One God, and love of the neighbour. These principles are found over and over again in the sacred texts of Islam and Christianity. The Unity of God, the necessity of love for Him, and the necessity of love of neighbour[62] is thus the common ground between Islam and Christianity.

The document proceeds to survey some of the qur'anic and biblical texts that elaborate these two principles, and it ends with a further quotation from the Qur'an, which includes the following:

We have assigned a law and a path to each of you. If God had so willed, He would have made you one community, but He wanted to test you through that which He has given you, so race to do good: you will all return to God and He will make clear to you the matters you differed about. [Q 5.48 *here in Abdul Haleem's translation*]

Conclusion

The aim of this present work has been to promote a better appreciation of our common Abrahamic inheritance, while raising a number of questions that need to be addressed. Some of the arguments and assertions made here are no doubt open to challenge; but, as Pope Francis has urged, it is better to make mistakes in the search for truth than not to search at all. It is

---

[62] Yet in August 2013 a young, seemingly moderate, convert from the Catholic faith to Islam wrote in the Guardian newspaper: 'I converted to Islam after learning about the religion's monotheistic foundation ... This made sense and was easy to comprehend. My conversion was further strengthened by learning that Islam recognised and revered the prophets mentioned in Judaism and Christianity ... Role models such as Malcolm X only helped to reinforce the perception that Islam enabled the empowerment of one's masculinity ... [whereas] "turning the other cheek" invites potential ridicule and abuse.' This begs the question, How far does 'love of neighbour' hold the same meaning in the different traditions?

certainly wise to admit, as does the Qur'an, that not all our questionings will be answered this side of Paradise.

Thus, the interaction between time and eternity itself surely remains a 'mystery' [cf. 1Cor 15.51]. While scriptural sources certainly indicate that the fulfilment of God's purposes for his creation is a developing process, yet scientific understanding of the origin and expansion of the universe is now so very different from that of 2000 years ago that theological thought in all the Abrahamic traditions has found it hard to keep abreast; hence one area where theologians could fruitfully collaborate across the religions is that of eschatology.

The greatest risk in the interpretation of scripture perhaps lies in employing a literalism that obscures deeper spiritual meanings (and so easily leads to forms of fanaticism). It can easily happen too that a text read only in translation can likewise be misleading, because certain resonances get lost — and that may well be a failing of the present work. As Thomas Carlyle observed of the Qur'an, the sheer beauty and poetry of the original Arabic can be far more powerful and uplifting than any more prosaic rendering in another language. Thus, while the study of texts can begin to promote better understanding of each other's faith, it needs in the end to be an exercise that engages in dialogue. What a particular scripture appears to say may not necessarily tell us how it really speaks to those who read it with the eye of faith or within their own living traditions.

Yet shared exploration of the scriptures is not simply for our mutual enrichment, but to enable God's Word to be proclaimed more clearly in a confused world that struggles to find its true direction. This study has drawn attention more than once to the apparently universal search for 'Paradise'; in these 'emerging scriptures' lie many divine hints as to where it may be found.